T0330087

Globalisation and International Trade Liberalisation

Globalisation and International Trade Liberalisation
Continuity and Change

Edited by

Martin Richardson

Associate Professor of Economics and Director, 1999 Foreign Policy School, University of Otago, New Zealand

Edward Elgar
Cheltenham, UK • Northampton, MA, USA

Published by
Edward Elgar Publishing Limited
Glensanda House
Montpellier Parade
Cheltenham
Glos GL50 1UA
UK

Edward Elgar Publishing, Inc.
136 West Street
Suite 202
Northampton
Massachusetts 01060
USA

A catalogue record for this book
is available from the British Library

Library of Congress Cataloguing in Publication Data

Globalisation and international trade liberalisation : continuity and change /
edited by Martin Richardson.
    Papers from a conference held in Dunedin, New Zealand in July 1999.
    Includes bibliographical references and index.
    1. International trade—Congresses. 2. Free trade—Congresses.
    3. International economic integration—Congresses. 4. Globalisation.
  I. Richardson, Martin, 1960–

HF1372.G585 2000
382—dc21

                          00–022626

ISBN 1 84064 350 1

Printed in the United Kingdom at the University Press, Cambridge

Contents

Figures

Tables

Contributors

Michael D. Bordo
Michael Bordo is a Professor of Economics at Rutgers University, NJ, and a Research Associate at the National Bureau of Economic Research, Cambridge MA in the USA. He is author of *Essays on the Gold Standard and Related Regimes* (Cambridge University Press, 1998) and editor, with Claudia Goldin and Eugene White, of *The Defining Moment: The Great Depression and the American Economy in the Twentieth Century* (University of Chicago Press for the NBER, 1998) among many other works.

Roderick Deane
Dr Roderick Deane is Chairman of Telecom NZ and was CEO and Managing Director from November 1992 to September 1999. Prior to that he was CEO of the Electricity Corporation of New Zealand Ltd (1987–92), Chairman of the State Service Commission (1986–87), Deputy Governor of the Reserve Bank of New Zealand (1982–86) and Alternative Executive Director of the International Monetary Fund. Dr Deane is also a former President of IHC New Zealand Inc. He is currently a Director of Fletcher Challenge Ltd and a Director of the ANZ Banking Group Ltd. He has a PhD and BCom (Hons) degrees in economics and is a Fellow of the NZ Society of Accountants, the Institute of Corporate Management and the NZ Institute of Management.

Barry Eichengreen
Barry Eichengreen is the George C. Pardee and Helen N. Pardee Professor of Economics and Professor of Political Science at the University of California at Berkeley, CA in the USA. He is author of *Golden Fetters* (Oxford University Press, 1990) and *Globalizing Capital* (Princeton University Press, 1996) among many other works.

Tim Groser
Tim Groser, currently the Executive Director of the Asia2000 Foundation, was previously NZ Ministry of Foreign Affairs and Trade's Principal Economic Adviser, and has had wide experience as a trade negotiator. Prior to being appointed as Ambassador to Indonesia, Tim was NZ's Chief Negotiator in the GATT Uruguay Round and spent some seven years of his professional

life on the Uruguay Round. Previously, and working originally out of the Treasury, Tim spent many years on developing the framework for NZ's economic relationship with Australia, culminating in the Closer Economic Relations negotiations. He is the principal author of the NZ Government's Trade Policy Strategy and, in his individual capacity, acts from time to time as an independent consultant to the WTO on trade disputes.

Tim Hazledine

Tim Hazledine has been Professor of Economics at Auckland University since 1992, when he returned to New Zealand after twenty years in Britain and Canada. He was born in Dunedin, NZ and educated at Otago and Canterbury Universities, before going to the University of Warwick, in England, to take his PhD. He has taught at Warwick, Balliol College Oxford, Queen's University and the University of British Columbia, where he was a professor in the Agricultural Economics Department for eight years before returning to NZ. He has worked in the public sector, for Agriculture Canada, in Ottawa, and at the Economic Council of Canada. Professor Hazledine has published widely on applied and policy issues, most recently in his book *Taking New Zealand Seriously: The Economics of Decency* (Harper Collins, 1998).

John F. Helliwell

John Helliwell has been a Professor of Economics at the University of British Columbia, Vancouver, Canada since 1971. He studied at the University of British Columbia and Oxford University, UK, and taught at Oxford before returning to UBC, which has been his base since 1967. His early research was mainly in applied macroeconomics, with special emphasis on energy and natural resource issues from the 1970s onwards. His recent research has emphasised comparative macroeconomics and growth (including especially the influence of openness and institutions), interdisciplinary research into the linkages among economic, social and human health (especially on the determinants and consequences of different measures of social capital) and evaluating and explaining the strikingly large importance of national borders. From 1991 to 1994 he was Mackenzie King Visiting Professor of Canadian Studies at Harvard, and in 1995–96 was back at Harvard as a Fulbright Fellow. He is a Research Associate of the National Bureau of Economic Research, a Fellow of the Royal Society of Canada and an Officer of the Order of Canada.

Douglas A. Irwin

Doug Irwin is a Professor of Economics at Dartmouth College, Hanover NH in the USA where he has been since 1997. Prior to joining Dartmouth he was on the Faculty of the Graduate School of Business at the University of

Chicago and before that was with the Division of International Finance at the Board of Governors of the Federal Reserve and an economist with the Council of Economic Advisers, Executive Office of the President. He has published widely in both international economics and economic history and is the author of *Against the Tide: An Intellectual History of Free Trade* (Princeton University Press, 1996).

Jane Kelsey

Jane Kelsey has degrees from Victoria University of Wellington, Oxford and Cambridge Universities and a PhD from the University of Auckland. She holds a personal chair in law at the School of Law, Auckland University and specialises in the area of law and policy, both domestic and international. Professor Kelsey is the author of four books on aspects of the restructuring of New Zealand's economic, political and social life since 1984, including *The New Zealand Experiment. A World Model for Structural Adjustment?* (Auckland University Press/Bridget Williams Books, 2nd edn, 1997). Her latest book, *Reclaiming the Future: New Zealand and the Global Economy*, (Bridget Williams Books) challenges prevailing views about globalisation and its implications for the future. Professor Kelsey travels extensively, talking on the New Zealand experience to a wide range of audiences, and is an active member of an international network of scholars who are critical of the global free market economy.

Patrick Lane

Patrick Lane has been a journalist with *The Economist* since November 1993. Having joined the newspaper as an economics correspondent, he became trade correspondent in April 1994. He switched to covering the British economy in September 1997. He wrote a survey of world trade ('Where next? Time for another round') which was published in the issue of *The Economist* dated 3 October 1998. He also deputises as editor of the Britain section of the newspaper. Between January 1990 and October 1993, Dr Lane was an economic consultant with Oxford Economic Research Associates, a consulting firm specialising in utility regulation. He holds a BA (Hons) in economics from Cambridge University, awarded in 1985. He went on to be a graduate student at Oxford, earning an MPhil in 1987 and a DPhil in 1991.

Rt. Hon. Don McKinnon

New Zealand's Minister of Foreign Affairs and Trade through the 1990s, from March 2000 Don McKinnon has been the Secretary-General of the Commonwealth. Elected to the NZ Parliament in November 1978, he became Junior Government Whip in October 1980, Senior Whip in February

1982 and Deputy Leader of the National Party in September 1987 when he also became Opposition spokesperson on Health and Defence. Mr McKinnon was sworn in as Deputy Prime Minister, Minister of Foreign Affairs and Minister of External Relations and Trade in 1990, adding to these Minister of Pacific Island Affairs in 1991 and Leader of the House of Representatives in 1993. As a member of the National-NZ First Coalition Government formed in 1996, he was reappointed Minister of Foreign Affairs and Trade and Minister of Pacific Island Affairs and appointed Minister of Disarmament and Arms Control. He was appointed a member of the Privy Council in 1992.

Allan I. Mendelowitz

Dr Allan Mendelowitz is currently a Vice President at the Economic Strategy Institute in Washington DC, USA where he has been since January 1999. Previously he has served as Executive Vice President of the Export-Import Bank of the United States, Managing Director for International Trade and Finance at the US GAO and Representative of the Comptroller General on the Chrysler Corporation Loan Guarantee Board. He has also been a Brookings Institution Economic Policy Fellow and an Assistant Professor of Economics at Rutgers University. Dr Mendelowitz has been a frequent expert witness before committees of the US Congress on international trade, finance, and competitiveness issues, lectured before audiences around the world, and has published articles in journals such as the *Journal of Policy Analysis and Management*; the *Journal of Business*; and the *National Tax Journal*. He holds PhD and MA degrees in Economics from Northwestern University and a BA in Economics from Columbia University.

Mike Moore

Mike Moore is the Director General of the World Trade Organisation based in Geneva, Switzerland. He became the youngest Member of the New Zealand Parliament ever elected when he won the Eden seat in 1972. Until taking his current position in 1999 he was a Member of the NZ Parliament for Waimakariri and Labour's spokesperson on Foreign Affairs and Trade. During his Parliamentary career, Mr Moore had responsibilities as spokesman on housing, regional, small town and community development, the environment, tourism, recreation and sport, overseas trade and marketing, external relations and trade and finance. He has been a Cabinet Minister in NZ in many portfolios: Foreign Affairs, Trade, Recreation and Sport and Tourism. He has been Prime Minister, Deputy Minister of Finance and Leader of the Labour Opposition and has led many trade missions around the world. He has written nine books including *A Brief History of the Future* (Shoal Bay, Christchurch NZ, 1998).

Martin Richardson
Martin Richardson has been an Associate Professor in the Department of Economics at the University of Otago, Dunedin NZ, since 1998. An Otago undergraduate, he received his BA (Hons) in Economics in 1982, a MEc from the ANU in 1984 and a PhD and MA from Princeton University in 1989. He taught at Georgetown University in Washington DC for a number of years before returning to Otago in 1995. He has published papers in the *European Economic Review*, *Oxford Economic Papers*, the *Journal of International Economics* and the *Review of Development Economics* as well as elsewhere. His principal current research interests are trade and competition policies, preferential trading areas and endogenous policy and recent NZ economic reforms.

David Robertson
Professor David Robertson was appointed to the John Gough Chair in the Practice of International Trade at the Melbourne Business School in early 1997. He has worked as an economist with Unilever Ltd in London, then with the European Free Trade Association Secretariat at Geneva. He has been an Assistant Commissioner of the Industries Assistance Commission and an Assistant Secretary of the Department of the Treasury in Australia. From 1984 to 1990 he was Deputy Director-General (Economic/ Executive) with the Office of National Assessment in Canberra, and has been Director, Trade and Development Program, the National Centre for Development Studies, at the Australian National University in Canberra. His current research interests include assessments of Uruguay Round agreements affecting developing countries, especially environment issues, international investment and competition policy. He has been a consultant with several international organisations (including the World Bank, the OECD, UN agencies and the Commonwealth Secretariat) and has published widely on international trade, finance and development issues.

Alex Sundakov
Alex Sundakov is the Director of the NZ Institute of Economic Research. His areas of interest span the labour market, macroeconomic forecasting, and the economics of institutions. He has consulted in public sector management issues both in New Zealand and overseas, and is also involved in a range of regulatory policy issues, including Commerce Act proceedings. He has been with the Institute since 1997. Prior to that he spent 5 years with the International Monetary Fund in Washington DC, including 3 years in Ukraine as a resident representative responsible for monitoring implementation of the agreed economic policy. He also acted as mediator in the Ukraine/Russia debt restructuring talks and assisted the government in

initiating public sector management reforms. Prior to his work with the IMF, Mr Sundakov worked for the New Zealand Treasury where, among other responsibilities, he was closely involved with the design and implementation of labour market reforms.

Kerrin M. Vautier

Kerrin M Vautier CMG is a consultant research economist specialising in competition policy and law. She is also a senior part-time lecturer in the Department of Commercial Law at the University of Auckland; a company director; Chair of the New Zealand Committee of PECC; a trustee of New Zealand's Asia 2000 Foundation; Advisory Board member of the Competition Law and Policy Institute of New Zealand (Inc.); former member of the Commerce Commission; former Chair of the NZ Institute of Economic Research (Inc.); and a past President of the NZ Association of Economists (Inc.). Recently published by Edward Elgar was Kerrin's second co-authored book with Professor Peter Lloyd: *Promoting Competition in Global Markets – A Multi-National Approach* (1999). Kerrin has also been convening the Competition Principles Project for PECC's Trade Policy Forum.

Acknowledgements

The chapters in this book are derived from invited presentations to the 34th University of Otago Foreign Policy School of which I was the Director and, as such, my indebtedness extends far and deep, to all of those who made the School possible and such a success. First, I am indebted to the distinguished authors themselves, of course, whose contributions are only partially captured in this book. Their questions and answers, their interaction with attendees at the School and their enthusiastic participation in the School do not show up here but were critical to its success and much appreciated by an anxious Director! Second, I am grateful to those people from all over New Zealand (and Australia, in fact) – academics, public servants, business people, diplomats, politicians, students, private citizens and others – who made the time and undertook the effort to spend a winter weekend in Dunedin at the School. Its intimate nature and the interaction amongst all these perspectives are what make the School unique in the New Zealand public affairs calendar and such a useful and special event.

Third, such an impressive line-up of contributors does not come together without a great deal of financial support and administrative effort. On the first of these I am extremely grateful to a number of financial supporters, some of whom have been great friends to the School over a number of years. I would like to thank the Australian High Commission, the British Council and British High Commission, the Canadian High Commission and the Association of Canadian Studies of Australia and New Zealand, the NZ Ministry of Foreign Affairs and Trade, the Dunedin South Rotary Club, Telecom NZ, the NZ Treasury and the NZ Association of Economists, the United States Information Service (USIS), the Division of Humanities at the University of Otago and Vincent George House of Travel, Dunedin. Two individuals particularly deserve special mention here: Lesley Haines of the NZ Treasury and Caryl Kirwan of the USIS. Both were wonderful to deal with and contributed to the success of the School in many ways.

As far as administrative effort is concerned, I have had tremendous support through the past year from the Academic Committee of the School: John Dawson, Bill Harris, Richard Jackson, Louis Leland, Robert Patman, Elena Poletti, Rob Rabel, Giora Shapira and Antony Wood. Their specific inputs are too numerous to mention – from planning the conference to stuffing envelopes to chairing sessions. The contributions of other session chairs are also appreciated: Professors Dorian Owen and Bob Catley and Sir Frank Holmes. One person who deserves repeated and special thanks is Pam Quin, nominally the School Coordinator but in practice the coordinator, organiser, Treasurer, administrator, secretary, liaison officer, and general keystone of the whole School. Wonderfully efficient, unwaveringly cheerful and encouraging, Pam made the running of the School a great deal smoother than it would otherwise have been and I owe her a tremendous debt of gratitude.

In putting the book together I have been greatly assisted by Dymphna Evans and her wonderful colleagues at Edward Elgar, Lou Leland and Nigel Zega. Finally I must thank the Economics Department at Otago for bearing some of the brunt of the time I have devoted to running this School and my wonderful family for bearing most of it! The impact this had on them became clear when James, aged eight, ran a small piece in his school newspaper on the problems I faced in organising the Conference. He made up a slogan: 'Economics: travelling everywhere, effecting everyone – including you!' and while I'm not so pleased with the grammar, I am very thankful for the great tolerance of my absences shown by James, his brother Emmett and his mother Debbie.

Martin Richardson

1. Globalisation and International Trade Liberalisation

Martin Richardson

APEC, GATT, MERCOSUR, NAFTA, PECC, the IMF, the OECD, the WTO, TRIPs and TRIMs. These and many other abbreviations and acronyms abound in modern current affairs discussion (and in the pages that follow!) and it would be surprising to find a reasonably-informed citizen of an OECD country who was not familiar with at least half of them. All of these are derived from the international institutions that govern and regulate economic relations amongst countries and it is a sign of our increased international interdependence (or, at least, of the increased attention paid to it) that these terms are so familiar. With New Zealand in the chair of APEC in 1999 and with a New Zealander – Mike Moore, a contributor to this volume – elected as Director General of the WTO in 1999, one might expect these abbreviations to be particularly familiar to New Zealanders. Appropriately, then, the theme of the 34th University of Otago Foreign Policy School, a residential conference held in Dunedin, New Zealand in July 1999, was *The Global Economy: Continuity and Change* and the School was designed to investigate the mechanics – and some of the consequences – of international interdependence. The chapters in this volume are based on invited presentations to that School.

The Secretary-General of the Commonwealth and NZ's Minister of Foreign Affairs and Trade through the 1990s, the Rt. Hon. Don McKinnon, raises (Chapter 2) two themes that occur throughout this volume. The first is that increased international integration has its base in trade. While McKinnon notes that interdependence has gone far beyond merchandise trade and that internationalisation reaches into most areas of human endeavour, it is nevertheless true that trade is the basis for much of it and one of the themes pursued in this volume is the difficulties and challenges surrounding international agreement on trade and trade-related issues. The second theme that is raised in McKinnon's chapter and that recurs throughout the book is globalisation and people. McKinnon stresses that international integration is not driven simply by what might be called supply-side factors – the

1

business strategies of multinational firms and mercantilist governments – but also by the demand side: consumers who want to travel, to have a wider choice of options, to shop on the Internet. On the other hand, a lot of grievances have been laid at the door of international integration and other chapters in this volume return to the question of how increased international interdependence may have negative consequences for some.

This interdependence has been termed 'globalisation' and, although this was a word deliberately avoided in constructing the conference, it nevertheless comes up frequently in what follows (and its ubiquity was recognised in titling this volume). The term was originally avoided so it would not have to be defined – as pornography was to US Supreme Court Justice Potter Stewart (*Jacobellis v. Ohio*, 378 U.S. 184 (1964)), so globalisation is to many others: we may not be able to define it but we know it when we see it.

Or do we? Doug Irwin, in Chapter 3, co-authored with Michael Bordo and Barry Eichengreen, notes that recently there has been some questioning of the extent to which globalisation today is really different to globalisation a century ago. So the US exports to GDP ratio in the late nineteenth century was around seven per cent and is around eight per cent today (and other countries show similarly undramatic changes); net capital outflows from Great Britain a century ago were higher as a percentage of GDP than today. Irwin *et al.* argue, however, that behind these aggregate figures lie strikingly different worlds, particularly in the composition of trade, its importance in particular sectors and in the importance of multinational corporations in facilitating trade. They suggest a number of reasons for greater commercial integration today than a hundred years ago and also argue that financial integration is much deeper today (largely for reasons of improved information flows.)

One aspect of greater international integration that is frequently stressed is that it constrains the actions of sovereign national governments. So fiscal restraint is imposed by the discipline of international financial markets, for instance, or labour standards are whittled away by a 'race to the bottom' of competing national jurisdictions. John Helliwell summarises a lot of recent research (his own and others') into the extent to which national borders do or do not matter and so the extent to which national policies are proscribed by a global environment (Chapter 4). Canadian evidence suggests that even when trade barriers are removed and distance and size are allowed for, trade between regions within countries is substantially larger than between countries. This suggests that borders are important: economic agents are more likely to deal with their compatriots, *ceteris paribus*, than with foreigners. Is this a bad thing – resisting globalisation – or a good thing? Helliwell goes on to ask why it might occur and looks at a number of possible explanations: social capital, democratic institutions, education and other factors that contribute to cohesion and growth. His conclusion is that it is not a bad thing but rather that it is evidence of the limits to global integration and thus to restrictions on the importance of domestic policies.

Those limits may only be temporary if Allan Mendelowitz' view of the world economy is accurate. He suggests that recent and ongoing changes in communications technology and the increasing spread of the Internet will change, fundamentally and irreversibly, many aspects of economic and social life. As more consumers get networked so more firms will be drawn to e-commerce and existing modes of commerce will disappear. In Mendelowitz' view this change is in every way as fundamental as was the Industrial Revolution and it renders economic geography much less significant than it has been in the past: producers need not locate near their consumers as every point in cyberspace is as close as every other point. So consumer information is improved, arbitrage can be immediate and frictionless markets finally move from the economics textbook to the real world.

The significance of international trade has long been greatest in small countries and its importance can only increase if Mendelowitz is correct. Rod Deane, chairman of NZ's largest company, Telecom NZ, considers the role of internationalisation in NZ's future (Chapter 6). He, too, sees it as inevitable and discusses earlier episodes in NZ's history in which governments' attempts to resist international pressures were costly and, eventually, futile. He argues that the discipline imposed on governments by the judgements of international capital markets is, on balance, desirable. He provides Telecom as a case study of a NZ company that not only faces competition from abroad but also competes in international markets, accesses global financial markets, adopts international technology and so on.

The next five contributions to the volume focus directly on trade and trade-related issues. However, Kerrin Vautier (Chapter 7) would rightly take issue with that characterisation: she considers multinational approaches to the design of competition policies and many economists increasingly think of trade policy as a subset of competition policy so describing the latter as a trade-related issue reverses the relative importance of the two. While the 'meta-objectives' of the two kinds of policy are the same, in practice they can differ significantly. Vautier describes and contrasts the various approaches that have been taken to competition policy from bilateral to regional to multilateral levels and discusses the treatment of competition policy in APEC. She outlines the PECC Competition Principles and looks at their relevance to the WTO Working Group on trade and competition policies.

One of the undisputed achievements of post-war multilateralism has been a great reduction in tariff barriers to international trade, particularly on industrial goods. This has raised the relative significance (and attraction) of non-tariff barriers to trade and it has also brought other policy areas into the negotiation forum. To achieve a world record in mixing metaphors (three in four words), this opens a whole new Pandora's kettle of worms. David Robertson examines these 'link issues' in Chapter 8 noting that they bring a new complexity to trade negotiations. With tariff reductions there is a (generally) accepted common goal of mutual liberalisation whereas there is no presumption that different countries will concur on an appropriate endpoint on environmental issues, labour standards, attitudes towards protection of intellectual property and so on. This makes log-rolling inevitable if progress is to be made on these sorts of issues; alternatively, they might simply fall into the 'too-hard' basket and be left off the agenda of future rounds. Robertson notes the role of non-governmental organisations in bringing these issues to the fore and notes, too, that while one might interpret this as greater 'democracy' in the international arena, one might also interpret it as exactly the opposite: the dictation of the agenda by non-elected and possibly non-representative groups and individuals. If nothing else, he suggests, link issues will shape future multilateral trade negotiations for good or bad through the irreversible introduction of private interest groups into the multilateral forum. Events in Seattle in December 1999 bear this out.

Another phenomenon that is likely to be of more significance in current and future multilateral rounds than in the past is the increased importance of regional and bilateral trading arrangements (which we might loosely call minilateralism). Tim Groser (Chapter 9) discusses the relationship between minilateralism and multilateralism. He notes that the general consensus ten years ago was that minilateralism threatened the multilateral GATT system as it was perceived as a substitute, an alternative means to liberalisation. He suggests that the experience of the last decade or so, however, has not borne this pessimism out. On the contrary, the so-called 'second wave' of regionalism has flourished as the GATT system has expanded and made considerable achievements, both actual as in the Uruguay Round and potential as in the Millennium Round discussed in Seattle in December 1999. Indeed, there is growing empirical evidence that many regional deals (Europe aside) have done little to enhance intra-bloc trade as opposed to increasing trade propensities generally (see Soloaga and Winters (1999)). Groser argues that a general perspective on regionalism and multilateralism is infeasible, however, as the potential for the former to undermine the latter is still there. What is critical is the nature of the regional agreement and whether it stems from a 'fortress' mentality.

Chapter 10 by Mike Moore looks more directly at multilateralism and the WTO as an organisation. Recognising that international interdependence goes well beyond trade alone, trade is nevertheless a 'key element in sustaining and spreading the benefits' of this interdependence, Moore argues, so the prognosis for the WTO, a critical medium for conveying trade liberalisation, is an important one. He sees a bright if uncertain future and considers it likely that the major issues to be faced are issues that have not even been thought of yet. The importance of an institution like the WTO, then, would lie largely in providing a forum and a set of rules and guidelines to which players adhere. Consequently, if the WTO were to lose the respect of its participants, major or minor, a lot of its value would be lost.

Chapter 11, the final directly trade-related chapter in this volume, by Patrick Lane, pursues this latter point directly and looks at the dispute settlement mechanism of the WTO. Often hailed as one of the most significant achievements of the Uruguay Round, the dispute settlement mechanism is really the cornerstone of the whole multilateral apparatus: without it (or if it is ignored) there is nothing to discipline governments determined to violate their undertakings or, just as significantly, to convince others that they will not do so. Lane discusses the evolution of the dispute-settlement mechanism and the stresses it is – and has been – under. He concludes that continued testing of it would likely undermine the WTO system (as ultimately the 'teeth' of the mechanism are the same as under the GATT: the right of the aggrieved to respond to protectionism with protectionism, albeit sanctioned by the WTO). It is only by engendering some faith in the system (and so going to sanctions less frequently) that this cornerstone of the multilateral system will survive.

Much of the focus on international institutions in this volume is on the institutions of trade. No less significant in recent years – particularly through recent crises in Russia, Brazil and Asia – have been the institutions of international finance, particularly the IMF. In Chapter 12 Alex Sundakov looks at the various roles that have been taken on by the IMF and World Bank, in particular, and assesses their future after the turmoil of the late 1990s. While the funds of the IMF are quite limited, Sundakov stresses its importance in catalysing private (and other) lending but suggests that its role in economic surveillance of countries is much less important than it once was. Further, the leverage over domestic policies that the IMF obtains by being a financier can exacerbate a short term focus in policy-makers, Sundakov argues, and he suggests that there is little evidence that these institutions have been particularly effective in financing 'good' policies. Nevertheless he concludes that they may still be valuable, if only in disseminating the so-called 'Washington consensus' on what constitutes good economic management.

Such dissemination would probably not constitute positive value-added for our final two contributors, both of whom are rather sceptical about the values of internationalisation. Indeed, in Chapter 13 Jane Kelsey suggests that the 'consensus' between the IMF and the World Bank on the advisability of the 'Washington consensus' is itself fractured. Kelsey argues that the economic liberalisation reforms of recent decades in many countries, perhaps most notably in New Zealand, have not 'worked' and that there is a growing mobilisation of people and communities, both internally and internationally, in opposition to such reforms. She refers to Karl Polanyi's (1957) analysis of globalisation and liberalisation in the first half of the twentieth century and so we return to our starting point in this volume, albeit with a rather different perspective than that of Irwin *et al.* Polanyi suggested that the novelty of economics in the late nineteenth/ early twentieth centuries was in seeing economic activity – conducted in efficient and impersonal markets – as isolated from other social and political spheres (whereas he saw it as 'normally' a *function* of the social order, an interesting contrast to the Marxist perspective that social relations are epiphenomena of economic relations). This led to a backlash, according to Polanyi, and an eventual breakdown of the 'self-regulation of the market'. Kelsey suggests that this scenario is being played out once more, both on the international stage and within New Zealand, as globalisation and economic liberalism lead to unacceptable social costs and losses of sovereignty at various levels.

The final contributor in this volume is Tim Hazledine who provides in Chapter 14 a personal overview of some of the other chapters. He echoes the themes of Jane Kelsey and takes up particularly the issue of social capital and liberalisation raised by John Helliwell. Hazledine suggests that economic reforms since 1984 in New Zealand have destroyed social capital, trust and informal institutions and that this might explain, at least in part, the disappointing subsequent performance of the NZ economy. He raises the possibility of a small tariff to put 'sand in the wheels' of increased integration (although it is interesting to note that NZ has relatively low levels of trade *vis-à-vis* similar countries and, from Hazledine's perspective, this would be considered a good thing).[1] He finishes on a summary note that seems very appropriate to this volume: there is more to the notion of globalisation – both in terms of meaning and desirability – than might be thought and dialogue and debate on policy options and goals is valuable; indeed, it is essential. The chapters in this volume all make valuable contributions to that debate.

NOTES

[1] Hazledine notes that modern production processes may involve nationals of many countries and may even involve multiple trans-shipments across countries (an observation which has

caused some concern through the ages: witness Sir Thomas Smith's complaint in 1581 that foreigners, 'make of our own commodities and send it us again, whereby they set their people awork and do exhaust much treasure out of the realm' (Irwin, 1996, p.28)).

REFERENCES

Irwin, D. (1996), *Against the Tide: an Intellectual History of Free Trade*, Princeton NJ: Princeton University Press.
Soloaga, I., and L.A. Winters (1999), 'Regionalism in the Nineties: what effect on trade?', Policy Research Working Paper #2156, The World Bank, Washington DC.

2.   The Global Economy: Continuity and Change

Don McKinnon

'The end of geography.' 'The borderless world.' These are two of the more provocative phrases used to describe the process of globalisation which underpins the world economy. They are phrases upon which I want to hang three key messages. First, that the forces of international integration are profoundly shaping the structures of the world. Second, that these forces present countries both with opportunities and challenges. And third, that the challenges are real, but not as malign as some suggest.

INTERNATIONAL INTEGRATION

Let me at the outset acknowledge that the pace of change, and its all-encompassing breadth, is a source of fear for some and unsettling for many. Even the most technologically adept of us feel the pressure to keep up. And as individuals grapple with globalisation, so governments are often portrayed as heartless, or ideologically driven, or both. It will not surprise you to learn that I reject these charges: in my experience, those involved in public policy, be they elected or appointed, are driven by a strong sense of national good.

Policymakers recognise that not all of us are well-equipped to cope with the pressures of adjustment. We know the need to carry the people in any debate that affects their future. We understand the sentiment whereby people want the benefits of globalisation, like cheaper imported cars, but are reluctant to pay the costs, like the closure of car assembly plants. But the role of government is clear. It is to mediate between those who want to move ahead faster and those who want to slow the process down, to balance the economic imperatives and the social, and to reconcile short-term pragmatism with long-term vision. I cannot deny that we sometimes get the mix wrong, but I dismiss any suggestion that our motives are any but the right ones.

In the fifty years or so preceding the first world war, international economic integration – or globalisation – rose dramatically on the back of falling transport costs and flows of migration and capital to new lands such as the Americas and Australia. Today integration is still being propelled by economic factors, but also by the revolution in information technology. This difference is important. The globalisation we are experiencing in 1999 is impacting on individuals in a way that is qualitatively different to that experienced 100 years ago. The figures are impressive. In the 45 years since 1950, world merchandise output multiplied over five times but world trade expanded by a multiple of 14. A similar trend is evident for capital flows. Two-way trade in goods and services today totals over NZ$6 trillion a year but gross capital movements may total that much in a week. The financial market shocks of Asia and elsewhere seem not to have shaken these trends.

Technological change is opening the way for new types of economic transactions. Firms are now able to locate different parts of their operation in different countries and to shift capital more quickly and more efficiently.

All this contributes to the changing nature of what might be termed the 'domestic' or 'national' economy, and it highlights the need for a broader definition of trade. The old model of manufacture in one country for sale in another has given way to a process of manufacturing, assembly, finishing and marketing which jumps national boundaries. If you want an example of this kind of economic integration, just consider a woman's fashion garment. Designed in New York. Manufactured in Mexico. Stock-controlled out of Rotterdam. Invoiced from Luxembourg. Merchandised by a mail-order company in the Cayman Islands. Advertised by commercials made in New Zealand. Why? To make the product more profitable.

The breadth of this integration, and the impact on our economic and cultural existence, is considerable. The cars we drive in New Zealand are likely to be the same models as those clogging up the motorways of Bangkok or Bristol. The television programmes we watch, or the music we listen to, will be playing the same day in New Delhi and New York. Kids here will be wearing the same baseball caps, turned around backwards, as those in Dublin or Dubai. The background music I heard recently in three international airports – Athens, Singapore and Johannesburg – was clearly from the same CD. And Pauly Fuemana's hit single 'How Bizarre' is, you'll be interested to know, used as background music in the foyer of the main hotel in Windhoek, Namibia!

Moreover it is no longer sufficient to think only in terms of merchandise trade. The analytical horizon must now be expanded to include services, physical capital investment, technology flows, and human capital. As firms have moved to become international, so national governments have been forced to develop new attitudes to economic management.

GLOBALISATION AND PEOPLE

At the end of the day, the reason governments by and large support globalisation is that it brings rewards to ordinary people. It's not simply an abstract ideology. Rather, it's a logical extension of what many people want in their daily lives: the bringing down of barriers to a better existence. People want to travel the world, cheaply and conveniently. They want freedom of movement across borders. They want a clear run through customs and immigration. They want to be able to live, work or study in the country or countries of their choice. They want to shop on the Internet. They want the right to move their savings offshore if they can't get a good return at home. My point is that people do not want to be hindered by national borders.

GLOBALISATION: OPPORTUNITIES AND CHALLENGES

At the heart of the global economy lies the reality of interdependence. This economic interdependence means that both policymakers and businesses must widen their focus – they cannot dismiss developments that were in past times far distant from national borders. Few countries can afford to ignore the economic reforms currently underway in China, or the emergence of Latin America as a major new region for economic growth, or the burgeoning development of regional trade or economic groupings.

The economic interests of individual nations have become closely knitted together to the point where the traditional distinction between domestic economic policy and foreign economic policy has become less meaningful. Firms still want to remove barriers between states (border restrictions such as tariffs and non-tariff measures). But they are increasingly interested in achieving liberalisation 'behind the border', with a particular focus on issues such as competition policy, investment policy, standards, intellectual property rights, and environmental regulations. This has put pressure on governments to implement 'best practice' policies and regulations.

One challenge facing policy-makers is that market developments can outpace the response of public policy. Perhaps the most graphic example of this in recent times has been the Asian financial shock and the consequential social and political upheavals. The free movement of capital has risks. We know this now better than we did in the mid 1990s. We also know that to mitigate these risks, supervisory controls and responsible market structures have to be in place.

The New Zealand economic reform programme has been described as the most comprehensive undertaken by any OECD country in recent decades. As most elements of the programme have involved the creation of more open and competitive product and factor markets, so they have also involved the increased integration of New Zealand with regional and international markets. This has meant a number of significant policy challenges for the New Zealand Government. Let me list three.

First, to stay ahead of the game. Other economies are reforming and the world's best practice is constantly evolving. If New Zealand is to prosper then we need to keep examining ways to become more efficient and more competitive while at the same time ensuring that the rewards of economic reform are enjoyed by the New Zealand people. Second, we need to influence the international trade and economic reform agenda so that we do not lose sight of our national interests. Third, we need to recognise the growing role of human capital as the source of comparative advantage. As economist Peter Drucker put it, 'the basic economic resource . . . is no longer capital . . . nor labour. It is rather knowledge'. Today often the most telling inequalities are not those between economies but those within economies, and so the low-skilled can sometimes feel marginalised.

These challenges are not unique to New Zealand. We share them with the rest of the international community. Those who benefit from globalisation want openness and liberalisation. Those who feel disempowered by the forces of globalisation, or impoverished by the strains of openness, want to try and put up protective barriers. It is the role of government to try and reconcile these differences in a way that promotes economic prosperity, cultural security, and social coherence. And this is not easy. The reactions from the various stakeholders can be extraordinarily visceral. Unlike some of our critics, however, we are not allowed the luxury of idealism. We must be realistic. Globalisation will not be turned back. People want more, not less, freedom. The forces of integration are remorseless. Our task, then, is to maximise the benefits and minimise the costs.

THESE ARE THE CHALLENGES: WHAT ARE THE OPPORTUNITIES?

Research conducted by the OECD and the World Trade Organisation (WTO), and the experiences of individual states like New Zealand, suggests that trade and investment liberalisation stimulates innovation, encourages efficiency and promotes growth. A recent study by the New Zealand Institute of Economic Research for the Ministry of Foreign Affairs and Trade (NZIER, 1999) shows that tariff reductions since 1987 have delivered real dollars to New Zealanders – more than NZ$1100 per annum, and rising, for a three person household. Over the same period, the policies of openness have seen the creation of 250,000 new jobs and a growth in real wages of eight per cent. It is right to acknowledge the adjustment costs of liberalisation and free trade, but let us also acknowledge the real benefits.

The results of this study are hardly surprising. Globalisation is making it easier to transfer capital and technology across borders, thereby giving lower-wage developing countries access to improved production techniques and so strengthening their economies. Likewise, it is not unreasonable to expect that as productivity rises in developing countries so too will wages or the real exchange rate. As this happens, those countries become significant markets for developed country goods.

To quote the just-retired Director General of the WTO, Renato Ruggiero,

> [M]any developing countries are opening up to the global market. And if we can help them succeed in opening up their economies and provide opportunities for them to market their products abroad, then they, in their turn, will become vigorous, demanding new markets for the exports of industrial and advanced developing economies. That is the way the global market is supposed to operate. (Address to World Economic Forum, Davos Switzerland, 1997.)

In this scenario all countries can win, especially if distortions in the marketplace are removed. But there is a responsibility on the part of the wealthy economies to assist the developing world to ride the wave of globalisation. I say this not only for moral reasons, but also because it is in our national interest to help lift the wealth and support the good governance of poorer countries.

If the benefits are to be reaped then domestic policy settings need to encourage and sustain the development of an efficient and competitive economy. And the international community must work to develop rules that are trade enhancing, which clear away trade distortions and restrictions including those behind national borders, and which are consistent with the imperatives of sustainable development. Only by working together can the international community address these issues of common interest.

In our own case, we have in Foreign Affairs and Trade a group of officials who in their diplomacy and negotiation have achieved some notable trade policy successes for New Zealand – not all of which have been recognised publicly. In the Uruguay Round for example, New Zealand played a key role in helping to bring the negotiations to a satisfactory conclusion. We were able not only successfully to advance our own trade and economic interests in the negotiations and achieve some substantial economic gains for NZ, but were often able to help other parties reach compromise solutions because we could perform an honest broker role and because our objective views were respected.

Foreign Affairs officials also had a major role to play in achieving the recent outcome on spreadable butter in the European Union (EU). It was their victory against the EU in the WTO that made possible a settlement which is worth many millions of dollars to New Zealand.

LOOKING FORWARD

Economic systems are increasingly being organised on a global and electronic basis while political systems remain local and geographical. People want the best of both these worlds. It is dealing with this asymmetry between economic systems and political systems which makes international organisations like the WTO (which now covers services, trade and investment, trade and competition, trade and the environment) and the OECD so important.

International agreements and international rules and disciplines bring with them the benefits of collective action and collective responsibility. While it may be true that they can lead in some cases to some diminution of national autonomy, this is balanced by the overall benefits that a freer and more open global economy is able to bring to the national jurisdictions within it. Every country has lost a degree of autonomy: but this must be balanced by the net gains brought to the populace.

The Uruguay Round was an endorsement by the international community of multilateralism: that the rules-based international trading system, grounded in the principle of non-discrimination, is vital if the world economy is to prosper. The immediate results for New Zealand were considerable. Examples of the achievements are: rules to govern agricultural trade; guaranteed beef access into the United States; more butter and chilled lamb into Europe. Those countries participating in the Uruguay Round also anticipated the road ahead. It was the first multilateral trade negotiation with significant involvement by less developed countries, especially from Asia and Latin America. And it established a framework for further trade and investment liberalisation via a built-in agenda of over 70 review and continuation provisions. On the basis of this agenda, the WTO Ministerial meeting in Seattle in November 1999, just after the APEC meetings, aimed to launch a new round of multilateral trade negotiations. The drive for prosperity through multilateral liberalisation will continue.

I should add that if the global trading environment is to continue along the path towards the elimination of all trade barriers then regional arrangements will also have a key part to play. And in this context, APEC provides a unique opportunity for the countries of the Asia Pacific region to foster their trade and economic links. New Zealand was in the APEC chair in 1999, and the agenda was a large and complex one. Our three themes for the year were: Expanding Opportunities for Business Throughout the Region; Strengthening Markets; and Broadening Support for APEC. These encapsulate what APEC (and globalisation) is all about – the progressive integration of Asia Pacific regional economies through the opening of markets and the creation of new opportunities for trade and investment.

APEC represents 70 per cent of world trade, so liberalisation of trade and investment among the APEC economies will have a major positive impact on the global economy as well. The going might be slow and sometimes the sceptics have much to be pleased about, but any progress in APEC can only benefit New Zealand. The political benefits alone – based around the dialogue between ministers and leaders – are considerable.

A WIDE VIEW: THE WORLD IS NOT JUST ABOUT TRADE

In this address I have focused on the economic impact of globalisation. But I want also to scan the wider horizon. It is important that we do not lose sight of the fact that our interests, and the impacts of globalisation, extend beyond trade and economic matters. We are bound together by much more than the forces of commerce. The most graphic example of this, perhaps, is the global environment. Forest fires in Sumatra, deforestation in the Amazon, the hole in the ozone layer, climate change – developments such as these affect all countries. There is little chance of New Zealand remaining clean and green if the rest of the world is becoming grimy and grey. More seriously, we owe it to ourselves and to future generations not to soil the only nest in which we live.

Another obvious example of the wider impact of globalisation is the international security environment. And I am referring to security in a broad sense. We have too many examples of how New Zealand tourists can be caught up in acts of violence and terrorism. Nuclear proliferation and the development of missile capability give an added drama to skirmishes in Kashmir. And we see nightly on our TV screens the horrors of famine in Africa, or violence in East Timor, or war crimes in Kosovo, or closer to home, deprivation and violence in Bougainville and the Solomon Islands. These events demand not only a moral response but also a recommitment on the part of all countries to the importance of international norms and international law.

Globalisation can also impact on our interests in more subtle ways. The movement of people for business, pleasure and for resettlement is happening on a scale never before seen. Education is becoming a global marketplace, with schools, universities and students increasingly expanding from their places of domicile to set up offshore. CNN, the Internet, e-mail, cheaper international telephone calls, Sky TV, international magazines and newspapers are all helping to shrink the world. These things bring with them advantages, not least a greater understanding and sharing of experiences between peoples. But they also provide significant challenges, both practical (for example, as policy-makers struggle to balance freedom and liberty on the Internet) and philosophical (as countries strive to maintain a distinctive cultural identity in the tidal flow of global culture).

Globalisation means that distance cannot insulate New Zealand from changes happening in other parts of the world. But nor is distance any longer a barrier to us grasping the opportunities or solving the problems. It is for this reason that bilaterally, and in regional bodies like the ASEAN Regional Forum or international bodies like the United Nations, we are working with others to advance our shared interests at the point of intersection between the national and the global.

CONCLUSION

John F. Kennedy once said that, 'our most basic common link is that we all inhabit this planet. We all breathe the same air. We all cherish our children's future. And we are all mortal.' What was true thirty years ago is even more so today. Put another way, as it is in a West African proverb, 'Rain does not fall on one roof alone'. What happens to our neighbours is increasingly of direct relevance to us, and these days what we might call our 'virtual' neighbours may be half a world away.

It has been suggested that we are entering an age where political or security schisms are no longer definable in geographic terms but rather are international phenomena based on increased discord between societies and civilisations. At worst, this could lead not to a global village but rather to a number of global villages each shallowly interconnected but deeply separated by resurgent nationalism and cultural and economic chauvinism. But at best the trend is towards integration and the convergence of government policies for mutual benefit. It is this pursuit of national interest within the context of mutual benefit which explains why a core theme of New Zealand's foreign and trade policy is to engage constructively with the forces of globalisation.

REFERENCES

NZIER (1999), Consumer Benefits from Import Liberalisation: A New Zealand Case Study, Wellington, NZ: Ministry of Foreign Affairs and Trade.

3. Is Globalisation Today Really Different from Globalisation a Hundred Years Ago?[1]

Michael D. Bordo, Barry Eichengreen and Douglas A. Irwin

The effects of globalisation – on the United States and more generally – is the topic of the day. Officials, academics and market participants all sense that the integration of national economies and the development of international markets have gone further than ever before. The idea that globalisation today is unprecedented is implicit in publications like Lawrence, Bressand and Ito (1996) and in much informed policy discussion. But there is also an undercurrent which recognises that there existed a previous period of globally integrated markets. A hundred years ago, it is suggested, prior to the disruptions of two world wars and the collapse of commodity and financial markets in a global depression, markets were every bit as internationalised as today. If we have just gone 'back to the future', simply matching the degree of economic integration experienced a century ago, globalisation may not be so unprecedented after all.

This view has been expressed by several prominent economists. Zevin (1992, p. 43), for example, believes that 'while financial markets have certainly tended toward greater openness since the end of the Second World War, they have reached a degree of integration that is neither dramatic nor unprecedented in the larger historical context of several centuries.' Sachs and Warner (1995, p. 5) argue that, 'the re-emergence of a global, capitalist market economy since 1950, and especially since the mid-1980s, in an important sense re-establishes the global market economy that had existed one hundred years earlier'. Rodrik (1998, p. 2) concludes that, 'in many ways, today's world falls far short of the level of economic integration reached at the height of the gold standard'.

Did globalisation a century ago create the same dilemmas as now? Or were markets not as profoundly integrated a hundred years ago as they are today, freeing governments of some of the dilemmas that now confront them? This chapter pursues the comparison of economic integration now and then for trade as well as finance, primarily for the United States but with reference to the wider world. We establish the outlines of international integration a century ago and analyse the institutional and informational impediments that prevented the late nineteenth century world from achieving the same degree of integration as today. We conclude that our world is different: commercial and financial integration before World War I was more limited.   Globalisation today raises new issues of governance not just because it is conjoined with a political system which gives a louder voice to special interests, but because the economic phenomenon itself is different: integration is deeper and broader than a hundred years ago.

COMMERCIAL INTEGRATION THEN AND NOW

The simplest measure of the importance of trade is its share in gross domestic product (GDP). Table 3.1 shows merchandise trade (average of exports and imports) as a share of GDP for selected countries for selected years over the past century.

Table 3.1. Ratio of Merchandise Trade to GDP (in per cent)

Country	1890	1913	1960	1990
Australia	15.7	21.0	13.0	13.4
Canada	12.8	17.0	14.5	22.0
France	14.2	15.5	9.9	17.1
Germany	15.9	19.9	14.5	24.0
Japan	5.1	12.5	8.8	8.4
Sweden	23.6	21.2	18.8	23.5
United Kingdom	27.3	29.8	15.3	20.6
United States	5.6	6.1	3.4	8.0

Source: Feenstra (1998), p. 33.

These figures have been interpreted either as showing that trade is roughly as important now as it was a century ago, or as showing that trade is more important now than it was a century ago.   For the United States, one interpretation points out that merchandise exports stood at about seven per cent of gross national product (GNP) in the late nineteenth century and are about eight per cent now, hardly a dramatic difference.   An alternative interpretation notes that the trade ratio has been rising since the mid-1980s and now exceeds any level achieved in the late nineteenth or early twentieth century.[2]

In our view, trade today is strikingly more important than a century ago. Three indicators sustain this view: (a) a higher share of trade in tradeables production, (b) the growth of trade in services, and (c) the rise of production and trade by multinational firms.

Trade in Goods

When the broad merchandise trade figures just mentioned are probed further, they reveal that trade is substantially more important now than a century ago for those sectors engaged in trade. The GDP denominator is typically disaggregated into the following sectors: agriculture, forestry, and fisheries; mining; construction; manufacturing; transportation and public utilities; wholesale and retail trade; finance, insurance, and real estate; other services; and government. Only agriculture, mining, and manufacturing are significant producers of goods that enter into standard merchandise trade statistics. For the United States, as in other countries, the sectoral composition of GDP has shifted away from the production of merchandise goods toward the production of services.[3] Broadly speaking, the share of tradeable goods in US national income has been sliced in half over the past century. In both 1899–1903 and 1950, agriculture, mining, and manufacturing comprised about 40 per cent of GNP; the comparable figure for 1997 was 20 per cent.[4] While the merchandise trade to GDP ratio a century ago was roughly comparable to what it is today, trade is now much larger as a share of tradeable goods production. In a sense, this means that trade is potentially less important than a century ago because non-traded goods loom larger in national production and consumer demand. (In the next subsection, however, we discuss how previously non-traded services have become increasingly tradeable and subject to international competition.) At the same time, however, the relatively constant share of merchandise trade to GDP masks the increasing importance of trade within the traded-goods sector.

Figure 3.1 illustrates the dramatic difference between the merchandise trade to GDP ratio and merchandise trade to merchandise output (value added) ratio for the United States. The modest change in the ratio of exports to GDP misses the post-war surge in merchandise exports as a share of merchandise production. While the ratio of exports to tradeables production was never much more than 20 per cent in the late nineteenth century, it is now more than 40 per cent.

Figure 3.1. Trade in the US Economy

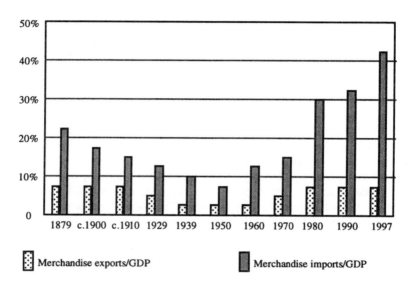

Table 3.2 shows that this same trend is evident in many, but not all, other OECD countries as well.[5] On the basis of the sheer volume of goods leaving and entering the country, therefore, the United States engages in significantly more international trade today. Before accepting these figures as demonstrating the greater importance of trade today, however, one caveat should be noted: the volume of goods exchanged between different markets may not reflect the degree of market integration. O'Rourke and Williamson (1999) suggest that, 'it is the cost of moving goods between markets that counts' and that therefore price differentials between markets should be examined.[6] Doing this for the late nineteenth century Atlantic economy, they find dramatic convergence in the prices of many commodities. In 1870, for example, the Liverpool price of wheat exceeded that in Chicago by about 60 per cent; by about 1912, that Liverpool/Chicago price gap had fallen to about 15 per cent. Today, basic agricultural commodities and raw materials such as wheat and petroleum are exchanged on organised global markets and these well-integrated international markets establish a base reference price (often in US dollars) for such commodities. The question is not whether there has been price convergence in recent years, but how closely the strictest test of market integration, namely the law of one price, holds.[7]

Table 3.2. Ratio of Merchandise Trade to Merchandise Value Added (in per cent)

Country	1890	1913	1960	1990
Australia	27.2	35.6	24.4	38.7
Canada	29.7	39.4	37.6	69.8
France	18.5	23.3	16.8	53.5
Germany	22.7	29.2	24.6	57.8
Japan	10.2	23.9	15.3	18.9
Sweden	42.5	37.5	39.7	73.1
United Kingdom	61.5	76.3	33.8	62.8
United States	14.3	13.2	9.6	35.8

Source: Feenstra (1998), p. 35.

Trade in Services

The previous section noted that the US economy has shifted toward producing more services. Once considered largely non-tradeable, services have of course become an increasingly important component of US trade. The value of US service exports (excluded from the merchandise trade figures considered above) now amount to about 40 per cent of the value of merchandise exports. The addition of trade in services raises our view of the economic importance of trade: in 1997, the broader figure of exports of goods and services as a percentage of GDP stood at 11.9 per cent, of which merchandise exports were 8.5 per cent and service exports were 3.4 per cent. In the 1960s, by contrast, service exports were just one per cent of GNP and amounted to about 30 per cent of merchandise exports.

There are no comparable figures for trade in services for the pre-World War I period, in part because such trade was significantly smaller than today. In 1900, shipping and tourism receipts amounted to just three per cent of US merchandise exports, according to balance of payments data from Simon (1960, pp. 704-5), compared to about 16 per cent of merchandise exports today. Shipping and tourism remain the two largest categories of US service exports, accounting for over 40 per cent of such exports. Data on other service exports are not readily available for the pre-1913 period, but those exports were probably minuscule. Services such as royalties and fees (receipts from intellectual property rights, such as trademarks, patents, and copyrights), education, finance, insurance, telecommunications, and business, professional, and technical services are the most rapidly growing category of US service exports, but they had no substantial counterpart a century ago.

We can also trace the rise of service exports as a share of services production, as we did in the case of tradeable merchandise. In 1960, the ratio of service exports to services value-added was 1.7 per cent. By 1997, that ratio had risen to 5.1 per cent. While low in comparison to the merchandise 'tradeables' sector, this ratio has been rising rapidly and portends even greater trade in services in the future.

The Role of Multinational Trade and Production

Production and exchange by multinational firms has been a force in global trade since the days of the East India Company. There has been a quantum leap, however, in the importance of multinationals from the pre-World War I era. While there were sizeable capital flows between countries in the pre-1913 world, as we discuss below, most of the flows were portfolio investment and not trade- or production-related direct investments. Multinational enterprises existed in the late nineteenth century, but they were exceptional.[8]   This situation has changed dramatically. The value of direct investments has soared since the early-1980s and is now a quantum leap above that of a century ago. Table 3.3 presents the value of direct investments, both by the United States in other countries and by other countries in the United States, as a share of US GNP. US direct investment abroad was remarkably similar in 1914, 1929, and 1960 at about six per cent of GNP, but since then has jumped by a factor of three. Similarly, foreign direct investment in the United States, although larger in 1914 than in 1929 or 1960, rose dramatically by the mid-1990s.

Table 3.3. US Foreign Direct Investment, Selected Years (as per cent of US GNP)

	US Direct Investment Abroad	Foreign Direct Investment in the US
1914	≈7	≈3-4
1929/30	≈7	≈1
1960	6	1
1996 market value	20	16

Sources: For 1914, Wilkins (1970), p. 201 and Wilkins (1989), p. 699. For 1929/30 and 1960, series U 26-39.   For 1996, Survey of Current Business, July 1998, available at http://www.bea.doc.gov/bea/

Direct investment can, in principle, complement or substitute for trade in goods. Collins, O'Rourke, and Williamson (1997) find that trade and capital flows were rarely substitutes and frequently complements in the late nineteenth century. Goldberg and Klein (1999) reach a similar finding for the present day. One reason is that multinationals are conduits for trade. A sizeable fraction of US trade is intra-firm trade conducted by multinationals. In 1994, about 36 per cent of US exports were intra-multinational transactions (sales to affiliates abroad), as were about 43 per cent of US imports (see Zeile, 1997). As we speculate below, multinational corporations mitigate informational barriers to exchange and thus serve to expand international trade.

Direct investments have increasingly exposed services to international competition. US firms can deliver their services to foreign customers either through cross-border transactions (service exports) or through sales by their foreign affiliates. To the extent that certain services cannot be directly traded across borders, direct investments enable US and foreign service providers to enter into each other's market and add an element of international competition to this 'non-traded' sector. The shift in US direct investments toward services marks another big difference from a century ago. Back then, the bulk of US investment abroad went into the development of natural resources and raw materials in other parts of the world. In 1914, over 40 per cent of US direct investment abroad was in the mining and petroleum sectors, and manufacturing and services (mainly railroads and utilities) each accounted for roughly 20 per cent of US direct investment. Today, about half of US direct investments are in services and another 35 per cent in manufacturing.

Thus, international direct investments serve as a powerful force for integration that was largely absent (or mainly confined to raw materials development) a century ago. Such investments not only facilitate trade but also bring about greater international competition in precisely those sectors whose services are difficult to exchange across borders.

WHY IS COMMERCIAL INTEGRATION GREATER TODAY?

Why is trade relative to the production of merchandise goods so much greater than a century ago? The simple answer is that the barriers that inhibit trade and prevent exchange from taking place are lower today than a century ago. Late nineteenth century integration was propelled by a rapid decline in transportation costs. These costs have remained low, and in the post-war period have been supplemented by policy measures to reduce tariff and non-tariff barriers to trade.

Transport Costs

In the second half of the nineteenth century, transportation costs fell significantly and were a major force for integrating world markets. O'Rourke and Williamson (1994) note that, between 1870 and 1913, the freight rate index on US export routes fell by more than 40 per cent when deflated by the general US price index. A wheat-specific freight index fell over 50 per cent over the same period. An equally large reduction in land transport costs took place due to railroads, which reduced interior-to-seaboard prices as much if not more than overseas routes. These transport cost declines set the stage for the convergence in traded-goods prices discussed above.

Transportation costs have not reversed course but have continued to fall. There is some dispute, however, about whether the postwar period has seen a reduction in transportation costs comparable to that a century ago. Lundgren (1996, p. 7) maintains that the post-war period has seen a sharp reduction in shipping costs. 'During the last 30 years merchant shipping has actually undergone a revolution comparable to what happened in the late nineteenth century.' Containerisation, bulk shipping, and other innovations have cut loading times and resulted in efficiencies that have propelled these cost reductions. Hummels (1999) disputes this conclusion. He finds that there has been little decline in shipping costs (perhaps even an increase), certainly not enough to have played a major role in accelerating international trade.

Air transport, however, has been displacing shipping as the means of moving goods in international trade. The share of US imports that arrives via air has risen from 8.8 per cent in 1974 to 19.0 per cent in 1996. Similarly, nearly a third of US exports (including aircraft) leave via air. Shipping via air has been largely a post-war phenomenon and has seen substantial cost reductions. Hummels (1999) finds that air cargo rates on long distant routes have declined by about 15–20 per cent (when deflated by US import price index) over the 1975–93 period.

Even if transport costs have not fallen as dramatically as they did in the late nineteenth century, they have remained low. In addition, technological changes have expanded the array of delivery mechanisms and cut the time to delivery in ways that have brought an ever-increasing variety of goods (cut flowers from Central America, lobsters from Maine) into world commerce.

Trade Barriers

Evidence on tariff barriers indicates that these have been dramatically reduced. Table 3.4 presents measures of average tariffs on manufactured goods for selected countries and years over the past century. Between 1875 and 1913, average tariffs crept up in most European countries, with the notable exception of that bastion of free trade, Great Britain. Germany imposed the 1879 'Bismark' tariff on manufactured goods, and such tariffs ratcheted up elsewhere as well. Tariffs on agricultural goods also rose across Europe as a result of the railroad-induced 'great grain invasion' of the 1870s. By the outbreak of World War I, average tariffs were in the 20 per cent range across many countries. As O'Rourke and Williamson (1999, p.29) note, '*all* the commodity market integration in the Atlantic economy after the 1860s was due to the fall in transport costs between markets, and *none* was due to more liberal trade policy'.

Table 3.4. Average Tariffs on Imported Manufactured Goods

	1875	1913	1931	1950	Pre-Uruguay Round	Post-Uruguay Round
France	12-15	20	30	18	–	–
Germany	4-6	17	21	26	–	–
Italy	8-10	18	46	25	–	–
United Kingdom	0	0	n.a.	23	–	–
European Union	–	–	–	–	5.7	3.6
Canada	n.a.	26	n.a.		9.0	4.8
United States	40-50	44	48	14	4.6	3.0

Source: Bairoch (1993), and Schott (1994) for last two columns.

In 1950 these barriers were still in the 20 per cent range, but had been supplemented by quantitative restrictions, exchange controls, and currency restrictions that had their origin in the interwar period. Multilateral trade negotiations, conducted under the auspices of the General Agreement on Tariffs and Trade (GATT), helped to reduce average tariffs to under 5 per cent. Import quotas and exchange controls that persisted into the early post-war period were also phased out or eliminated. Furthermore, whole geographic areas have become, if not pure free-trade zones, at least zero tariff areas, such as Europe with the European Union (EU) and North America with the North American Free Trade Agreement (NAFTA).

As is well known, however, even as tariffs have fallen, other measures have been adopted to protect domestic producers from import competition.

Antidumping actions, voluntary restraint agreements, and other forms of protectionism persist and are not adequately reflected in these tariff measures. These caveats prevent us from making definitive statements about the comparability of trade barriers now and a century ago. But they do not prevent us from suggesting that, broadly speaking, trade barriers have fallen substantially in the post-war period and today are quite likely lower than a century ago.

Informational Barriers to Exchange

In addition to transportation costs and trade barriers, informational barriers to exchange can limit the extent of market integration. Consumers are likely to have better information about the attributes of goods produced locally, while producers are likely to have better information about local tastes and demands. A century ago, before the age of mass communications, the difficulty of transmitting and receiving information about these attributes was plausibly greater than today.

To an extent, of course, these informational barriers to exchange could be overcome through network mechanisms. The high level of migration, including reverse and seasonal migration, that characterised the late nineteenth century was an important channel for the flow of such information. Italian workers who travelled to the New World for a few years, or even just for the planting and harvest seasons, before returning to their home town in Italy formed an obvious network for information about supplies and demands in the Americas.[9] Multinational corporations similarly established (in their case, proprietary) networks for conveying such information across borders.[10] But the presence of these mitigating factors does not change the conclusion that information relevant to product-market outcomes was more difficult to transmit and receive from abroad prior to 1913.

Since multinationals were not as prevalent a century ago, their recent rise has acted to overcome reputational and informational barriers to trade. This points up an important contrast with a century ago. As alluded to in our introduction, recent observers have recalled the late nineteenth century as being a time of common values and institutions. Colonialisation forced other countries in the world to adopt legal systems and commercial codes that, in some sense, provided for harmonised economic policies across countries; indeed Rauch (1999), among others, has found that countries with colonial ties continue to trade unusually highly with one another long after independence has been established. As former colonies have regained their sovereignty, they have chosen to implement their own systems, which may account for their attenuated commercial links to developed countries.

The globalisation of production has not forced such a convergence of domestic policies and institutions, but it has promoted greater integration. Could this intimacy potentially breed friction and conflict rather than accord and harmony?

CONTAINING TRADE TENSIONS

As trade expanded in the years leading up to World War I, aggrieved interests sought redress. Jeffrey Williamson (1998) argues that this 'globalisation backlash' manifested itself in increased political pressure to raise trade barriers, halt immigration, and stifle capital flows. Could the current wave of globalisation generate similar pressures to retreat from the global economy? Or do we now have institutional safeguards that can relieve such anti-globalisation pressures and preserve political support for an open world economy?

While the extent of the globalisation backlash prior to 1913 should not be exaggerated, there was continual pressure in the United States to restrict immigration starting in the 1880s, and protectionist pressure throughout the industrialising world, especially in the period 1880–1895. By no stretch of the imagination was the open international system on the verge of collapsing upon itself by 1914, but pressure to restrict trade and immigration was more intense than today. We suggest three reasons why trade tensions were greater despite the fact that the extent of product-market integration was, if anything, less.

Macroeconomic Performance

First, macroeconomic performance – both growth and stability – is important to maintaining support for an open trade regime, and cyclical instability was, by most measures, more of a problem. Up to the outbreak of World War I, protectionist pressures were most pronounced during the 'Great Depression' of the 1870s when cheap grain from the United States and Russia caused distress among European farmers and slower growth prompted manufacturers (even in Britain) to demand higher tariffs. This was well before greater integration that had emerged by the end of the century. Indeed, in the 15 years or so preceding the outbreak of war, there was little resurgence of protectionism. One factor that contributed to this outcome was the worldwide economic boom from the mid-1890s up to World War I.

For the developed economies in general, the post-war period has been one of economic expansion and cyclical stability. Such an environment is conducive to efforts at trade liberalisation. The lesson is trite but true: while global integration undoubtedly creates sectoral pressures, those pressures are muted in an environment of steady economic growth and low unemployment.

Social Insurance

Second, there were few forms of social insurance in place a century ago to mitigate the effects of surges in import competition.   Unemployment insurance and adjustment assistance did not exist.   Workers seeking compensation from foreign competition thus had no choice but to lobby Congress for higher tariffs.   Congress was sympathetic to such pleas, although it could not always accommodate them quickly due to the political coordination costs of passing tariff legislation.

To be sure, limited insurance mechanisms did exist. As Feldman (1993) notes, many late nineteenth century US tariffs (particularly for iron and steel products and textiles and apparel) were set higher than necessary to ensure effective autarky (a phenomenon known as 'putting water in the tariff'). Redundant tariffs arise not for insurance reasons in Feldman's particular framework, but the insurance motive clearly could play a role in creating demands for high tariffs in the absence of other institutional mechanisms to provide temporary protection in the face of negative import price shocks.

Moreover, the particular tariff form adopted, namely specific duties, provided another form of insurance. The *ad valorem* equivalent of specific duties – a particular dollar amount charged per imported quantity – is inversely related to the price of imports.   Thus, if import prices fell as a result of some technological innovation (railroads bringing new sources of supply into the market, for example) or other development, the *ad valorem* tariff equivalent would automatically rise without requiring government action.   This insured domestic producers and the political system against pressure for higher tariffs in the face of trade-related distress.

When the United States shifted away from this system, an even more extensive insurance mechanism was created to provide a safety valve for distressed industries. When protectionist elements in the Republican Party sought to halt the Geneva GATT negotiations in early 1947, the Truman administration issued an executive order requiring an escape clause to be included in all future trade agreements. It allowed the United States to withdraw or modify tariff concessions 'if, as a result of unforeseen developments and of the concession granted by the United States on any article in the trade agreement, such article is being imported in such increased quantities and under such conditions as to cause, or threaten, serious injury to domestic producers of like or similar product. . .'

The executive order placated Congressional concerns and allowed the United States to complete the GATT negotiations. And at US insistence, the escape clause was included as Article XIX of the GATT. While the leading interpretation of the escape clause is that it is a necessary political compromise to obtain greater support for trade agreements, others have thought that these are merely protectionist 'loopholes.'[11]

Clearly, the challenge for policy-makers operating in an era of greater economic integration is one of balance – making safeguards available, but without compromising open markets. As Lawrence and Litan (1986, p. 79) point out, 'if the standards for obtaining import-related remedies are too restrictive, the escape clause mechanism cannot serve as an effective shock absorber for protectionist pressures. On the other hand, if the eligibility criteria are too weak, any domestic industry that faces import competition may become eligible for temporary protection.' They called for adjusting the escape clause and trade adjustment assistance policies as a result of the trade frictions of the early 1980s, and their proposals may need to be dusted off in the future if globalisation leads to a resurgence of such pressures.

The Growth of Countervailing Interests

Finally, while increased integration can threaten the economic interests of certain aggrieved groups, it also creates countervailing groups whose interests are enhanced. As noted above, much of the increased trade in recent years has been in intermediate goods. While domestic intermediate goods producers may be harmed by lower import prices, the competitive position of other domestic producers may depend upon those lower prices. In recent years, steel-using firms have successfully fought off efforts by the integrated steel producers to obtain extended protection, and semiconductor-using firms have successfully fought off efforts by semiconductor producers to obtain protection. Direct investments and international diversification by domestic producers in such sectors as automobiles has also muted national pressures for protection against foreign competition.

Given the greater trade integration that exists today compared to a century ago, one might have anticipated that much stronger protectionist pressures would be evident. That they are not suggests that stable macroeconomic management, the existence of escape clauses, and the rise of pro-trade economic interests have been capable of sustaining political support for an open trading system.

FINANCIAL INTEGRATION THEN AND NOW

The typical 'back to the future' story about capital markets before 1913 emphasises the magnitude of net flows from the core countries of Western

Europe to peripheral Europe and the overseas regions of recent European settlement. These flows were large relative to GDP – indeed, larger than today – suggesting high levels of financial integration a hundred years ago. At the same time, the range of sectors and activities to which this foreign investment was directed was narrower than today. For investment as for trade, the volume was large but the range of affected activities was small.

The net capital outflow ranged as high as 9 per cent of GDP on an annual average basis for Britain and scaled comparable peaks, at least briefly, in France, Germany and the Netherlands.[12] Current account deficits exceeded 10 per cent of GDP in Australia, Canada and Argentina for significant portions of the three decades preceding 1913 and sometimes exceeded 5 per cent of GDP in Finland, Norway and Sweden. (For comparison, recall that Thailand's 'dangerously large' current account deficit in 1996 was eight per cent of GDP.) Regression-based studies on a larger sample of countries, designed to deal with sample-selection bias, find lower savings-investment correlations before 1945 than today, reinforcing the conclusion that capital flows were large relative to savings, investment and GNP.[13] Current account surpluses and deficits were also more persistent prior to 1914 than in recent decades.[14]

Fishlow (1985) summarises the conventional wisdom on this subject as follows. In the overseas regions of recent settlement to which the bulk of European lending flowed, external resources were invested in infrastructure projects, which enhanced the borrowing country's capacity to export. Foreign funds were used to construct port facilities, railway networks and other internal improvements'. At the same time, the lending countries (particularly Britain) provided open markets for the raw materials and agricultural commodities produced and exported by these newly settled regions. In this way, foreign borrowing generated a stream of export revenues sufficient to service and repay the borrowed funds.

Upon scrutinising it more closely, one discovers several blemishes on this smoothly-complexioned history. For one thing, infrastructure investment was not always productive, a point that any observer of the Thai economy in the 1990s would be quick to appreciate. For more than a few countries, the story of railway investment in the late-19th century was a story of fraud, bankruptcy and debt default. Nor were railway enterprises and other companies supplying infrastructure services the only borrowers. Governments too had voracious appetites for external finance. A non-negligible share of public spending took the form of subsidies for the construction of railways and infrastructure projects, but governments that borrowed abroad typically did so, as Fishlow emphasises, not to finance public investment but to underwrite public consumption. And financial crises and sharp reversals in the direction of capital flows, culminating in debt default, were anything but rare, as we describe below.

What is clear is that foreign borrowing meant almost exclusively borrowing by railways and borrowing by governments. Consider the composition of pre-1914 portfolio investment by Great Britain, the leading creditor country of the period.[15] Early estimates suggest that fully 40 per cent of British overseas investments in quoted securities were in railways, 30 per cent were in the issues of governments (national, state and municipal), ten per cent were in resource-extracting industries (mainly mining), and five per cent were in public utilities.[16] Note that portfolio investment in commercial, industrial and financial activities is absent from this list. Six out of every seven pounds sterling of portfolio investment was in securities of debtors with relatively tangible, transparent assets (the ability to tax in the case of governments, trunk and branch lines and rolling stock with a well-defined revenue-raising capacity in the case of railways, mineral reserves in the case of mining companies). Davis and Gallman (1999), focusing on the 'nineteenth century emerging markets', found that nine of every ten pounds of British investment in Argentina, Australia, Canada and US between 1865 and 1890 went into railroads and government bonds.

Table 3.5. Bank and Bond Market Lending to Emerging Markets

Functional Sectors	Number of bonds	Value of bonds (US$000m)	Number of loans	Amount of loans (US$000m)
Central Bank	77	18.156	147	24.897
Other Government	368	128.08	294	39.122
Infrastructure Investment	385	67.695	879	110.845
Oil/Coal/Gas	153	28.047	315	56.227
Energy-Utility	107	21.951	233	30.414
Others	125	17.623	331	24.204
Mining	10	0.664	87	10.717
Finance (banks etc.)	1302	161.61	1769	132.049
Manufacturing	415	38.504	946	66.997
Service	241	26.262	867	76.545
TOTAL*	**3183**	**508.593**	**5868**	**572.017**

* Columns may not sum to totals due to rounding.

Source: see text.

Data for portfolio capital flows to emerging markets in the 1990s paint a different picture. We have tabulated these in Table 3.5 by recipient sector for both bank lending and bonds from Capital Data's Bankware and Bondware, respectively. Admittedly, one way of reading these figures is, 'the more things change, the more they remain the same'. But to many readers they will suggest the growing importance of lending to the financial-services sector (banks, etc.), to enterprises producing commercial services, and to manufacturing. The kind of statement made by Madden (1985, p. 73) with reference to the late nineteenth century, that 'British investment in [US] banks . . . and industry was of little importance in this period', would scarcely be made of portfolio investment in emerging markets today.

Less information exists on the volume of short-term capital flows prior to 1914, but everything we know points to a lower level than today, even adjusting for the smaller size of the world economy. Bloomfield's (1963) discussion suggests that short-term flows were significantly smaller than long-term flows, in sharp contrast to today: Bank for International Settlements data on turnover in foreign exchange markets suggest that gross flows are in the range of US$1.25 trillion a day, or more than US$250 trillion a year, much larger than corresponding figures for long-term capital flows.

WHY IS FINANCIAL INTEGRATION GREATER TODAY?

These differences in the scope of market integration are readily understood as consequences of information asymmetries, which were even more pervasive 100 years ago than today.

Any discussion of information flows must start with the communications technology of the day. The transatlantic cable was laid in the 1860s, coming into operation in 1866. Prior to its opening, it could take as long as three weeks for information to travel from New York to London. With the inauguration of the cable, this delay dropped to one day. By 1914 the time for cable transmission was down to less than a minute. Garbade and Silber (1978) compare the London and New York prices of US bonds four months before and four months after the cable and find a significant decline in the mean absolute difference. There is every reason to think that the cable had a comparable impact on other markets.[17]

The radio telephone was the next breakthrough. Like the telegraph, it first linked the national financial centre (London or New York) to the hinterlands and regional exchanges before linking up those centres internationally (linking Europe with North America by 1900).

It should be apparent why this information and communications technology translated into a smaller volume of short-term capital flows. Today currency traders respond almost instantaneously to minute-to-minute changes in currency values. Prior to 1870, when it might take weeks for this information to cross the Atlantic, and even after the advent of the cable and the radio telephone, news arrived at longer intervals.

Long-term lending to manufacturing, commercial and financial concerns was deterred not so much by the limitations of the communications technology as by the difficulty of assembling and evaluating the information to be communicated. Lenders were reluctant to lend because of the difficulty of distinguishing good and bad credit risks. This information asymmetry created adverse selection (where the average credit quality of the pool of borrowers declines with increases in the interest rate) and therefore credit rationing. Overseas investors were further deterred by the difficulty of monitoring and controlling management's actions *ex post* – of detecting malfeasance and rent dissipation and preventing owner-managers whose downside risk was truncated by limited liability from devoting borrowed funds to riskier projects.

Several already-noted characteristics of late nineteenth century international capital markets are explicable in terms of obstacles to information flows. For example, asymmetric information can explain the disproportionate share of railway bonds in foreign investment portfolios. To be sure, information asymmetries were not the only factor contributing to disproportionate importance of railway securities. America's transcontinental railways were built only once, in this period. Private as well as social returns on railway investment were attractive (Fogel (1964)). But the manufacturing, financial and commercial sectors of the economy were growing every bit as fast as transportation, and foreign investment in these sectors was less; information asymmetries explain this fact. It was relatively easy to monitor the actions of a railway company's management: investors could verify how much track had been laid, where it had been laid, and how much traffic it carried more easily than they could verify and evaluate the investment decisions of managers of concerns in these other sectors. These considerations explain the particular preference of British investors for 'coal roads,' that is, railways whose traffic was disproportionately comprised of coal haulage, since this made it relatively straightforward to forecast operating revenues.

Obstacles to the flow of information can also explain the disproportionate importance of debt as opposed to equity in foreign investment portfolios (Baskin, 1988), since debt reduces the risk to investors when imperfect information creates agency problems. The pattern persists today (see, for example, Eichengreen and Mody, 1998), but a century ago it was if anything more pronounced.[18]

Information asymmetries can explain the disproportionate importance of family groups (the foreign branches of the Rothschild and Morgan families, for example) and of the merchant and investment banks that grew out of them, which underwrote foreign bond issues and served as conduits for foreign investment, acting as delegated monitors and emitting signals of borrower credit worthiness. They can explain the well-known 'Kuznets cycle pattern' in which immigration and financial capital tended to flow in the same direction (what Hatton and Williamson (1992) refer to as the tendency for capital to chase after labour), as the migrants provided the European sending countries with valuable information about local conditions. They can explain the 'sovereign credit rating departments' established by intermediaries like Credit Lyonnais (Flandreau, 1998). They can explain the development of investment trusts (the nineteenth century analogue of modern mutual funds), to whom investors delegated information-gathering and analysis functions. They can explain the explosive growth of insurance companies, investments in which were attractive to households partly because they could offer an attractive rate of return as a result of their comparative advantage in gathering information from far-flung regions (Snowden, 1995). They can explain the popularity of specialised publications like *The Investor's Monthly Manual, Burdett's Stock Exchange Official Intelligence, Poor's Manual of Railroads,* and *Herapath's Railway Journal.* They can explain the practice by established railroads of guaranteeing the bonds of feeder lines.

Finally, information asymmetries can explain the surprisingly limited importance of foreign direct investment (FDI) prior to 1913 and the importance of the freestanding company as the vehicle for foreign direct investment. A considerable majority of foreign investment prior to 1913 took the form of portfolio investment, whereas direct investment and portfolio investment are of roughly equal importance today.[19] And whereas nineteenth century FDI was undertaken mainly by freestanding companies (companies incorporated in Britain, France, Belgium and other Western European countries for the sole purpose of investing and doing business in an emerging market), it takes place today through the agency of multinational enterprises that establish foreign branches and foreign subsidiaries.[20] Freestanding companies, in the words of Wilkins (1998, p. 13), 'were structured to solve the problem posed earlier; business abroad was risky; it was hard to obtain adequate and reliable information about firms in distant lands; returns were unpredictable; but there were clearly opportunities abroad; a company organised within the source-of-capital country, with a responsible board of directors, under source-of-capital country law, to mobilise capital (and other assets) and to conduct the business in foreign countries could take advantage of the opportunities, while reducing the transaction costs by providing a familiar conduit'.

In part, these information problems can be understood in terms of sheer physical and cultural distance. The anecdote about the dinner in London at which a British investor, encountering an American guest, inquired whether Cincinnati or Ohio was the larger city may be apocryphal but the story has a point: lack of familiarity with the regions that the railways were penetrating was an impediment to capital flows. Madden (1985, p. 317) notes that while some two-thirds of all American railroad bonds issued publicly between 1860 and 1880 were for what he calls 'developing' and 'underdeveloped' (as opposed to already developed) parts of the country, only one-third of those purchased by British investors were for those regions.[21]

FINANCIAL CRISES

The Victorian age of capital flows to emerging economies, like our era, was marred by banking and currency problems and abrupt reversals of capital flows. The important question is how serious their economic consequences were.

To compare the severity and longevity of crises, we examine changes in the annual rate of growth of real GDP. We calculate the growth rate and assess its behaviour before, during and after crises for 15 'emerging markets' in the period 1880–1914.[22] We then make similar calculations for ten well-known emerging countries (Argentina, Brazil, Chile, Indonesia, Korea, Malaysia, Mexico, Philippines, Singapore and Thailand) that have experienced crises in the past 25 years.

We identify currency and banking crises from a survey of the historical literature.[23] For an episode to qualify as a banking crisis, we must observe either bank runs, bank failures and the suspension of convertibility of deposits into currency (a banking panic), or else significant banking-sector problems (including failures) that are resolved by a fiscally-underwritten bank restructuring.[24] For an episode to qualify as a currency crisis, we must observe a forced change in parity, the abandonment of a pegged exchange rate, or an international rescue. An alternative measure of currency crises that we also use is an index of exchange market pressure (EMP), calculated as a weighted average of the percentage change in the exchange rate with respect to the core country (the UK before 1914, the US thereafter), the change in the short-term interest rate differential with respect to the core country, and the difference of the percentage change in reserves of a given country and the percentage change in reserves of the core country.[25] We count an episode as a currency crisis when it shows up as positive according to either or both of these indicators.

Table 3.6 presents averages for the individual country episodes in the pre-1914 era and the recent period.[26] For each country we calculate the growth rate in the crisis year relative to the five-year-average growth rate preceding the crisis; the growth rate in the crisis year relative to the three-year-average growth rate preceding the crisis; the difference between the crisis-year growth rate and the preceding year's growth rate; the difference between growth the year following the crisis and the crisis-year growth rate; the difference between the three-year-average growth rate following the crisis and the crisis-year growth rate; and finally the difference between the five-year-average growth rate following the crisis and the crisis-year growth rate. Assuming that the economy is at its trend growth rate five years before the crisis, this gives a rough measure of the extent to which growth deviated from trend and then recovered.[27]

Table 3.6. Fluctuations in Growth Around the Time of Crises, 1880–1998

Part A: All crises

	1880–1913 (22)	1973–1998 (30)	Recent (7)
t-5	0.01	-0.03	-0.05
t-3	0.00	-0.03	-0.06
t-1	-0.02	-0.03	-0.06
t+1	0.00	0.02	0.01
t+3	0.01	0.02	0.04
t+5	0.01	0.03	

Part B: Twin crises

	1880–1913 (11)	1973–1998 (14)	Recent (6)
t-5	-0.02	-0.05	-0.05
t-3	-0.02	-0.05	-0.06
t-1	-0.02	-0.05	-0.06
t+1	0.00	0.03	-0.01
t+3	0.01	0.05	0.04
t+5	0.02	0.05	

Part C: Banking crises

	1880–1913 (8)	1973–1998 (12)	Recent (0)
t-5	-0.02	-0.03	
t-3	-0.02	-0.03	
t-1	-0.03	-0.02	
t+1	-0.03	0.02	
t+3	0.00	0.02	
t+5	0.05	0.01	

Part D: Currency crises

	1880–1913 (5)	1973–1998 (4)	Recent (1)
t-5	0.00	-0.02	-0.05
t-3	0.03	-0.01	-0.05
t-1	-0.01	0.00	-0.04
t+1	-0.03	0.01	
t+3	0.02	0.00	
t+5	0.00	0.01	

A key fact emerging from Table 3.6 is that while banking and financial crises with serious recessionary effects are not new phenomena, those output effects were on average somewhat less serious before 1914 compared to today. This holds for banking crises, currency crises and twin crises alike. Thus, while output declined by three per cent relative to trend in the average post-1972 crisis, the comparable number for the pre-1914 period was only two per cent. The contrast is especially sharp for crises with both banking and currency components, which have been exceptionally disruptive since 1972 (when the average drop in output was five per cent) but were less so prior to 1913 (when that drop was 'only' two per cent).

Relative to these averages, the drop in output in the Asian crises of the late 1990s was especially steep: Korea's growth rate declined seven percentage points below its pre-crisis five-year-average growth rate, eight percentage points below its three-year pre-crisis average and seven percentage points from the year preceding the crisis. Indonesia's performance was similar, while Thailand's was the worst (at minus 13, 13 and 11 per cent respectively).[28]

How does this compare with the worst of the pre-1914 era? In fact, the two most infamous pre-World War I episodes, the US in 1893 and Argentina in 1890, were even worse than Asia in recent years. For the US, growth during the crisis years declined by nine percentage points relative to its previous five-year average, 12 percentage points below its three-year average, and 14 percentage points from the pre-crisis year. However, the growth rate recovered to its pre-crisis level within 5 years. For Argentina the numbers are dramatic: minus 17 per cent, 20 per cent and 24 per cent, with recovery in growth not complete after five years. Clearly, generalisations about the pre-1914 period should be drawn cautiously, since that period appears to have featured a small number of exceptionally severe crises along with a larger number of milder episodes.[29]

Generalising about the post-crisis recovery is even more difficult. On the one hand, the recovery from currency crises is quicker prior to 1914. Then, growth rose by two percentage points between the crisis year and the three years following, whereas since 1972 there has been essentially no post-crisis recovery until after three years. The recovery from currency crises both began earlier and continued more rapidly prior to 1913. DeLargy and Goodhart (1999) find a similar pattern and interpret it in terms of the resumption rule. Prior to 1913, countries driven off the gold standard generally intended to restore convertibility at the previously prevailing exchange rate once the crisis passed. While investors who held domestic-currency-denominated assets suffered losses when the currency collapsed, they anticipated gains as the currency recovered to its traditional parity. To put the point another way, there was little reason to fear that abandonment of the currency peg would unleash uncontrolled inflation, since the authorities were committed to reestablishing the previous rate of exchange. Hence, devaluation did not unleash persistent capital flight. Rather, gold and capital began flowing back in at a relatively early date, stabilising the economy and stimulating recovery.

In contrast, the recovery from banking crises starts earlier in the modern period, in the first post-crisis year as opposed to the second or third post-crisis year. This is true whether or not banking crises are accompanied by currency crises. A likely explanation is the absence of an effective lender of last resort at the periphery in the pre-1914 era to quickly restore depositor confidence, stabilise supplies of money and credit, and sustain the provision of intermediation services. The US crises of 1893 and 1907, which were greatly aggravated by the absence of effective last-resort lending (leading in turn to the establishment of the Federal Reserve), clearly make this point. One can argue that regulatory forbearance and central bank bailouts have adverse long-term effects by weakening market discipline and leading to a less efficient allocation of capital. Indeed, there is some suggestion of this in the data: while recovery from banking crises is initiated earlier in the post-1972 period, the subsequent expansion accelerates less dramatically and is sustained less successfully, as if market discipline and the efficiency with which credit is allocated are less (than in comparable episodes a hundred years ago).

Automatic stabilisers were also absent prior to 1914. Some recent commentators have noted that the Asian crisis countries (and other emerging markets) found their use of automatic stabilisers constrained by a lack of confidence and the existence of high capital mobility. That may be true, but the comparison suggests that they still have been able to adopt a more concerted response than their counterparts a century ago. Other commentators have been critical of regulators for failing to force through an earlier resolution of banking problems. Again, they have a point, but the striking fact is that recovery from banking crises has tended to begin earlier in the recent period than in the typical crisis episode a hundred years ago. A final point is that there were no international rescue packages available to emerging economies prior to 1913, whereas such rescues are a prominent feature of the international financial landscape today.[30] Some would argue that these international rescue operations may have themselves contributed to the severity of recent crises by aggravating the problems of moral hazard accompanying the provision of a safety net, but it is also possible that international efforts to encourage the quick resolution of banking crises and to provide resources for recapitalisation have contributed to the earlier initiation of recovery from banking crises.

Thus, while the crisis problem is hardly new, there are some new and distinctive features of recent crises. The drop in output following their outbreak is even more dramatic. And for currency crises, the subsequent recovery is slower. In this respect as others, there are aspects of our current age of globalisation that are both unprecedented and disturbing.

CONCLUSION

We have sought in this chapter to emphasise a small number of general points. First, the globalisation of commodity and financial markets is historically unprecedented. Facile comparisons with the late nineteenth century notwithstanding, the international integration of capital and commodity markets goes further and runs deeper than ever before.

Second, that the advent of highly integrated commodity and financial markets has been accompanied by trade tensions and problems of financial instability should not come as a surprise, for the earlier period of commodity- and financial-market integration that is our basis for comparison was also marked by trade tensions and financial instability. The surprise is that these problems are not even more severe today, given that the extent of commodity- and financial-market integration is so much greater.

One possible explanation for this contrast is the stabilising role of the institutions built in the interim. At the national level this means social and financial safety nets. At the international level it means the WTO, the IMF, the Basle Committee of Banking Supervisors. These institutions may be far from perfect, but they are better than nothing, judging from the historical correlation between the level of integration on the one hand and the level of trade conflict and financial instability on the other. The financial safety net may create moral hazard, but it at least prevents financial catastrophe. Contingent protection may prevent the full gains from trade from being realised, but it at least sustains a critical mass of political support for open markets. Global markets without global governance may create problems, but these multilateral institutions would appear to provide at least an imperfect substitute for some of the functions of the latter, or so outcomes would suggest.

Lest we be accused of being Panglossian, we should emphasise that current problems of trade conflict and financial instability are real and pressing, especially for smaller, more open, lower-income countries with the least ability to protect themselves from the consequences. Governments seeking to make the world safe for global capitalism still have a way to go.

NOTES

[1] This chapter draws on a longer manuscript prepared for the Brookings Trade Policy Forum (Collins, 2000) portions of which are reproduced by permission.

[2] Krugman (1995, p. 331) presents a balanced interpretation of such figures when he writes: 'the general picture of world integration that did not exceed early-twentieth century levels until sometime well into the 1970s is thus broadly confirmed. In the last decade or so, the share of trade in world output has finally reached a level that is noticeably above its former peak. Nonetheless, it would be hard to argue that the sheer volume of trade is now at a level that marks a qualitative difference from previous experience.'

[3] The more rapid productivity growth in goods-producing sectors, a shift in demand toward services (such as health care), and the rise of government spending have all contributed to this result.

[4] US Bureau of the Census (1975), series F250-254, F130-134. Council of Economic Advisers (1999), Table B-12.

[5] The export figures are measured on the basis of gross value, while the production data (for agriculture, mining and manufacturing) from the national income accounts are based on value added data. It would therefore be incorrect to say that over 40 per cent of US merchandise production was exported in 1997. The value of trade relative to production may be inflated if intermediate products cross international borders multiple times in the production process. Hummels, Rapoport, and Yi (1998) examine the increasing trade in intermediate products and components ('vertical specialization') and conclude that it accounts for only a part of the recent growth in trade.

[6] They argue that the volume of trade is an unsatisfactory index of commodity market integration because 'trade volumes can increase for reasons completely unrelated to

commodity market integration and they can decline for reasons completely unrelated to commodity market disintegration' (p. 31).

[7] Goodwin (1992) examines wheat prices at five major markets – the United States Gulf export price, Canada's Pacific Coast export price, at the Netherlands' Rotterdam exchange, Australia's export price, and Japan's import price – and finds that, after accounting for freight rates, the law of one price holds. Local market prices, of course, may differ due to import tariffs, domestic price supports, or transportation charges. In manufactured goods, such price comparisons are difficult to undertake due to the difficulty of uncovering data on like goods.

[8] As Wilkins (1970, p. 207) concludes: 'The skeptic's claim that for major US enterprises of the pre-World War I years foreign business was simply peripheral to domestic investment seems to be supported by the evidence. It does seem that with the exception of Standard Oil of New Jersey, Singer Sewing Machine, International Harvester, New York Life, and perhaps a handful of other large companies, foreign activities did not make a substantial contribution to the profits of US enterprises. In 1914 the vast majority of American corporations were *not* multinational (this is true today [1970] as well).'

[9] Rauch and Casella (1998) distinguish between homogeneous commodity goods in which organized exchanges (markets) set international reference prices and differentiated manufactured goods in which information networks appear to be important. Rauch (1999) presents evidence that search barriers to trade are higher for differentiated than for homogeneous products.

[10] Rangan and Lawrence (1999) argue that multinationals that pursue cross-border exchanges have advantages regarding the informationally-intensive activities of search (identifying potential exchange partners) and deliberation (assessing their reliability and trustworthiness).

[11] Hoekman and Kostecki (1995, p. 161) write that, 'Safeguard provisions are often critical to the existence and operation of trade-liberalizing agreements, as they function as both insurance mechanisms and safety-valves. They provide governments with the means to renege on specific liberalisation commitments – subject to certain conditions – should the need for this arise (safety valve). Without them governments may refrain from signing an agreement that reduces protection substantially (insurance motive).'

[12] See Bairoch and Kozul-Wright (1998) for estimates for these and other countries. For comparison, note that Japan and Germany's current account surpluses in the 1980s never exceeded five per cent of GDP.

[13] See for example Bayoumi (1990), Eichengreen (1990) and Taylor (1996). Price-based studies paint the same picture.

[14] As measured by the Phillips-Perron Z statistic. This is true for surplus and deficit countries alike.

[15] British investors held approximately 40 per cent of the stock of long-term foreign investments outstanding in 1913, and there is no reason to think that the composition of British investment is unrepresentative in terms of its concentration in the railway and public sectors. Fishlow (1985) suggests that French and German foreign investment may have been more heavily directed toward governments and less toward railways, but this does not undermine our central point.

[16] See e.g. Royal Institute for International Affairs (1937).

[17] The cable reached Buenos Aires in 1878 and Tokyo in 1900.

[18] The 1997 issue of the World Bank's *Global Development Finance* suggests that stocks and bonds are now of roughly equal importance in international portfolio capital flows to emerging markets, after a long period in which debt instruments (bonds and bank loans) dominated purchases of equities.

[19] Bloomfield (1968), pp. 3-4.

[20] See Wilkins (1998).

[21] Madden's developed regions were New England and the North East, his developing regions the East Central and South, and his underdeveloped regions the North Central, Central and Far West.

[22] The countries are those used in Bordo and Schwartz (1996): Argentina, Australia, Brazil, Canada, Chile, Denmark, Finland, Greece, Italy, Japan, Norway, Portugal, Spain, Sweden, United States. Our criteria for classifying a country as emerging are (i) whether it was primarily a recipient of capital flows and (ii) its level of per capita income. Thus, in the pre-1914 era a number of the 20th century's most advanced countries (the US, Japan, and the Scandinavians) are classified as emerging markets. A similar comparison is made by DeLargy and Goodhart (1999). Their empirical base is more limited, however; they concentrate on the behaviour of a number of famous crisis episodes in the pre-1914 era in 5 emerging countries: the US, Australia, Argentina, Italy and Austria, with similar evidence for victims of the recent Asian crisis. An alternative metric would measure the wealth losses associated with the resolution of the crises. This is the approach taken by Caprio and Klingbiel (1996). By this metric the losses associated with banking crises in the 1980's and 1990's is likely to be larger than before 1914 (Calomiris, 1999).

[23] The resulting chronology is presented in a companion paper (Bordo and Eichengreen, 1999).

[24] This allows us to distinguish between liquidity crises before 1914 in which lender of last resort intervention was either absent or unsuccessful, and more recent events where a lender of last resort or deposit insurance is in place and the main problem has been bank insolvency. In fact, however, a number of banking crises which occurred in Europe before 1914 did not involve panics and in this respect were not dissimilar from episodes occurring more recently.

[25] This builds on the exchange-market-pressure model of Girton and Roper (1977), following the methodology in Eichengreen, Rose and Wyplosz (1995, 1996).

[26] The individual cases are tabulated and described in Bordo and Eichengreen (1999).

[27] To illustrate, this generates the following picture for the US around the crisis of 1893. Real GDP dropped five per cent in the crisis year, declined relative to the average of the preceding five years by nine per cent, declined relative to the average of the preceding three years by 12 per cent, and declined relative to the year before the crisis by 14 per cent. In the three years following the crisis, growth increased on average to two per cent, so the deviation of the crisis year from the three-year average that we calculate is seven per cent. Finally, in the five years following the crisis, growth recovered by nine per cent relative to the crisis. Thus it took the US five years to return to its pre-crisis growth rate.

[28] In contrast to the Asian cases, real GDP declined only modestly in the Mexican crisis of 1994 with output only declining by one per cent below its five-year average during the crisis year, less than one per cent below its three-year average and two per cent in the crisis year. It recovered three per cent a year after the crisis and four per cent after three years.

[29] Another reason for caution is that the results change when we include the crises that erupted in 1914 due to the outbreak of World War I. These are numerous; including them increases the size of our sample by about half. They are also relatively severe, since the disruption to international financial relations due to the outbreak of the war was extensive. Including these episodes in the averages makes the immediate post-crisis drop in output slightly *more* severe prior to 1915 than after 1972. While there is good reason to regard these wartime shocks as special (and for therefore not including them in the comparison with our day), this is another reminder of the difficulty of generalising about financial stability in the last age of globalisation.

[30] The Belmont-Morgan loan arranged for the US Treasury in the 1890s being a prominent exception.

REFERENCES

Bairoch, Paul (1993), *Economics and World History*, Chicago: University of Chicago Press.

Bairoch, Paul and Richard Kozul-Wright (1998), 'Globalization Myths: Some Reflections on Integration, Industrialization and Growth in the World Economy', in Richard Kozul-Wright and Robert Rowthorn (eds), *Transnational Corporations and the Global Economy*, New York: St. Martin's Press.

Baskin, Jonathan B. (1988), 'The Development of Corporate Financial Markets in Britain and the United States, 1600–1914: Overcoming Asymmetric Information', *Business History Review* 62, 197–237.

Bayoumi, Tamim (1990), 'Saving–Investment Correlations: Immobile Capital, Government Policy, or Endogenous Behavior?', *IMF Staff Papers* 37, 360–87.

Bloomfield, Arthur I. (1963), 'Short-term Capital Movements Under the Pre-1914 Gold Standard', *Princeton Studies in International Finance No. 11*, Princeton, NJ: International Finance Section, Department of Economics, Princeton University.

Bloomfield, Arthur I. (1968), 'Patterns of Fluctuation in International Finance Before 1914', *Princeton Studies in International Finance No. 21*, Princeton, NJ: International Finance Section, Department of Economics, Princeton University.

Bordo, Michael and Barry Eichengreen (1999), 'Plus ça Change: A Century of Banking and Currency Crises', unpublished manuscript, Rutgers University and University of California, Berkeley.

Bordo, Michael D. and Anna J. Schwartz (1996), 'The Operation of the Specie Standard: Evidence for Core and Peripheral Countries, 1880-1990', in Jorge Braga de Maceda, Barry Eichengreen and Jaime Reis (eds), *Currency Convertibility: The Gold Standard and Beyond*, New York: Routledge, pp. 11–83.

Calomiris, Charles (1999), 'Victorian Perspectives on the Banking Collapse of the 1980s and 1990s', Columbia University (mimeo).

Caprio Jr., Gerard and Daniela Klingbiel (1996), 'Bank Insolvencies: Cross Country Experience', *World Bank Policy Research Working Paper No. 1620*, Washington DC: World Bank.

Collins, Susan.(ed.) (2000), *Brookings Trade Forum 1999*, Washington DC: The Brookings Instituion.

Collins, William J., Kevin H. O'Rourke, and Jeffrey Williamson (1997), 'Were Trade and Factor Mobility Substitutes in History?' *NBER Working Paper No. 6059* (June).

Council of Economic Advisers (1999), *Economic Report of the President*, Washington, DC: GPO.

Davis, Lance E. and Robert Gallman (1999), 'Waves, Tides, and Sandcastles: The Impact of Foreign Capital Flows on Evolving Financial Markets in the New World, 1865-1914', unpublished manuscript, Caltech and University of North Carolina, Chapel Hill.

DeLargy, P.J.R. and Goodhart, Charles (1999), 'Financial Crises: Plus ça change, plus c'est la même chose', *LSE Financial Markets Group Special Paper No. 108*, London: London School of Economics.

Eichengreen, Barry (1990), 'Trends and Cycles in Foreign Lending', in Horst Siebert (ed.), *Capital Flows in the World Economy*, Tubingen: Mohr, pp. 3–28.

Eichengreen, Barry and Ashoka Mody (1998), 'What Explains the Changing Spreads on Emerging-Market Debt: Fundamentals or Market Sentiment?', *NBER Working Paper No. 6408* (February).

Eichengreen, Barry, Andrew Rose and Charles Wyplosz (1995), 'Exchange Market Mayhem: The Antecedents and Aftermath of Speculative Attacks', *Economic Policy* **21**, 249–312.

Eichengreen, Barry, Andrew Rose and Charles Wyplosz (1996), 'Speculative Attacks on Pegged Exchange Rates: An Empirical Exploration with Special Reference to the European Monetary System', in Matthew Canzoneri, Wilfred Ethier and Vittorio Grilli (eds), *The New Transatlantic Economy*, New York: Cambridge University Press.

Feenstra, Robert C. (1998), 'Integration of Trade and Disintegration of Production in the Global Economy', *Journal of Economic Perspectives* **12**, 31–50.

Feldman, David H. (1993), 'Redundant Tariffs as Rational Endogenous Protection', *Economic Inquiry* **31**, 436–447.

Fishlow, Albert (1985), 'Lessons from the Past: Capital Markets During the 19th Century and the Interwar Period', in Miles Kahler (ed.), *The Politics of International Debt*, Ithaca, NY: Cornell University Press, pp. 37–94.

Flandreau, Marc (1998), 'Caveat Emptor: Coping with Country Risk without the Multilaterals, 1870–1914', *CEPR Discussion paper No. 2004* (October).

Fogel, Robert (1964), *Railroads and American Economic Growth*, Baltimore: Johns Hopkins University Press.

Garbade, Kenneth D. and William L. Silber (1978), 'Technology, Communication and the Performance of Financial Markets, 1840–1975', *Journal of Finance* **33**, 819–832.

Girton, Lance and Donald Roper (1977), 'A Monetary Model of Exchange Market Pressure Applied to Postwar Canadian Experience', *American Economic Review* **67**, 537–48.

Goldberg, L. and Michael W. Klein (1999), 'International Trade and Factor Mobility: An Empirical Investigation', *NBER Working Paper No. 7196* (June).

Goodwin, Barry K. (1992), 'Multivariate Cointegration Tests and the Law of One Price in International Wheat Markets', *Review of Agricultural Economics* **14** (June), 117–124.

Hatton, Timothy J. and Jeffrey G. Williamson (1992), 'International Migration and World Development: A Historical Perspective', *Harvard Institute of Economic Research Discussion Paper No. 1606* (August).

Hoekman, Bernard, and Michel Kostecki (1995), *The Political Economy of the World Trading System: From GATT to WTO*, New York: Oxford University Press.

Hummels, David (1999), 'Transportation Costs and International Integration in Recent History', unpublished manuscript, University of Chicago.

Hummels, David, Dana Rapoport, and Kei-Mu Yi (1998), 'Vertical Specialization and the Changing Nature of World Trade', *Economic Policy Review*, Federal Reserve Bank of New York (June), 79–94.

Krugman, Paul (1995), 'Growing World Trade: Causes and Consequences', *Brookings Papers on Economic Activity* **1**, 327–362.

Lawrence, Robert Z., Albert Bressand and Takatoshi Ito (1996), *A Vision for the World Economy: Openness, Diversity and Cohesion*, Washington, DC: The Brookings Institution.

Lawrence, Robert Z., and Robert E. Litan (1986), *Saving World Trade: A Pragmatic Approach*, Washington, DC: The Brookings Institution.

Lundgren, Nils-Gustav (1996), 'Bulk Trade and Maritime Transport Costs: The Evolution of Global Markets', *Resources Policy* **22**, 5–32.

Madden, John J. (1985), *British Investment in the United States, 1860-1880*, New York: Garland Publishing.

O'Rourke, Kevin H., and Jeffrey G. Williamson (1994), 'Late Nineteenth Century Anglo-American Factor Price Convergence: Were Heckscher and Ohlin Right?' *Journal of Economic History* **54** (December), 892-916.

O'Rourke, Kevin H., and Jeffrey G. Williamson (1999), *Globalization and History: The Evolution of a 19th Century Atlantic Economy*, Cambridge: MIT Press.

Rangan, Subramanian and Robert Z. Lawrence (1999), *A Prism on Globalization: Corporate Responses to the Dollar*, Washington, DC: The Brookings Institution.

Rauch, James (1999), 'Networks versus Markets in International Trade', *Journal of International Economics* **48** (June) 7–35.

Rauch, James and Alessandra Casella (1998), 'Overcoming Informational Barriers to International Resource Allocation: Prices and Group Ties', *NBER Working Paper No. 6628* (June).

Rodrik, Dani (1998), 'The Debate Over Globalization: How to Move Forward by Looking Backward', unpublished manuscript, Harvard University.

Royal Institute for International Affairs (1937), *The Problem of International Investment*, London: Oxford University Press.

Sachs, Jeffrey and Andrew Warner (1995), 'Economic Reform and the Process of Global Integration', *Brookings Papers on Economic Activity* **1**, 1–118.

Schott, Jeffrey J. (1994), *The Uruguay Round: An Assessment*, Washington, DC: Institute for International Economics (November).

Simon, Matthew (1960), 'The United States Balance of Payments, 1861–1900', in *Trends in the American Economy in the Nineteenth Century*, Vol. 24, Studies in Income and Wealth, Princeton: Princeton University Press for the National Bureau of Economic Research.

Taylor, Alan M. (1996), 'International Capital Mobility in History: The Saving–Investment Relationship', *NBER Working Paper No. 5743* (September).

US Bureau of the Census (1975), *Historical Statistics of the United States*, Washington, DC: GPO.

Wilkins, Mira, (1970), *The Emergence of Multinational Enterprise: American Business Abroad from the Colonial Era to 1914*, Cambridge: Harvard University Press.

Wilkins, Mira (1989), *The History of Foreign Investment in the United States to 1914*, Cambridge: Harvard University Press.

Wilkins, Mira (1998), 'Conduits for Long-Term Investment in the Gold Standard Era', unpublished manuscript, Florida International University.

Williamson, Jeffrey G. (1998), 'Globalization, Labor Markets and Policy Backlash in the Past', *Journal of Economic Perspectives* **12**, 51–72.

Zeile, William J. (1997), 'US Intrafirm Trade in Goods', *Survey of Current Business* (February), 23–38.

Zevin, Robert (1992), 'Are World Financial Markets More Open? If So, Why and With What Effects?' in Tariq Banuri and Juliet B. Schor (eds), *Financial Openness and National Autonomy*, Oxford: Clarendon Press, pp. 43–83.

4. Balanced Growth: The Scope for National Policies in a Global Economy

John F. Helliwell [1]

Is there scope or need for national economic and social policies in today's global economy? Many commentators have argued that national economies have disappeared, with their former powers and functions being usurped from the one side by the global economy and from the other side by cities and regions. Thus Kenichi Ohmae (1995) treats regional economies and multinational firms as the chief building blocks of the modern global economy. If this is true, then we would expect to find that national borders no longer mark separations in economic space. This paper assesses the facts of the matter, searches for their implications for national economies, and considers the scope and need for local and national policies that provide a basis for balanced growth. This will be done in two main sections. The first will summarise the evidence and implications leading to the conclusion that there is still great scope and need for national policies. In some ways, increasingly open international markets place even greater importance on the development of national policies to develop domestic institutions that are robust enough to deal with the consequences of international disturbances. The second section will consider some specific domestic policies that can help to support balanced growth. The range considered will be far broader than the usual list of economic policies, because there is increasing evidence that sustainable economic growth depends of a whole range of social and political institutions. The emphasis will be on those institutions that can help to support growth that is socially, politically and environmentally balanced, and thereby sustainable.

COMPARING NATIONAL AND GLOBAL ECONOMIC LINKAGES

Evidence[2]

Only in recent years has it been possible to measure the relative strengths of domestic and international economic linkages. Even now, most countries have no systematic measures of internal trade flows, and hence no empirical basis for comparing domestic and international trading intensities. Canada remains the only country with a full set of inter-provincial trade data that can be compared with trade flows between Canadian provinces and US states. The first use of these data to compare the strengths of domestic and international trading intensities was by John McCallum (1995), who came to the startling conclusion, based on a gravity model of trade flows, that in 1988 Canadian provinces traded twenty times as intensely with each other as with US states of comparable size and distance.

The gravity model assumes that trade flows increase proportionately with the economic size of the trading partners, and decrease proportionately with the distance separating them. These adjustments are essential if domestic and international trade densities are being compared, because the important effect of distance on trade would lead us to expect greater trade flows within a country just because of the greater distances involved in foreign trade. Over recent decades the gravity model, always a great empirical success, has gone from being a theoretical orphan to being the favoured child of all main theories of international trade.[3] This makes it a solid tool for the evaluation of border effects, even if it cannot easily be used to discriminate among competing theories of international trade.

To ensure that McCallum's startling finding is not some mysterious result generated by some feature of the model used for estimation, it is useful to see if it matches the data for specific pairs of provinces and states. For example, Ontario is almost equidistant from British Columbia, Washington State, and California. In 1990 the Californian economy was almost twelve times larger than that of British Columbia, and thus should have provided, without border effects, a market almost twelve times as large. Ontario merchandise shipments to British Columbia were actually almost twice as large as those to California, for a total border effect of 21. Washington State GDP was more than one-third larger than that of British Columbia, but Ontario's exports to British Columbia were more than twelve times larger than exports to Washington, for a total border effect of 21.

In Helliwell (1996b) I extended the sample to include data for 1989 and 1990, found an increase of the border effect from 1988 to 1990, and showed that the preference for Canadian over US markets applied as much to Quebec as to the other provinces. Since that time, there has been additional work by Statistics Canada to improve the province-state data to make them match more closely the concepts used in the construction of the inter-provincial trade data, and to refine the assignment of trade to its province of origin or destination. In addition, the data have now been extended through 1996, permitting the consequences of the US-Canada Free Trade Agreement (FTA) to be assessed.

Results for 1988 to 1996, including disaggregation by province, by industry, and by direction of trade, are all reported elsewhere (Helliwell, 1998, Chapter 2). The best summary measure of the results is for total merchandise trade, along with some more approximate calculations for trade in services. The estimated border effects, shown separately for merchandise and for services, for each year from 1988 to 1996, are pictured in Figure 4.1.

Figure 4.1. Canada–US border effects 1988–96

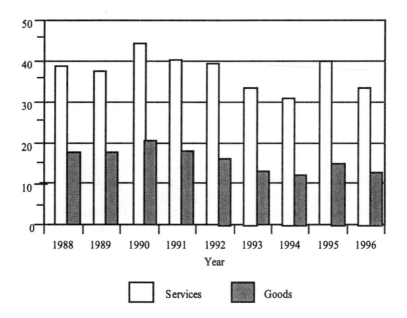

The improvements in the classification of province-state trade flows for 1990 have lowered the estimated border effect for merchandise trade for that year from a previously estimated 21 to about 17. The subsequent sharp drop in the border effect from 1990 to 1993, coupled with its rough constancy since, at a level of about 12, suggests that the major adjustments of trade patterns following the FTA may have been completed.

The estimated border effects for services are in every year much larger than those for merchandise trade, and do not show the same evidence of sharp reduction in the wake of the FTA. The high values of border effects for services are not simply caused by the fact that services are generally traded less than goods, since the border effects being estimated relate only to those services that do enter trade, whether inter-provincial or between provinces and states. Intra-provincial consumption of goods and services does not enter these calculations, although it is perhaps worth noting, in the light of all the discussion about inter-provincial trade barriers, that attempts to estimate inter-provincial border effects show them to be small and insignificant (Helliwell, 1998, Chapter 2).[4]

Thus Figure 4.1 is consistent both with the large increase in north–south trade flows in the 1990s, and with continuing national border effects of about twelve for goods and about twice that for services. Two features of the post-FTA changes in border effects are worth further discussion here. First, the post-1990 increases in north–south trade are more than twice as large as those that were predicted in various studies before the FTA came into effect.[5] Second, the forecast productivity gains have not materialised to any significant degree. This combination poses a puzzle for future research, but in the meantime provides some evidence to support the tentative conclusion of the next section – that the continuing high levels of national economic densities, relative to international ones, may not suggest that there are large productivity gains thereby lost.

The finding of large border effects for Canadian merchandise trade led to attempts to develop data that could lead to replication, or not, of these results in an international setting. Unfortunately, domestic inter-regional trade data are not available for other countries, so that it is necessary to estimate total domestic sales (using data from input–output tables, not available even for all of the OECD countries) and then to use some plausible procedure for guessing what might be the typical internal trade distances. This is no mean feat, since the estimate hinges a great deal on how much internal trade goes on within rather than between the large cities and industrial areas. Wei (1996) assumed that internal trade distances were generally one-quarter those between the capitals of a country and its nearest neighbour. On this basis, the latest estimates of 1992 border effects for merchandise trade within and among the OECD countries is about ten for countries not sharing a common language or membership in the European Union (Helliwell, 1998, p.51). Sharing a common language increases trade densities by more than 60 per cent, while EU membership increases trade between member countries by about 40 per cent. This 40 per cent is a significant effect, but it emphasises once again the surprisingly large size, almost equivalent to the cumulative EU effect, of the trade-increasing effects of lowering or removing the relatively small pre-FTA tariff rates on trade between Canada and the United States.

Comparable estimates of border effects for developing countries show them to be up to 100 or more, with a strikingly tight relation between GDP per capita and the size of the border effect. If a gravity model is fitted to merchandise trade data for the OECD countries plus a sample of other countries for which suitable data are available, the wide variety of border effects is successfully explained by the hypothesis that international differences in border effects are entirely due to international differences in real GDP per capita. These international results, along with further discussion of their trends and implications, are reported in Helliwell (1998, Chapter 3).

Engel and Rogers (1996) reasoned that if trade densities are greater within than between national economies, then it should also be true that inter-city price differentials are larger and more enduring internationally than within the same country, for city pairs of the same distance from one another. Using data for the inter-city co-variability of components of the consumer price index, for a sample of Canadian and US cities, they found that this was indeed the case, and calculated that the implied width of the US-Canada border was more than 2000 miles. Subsequent research using their data (and reported in Helliwell (1998, Chapter 4)) has shown the result to be even starker, since there is no evidence of cross-border price arbitrage for city pairs of any distance, making the border of infinite width in terms of their calculations. Of course, there is no doubt a lot of cross-border price competition, but it does not show up in month-to-month changes in the components of the consumer price index. National economies are so much tighter than the international economy that arbitrage of these prices among domestic city pairs does show up even using the short-term data for components of the consumer price index, but not across national borders.

Turning to capital markets, there was an important finding by Feldstein and Horioka (1980) that domestic saving and national investment rates are correlated across countries, leading them to conclude that capital markets are separated rather than integrated. To avoid such correlation entirely would require that markets for goods and capital both be tightly integrated. If provincial markets are tightly integrated, but national ones are not, then the Feldstein-Horioka result should be less evident, or disappear entirely, using inter-provincial data. Helliwell and McKitrick (1998) pooled OECD and provincial data, and confirmed the Feldstein-Horioka result among the OECD countries, with the effect being completely reversed for the provincial data. This is a strong confirmation of the Feldstein-Horioka interpretation, and shows that the inter-provincial markets for goods and capital are tightly knitted together, while international ones are not.

Border effects for migration, at least that from states to provinces, are even greater than for goods and services. Inter-provincial migration is about a hundred times more likely than is migration from a US state to a Canadian province, after taking due account, using the gravity model, of population, distance, and the economic incentives for migration (Helliwell, 1998, Chapter 5). The border effect is much smaller for migration from Canada to the United States, reflecting the greater southbound flows of migrants and the high inter-provincial migration flows.

Finally, even though Coe and Helpman (1995) have provided convincing evidence that research and development spending has important productivity-enhancing effects both at home and abroad, the implied border effects are even larger than those for goods, services and population (Helliwell, 1998, Chapter 6).

Implications

If the evidence presented above is to be believed, the economic fabric of nation states has a much tighter weave than previously thought. Is this good or bad, and what does it suggest for current and future national policies?

Many studies have shown that among developing countries, and to a lesser extent among OECD countries, those countries that are more internationally open have had higher rates of growth of productivity and of incomes per capita. The basic intuition behind this result is that developing countries gain most by learning from the successes and failures of other countries, and tailoring the best of foreign ideas to suit domestic conditions. This is also consistent with studies of R&D spillovers, which find them to be larger for countries that have higher degrees of openness. If some degree of openness is a good thing for economic development, is much more openness even better? If so, then the fact that economic densities are much higher within than among national economies means that there is more to be gained from further increases in international linkages.

On the other hand, if some degree of openness is sufficient to achieve the major gains from international exchange, specialisation, and the acquisition of fresh ideas, then there may be diminishing returns to openness. If so, and if there are some efficiency effects offered by the partial segmentation of global markets into national pools, then there may be some right amount of openness that may not differ much from the levels already achieved among the industrial countries.

What is the available evidence on these issues? First, as already noted, there is evidence that some degree of openness is good for growth. However, if further increases in openness, beyond those already achieved by the richer OECD countries, promised great efficiency gains, then we would expect to find that bigger countries (in terms of GDP, not hectares) would have substantially higher levels of real GDP per capita, since they already have much larger trading networks, given the fact that trade is much denser within than among nation states. However, there is no systematic evidence that larger countries have higher levels or rates of growth of productivity.

If income levels are not significantly higher in larger countries, and yet economic relations are much denser within than between countries, there are two broad types of explanation possible. One possible explanation is that while there are initially large gains from trade, both to exploit comparative advantage and to achieve efficient levels of scale in production, these gains have been largely reaped by the time international linkages have become as tight as they now are among the industrial countries. There may be more scope for increased openness to lead to temporarily higher growth rates in the developing countries, since there is still much for them to learn from elsewhere, but even here it is clear, as is evident from the late 1990s experiences of cascading loan defaults across Asia, that interdependence may have costs as well as benefits.

The second possible reason why the insular nature of national economies may not be costly is that national boundaries may provide fairly efficient means of segmenting impossibly large markets into manageable chunks. It is well known that in a fully informed and frictionless world of a seamless global market place there would be no need for borders, for firms, or for most of the other institutions of the old and new worlds. But the real world has frictions; knowledge is tough to acquire and becomes obsolete; people cannot always be trusted; contracts are not always what they seem to be; one bad apple can spoil the whole bushel; and Murphy's Law may be the only one that applies without an expensive legal process. In such a world, which is the only one on offer, not everyone is equally informed, and people are best informed about the events, institutions, and people they know best.

To deal with those you know and trust, under shared and well-understood rules and institutions, can mean lower costs and lower risks for all participants. Those who understand a market better are more able to guess its moods and changes, and to adapt flexibly to new patterns of demand and new technologies. To the extent that national boundaries enclose communities that have common institutions and shared views, local businesses are likely to be able to meet local market needs at lower cost than are their foreign or global competitors. There are limits to this, of course, set on the one hand by economies of scale and on the other by the possibility of exporting tastes and preferences, thus building a global market from scratch. Even the most successful global products, however, often have national systems of production and distribution, and characteristics specially put in to suit national tastes. What is surprising, in the latest evidence about the strength of national economies, is that the global market is very much the exception, and the national market the rule.

How does this view of tightly woven national economies tie in with the re-discovery of local economies as poles of growth? There is one strong link between the two. The benefits of close interaction, and the bonds of trust that are built up among those who have many repeated dealings underlie the logic of local economies and the strength of the national economy. Distance is costly, and tends to cause economies to cluster. The regional literature focuses on the effects of distance and also on whatever historical events may have led to a city getting started in the first place. The national borders results, on the other hand, show that distance has many more dimensions than simply kilometres or miles. To whatever extent history, politics and geography have spread people around in groups with different institutions, values and networks, their economic relations will follow similar patterns. This may be partly because patterns, once started, are costly to change, but also reflects the cost advantages possessed by those who are nearby, well-informed, and well-trusted. Physical distance is indeed an important separating device, but national boundaries are also important. One of the findings from recent research is that for different markets the effects of national borders can be interpreted in terms of distance, and the implied numbers are strikingly large, often in the order of thousands of miles.

NATIONAL INSTITUTIONS TO SUPPORT STABLE GROWTH

Social Capital

What are the most relevant ways of measuring those aspects of the political and social system that might influence the operation of a modern economy? In their pioneering comparative empirical study of post-war democracies, Almond and Verba (1963) 'concluded that interpersonal trust is a prerequisite to the formation of secondary associations, which in turn is essential to effective political participation in any large democracy' (Inglehart, 1990). Over the forty years since their empirical work in the 1950s, researchers in many countries have probed the extent of interpersonal trust, and examined the extent to which individuals participate in, and contribute their efforts to, voluntary associations. There have also been attempts to establish the extent to which interregional differences in these variables, described sometimes as measures of social capital or of civic culture, are linked with the extent to which citizens in the regions of a country are satisfied with the efficiency of their regional governments (Putnam, 1993), and in turn whether there are subsequent payoffs in terms of conditionally higher growth in those regions with higher levels of social capital. For the regions of Italy, where detailed research had been carried out for more than twenty years, the results were fairly supportive of the notion that there was a causal linkage running from high levels of trust and engagement to higher levels of regional government performance and in turn to higher levels of economic performance, and higher rates of upward convergence towards best practice levels of efficiency (Helliwell and Putnam, 1995).

Subsequent attempts to use World Values Survey (Inglehart, 1990) measures of trust to explain subsequent differences in growth rates among industrial countries and among Asian economies (Helliwell, 1996a) have had mixed results, although Knack and Keefer (1997) have found stronger evidence supporting the view that better social institutions do support higher levels of growth among a sample of countries including both industrial and developing countries. Their use of a larger sample, covering a broader range of institutional quality, was probably an important reason for their finding.

Democracy

Proponents of democracy often argue that it is good for everything, including economic growth, while sceptics have argued that populist electoral pressures within a democracy are likely to destroy economic policy discipline, and then lead to budget deficits, inflation, and ultimately to political and economic instability. The relationship is difficult to unravel, since there is reason to expect that higher levels of income will increase the demand for democracy, thus making it difficult to untangle the reverse influences running from democracy to subsequent economic growth. My best attempts to sort out these two-way relations (Helliwell, 1994) indicate that there is indeed a strong linkage running from the level of real per capita GDP to the existence of a democratic regime. As for the reverse line of causation, from democracy to economic growth, it is of uncertain sign, and in any event very weak. Thus it would appear, based on more than twenty years' experience from almost 100 countries, that countries tend to become more democratic as they get richer, while the attainment of democratic institutions does not itself either damage or ensure subsequent economic growth.

In the light of this evidence that democracy does not hinder economic growth, how are we to interpret the sharply contrasting experience of Russia and China over the 1990s? In mid-1989, as President Gorbachev arrived in

Beijing, to be greeted by students eager to see Glasnost and democracy imported into China, it seemed as though democracy was poised to spread in both countries. In the event, democracy was established in Russia while being suppressed in China. The growth experiences of the two countries diverged dramatically over the following decade, with Russian GDP at the end of the century about half what it was in 1990, while that of China more than doubled over the same period. Is this a black mark for democracy?

At the time the transition in Russia and Eastern Europe was just beginning, policy-makers and analysts drawn together for an OECD conference (Marer and Zecchini, 1992) were inferring the lessons to be drawn from previous transitions to market economies, including, among others, post-war experience in Germany and Japan, later industrialisation in Spain, and the development experience of Korea. Nothing in those earlier experiences hinted at the many years of economic decline in Russia and Ukraine. What went wrong? The studies done in 1990 did raise the difficulties posed by the institutional gaps in the former USSR – the lack of a rule of law, of standards of commercial practice and contracts, and even of basic levels of social and interpersonal trust – but did not begin to predict the full consequences of these institutional gaps. Perhaps it should have been possible to predict that in these circumstances even the most likely of commercial ventures would be mired in corruption and delays, while the most striking growth would be of criminal activities expanding to fill the institutional vacuum. The result was one of the twentieth century's most dramatic displays of the central importance of the institutions of civic society.

Is it reasonable to attribute the tumult and decline to the existence of a democratic system? Surely not, but it is reasonable to ask if it was unrealistic to expect that the institutional, political, social and entrepreneurial vacuums would be filled appropriately by some magical operation of the invisible hand. Russia's continuing lack of success is being blamed on too much reform, too little reform, political instability, criminality, and other plausible and implausible candidates. What is clear is that the institutional needs would have been easier to fill had they been more clearly foreseen, and if the process had been launched earlier and more effectively. If trust levels start low, and then fall sharply lower, the process of recovery is bound to be more difficult. There is some reassurance from polling evidence that electoral support for continuing economic and political reform is more robust among the pro-reform voters in Russia than is the anti-reform support, which has been easier to erase if and when economic times improve. The earlier studies of democracy would suggest that effective support for reforms might erode as per-capita incomes fell. The fact that this has not happened, and that reforms have even tended to survive changes in government in several of the transition economies, suggests that bad memories of the previous regime are still strong enough to provide continuing support for democracy.

In China, by contrast, the process of gradual economic liberalisation was continued in the context of a tight political regime and widespread restrictions on freedom of speech and on personal freedoms and mobility. From the earlier studies linking income with democracy, the continuing high rates of economic growth are likely to have strengthened the effective demand for democracy. However, the experience in Russia, to the extent it is widely known in China, may provide a broader base of public support for continuing official attempts to halt substantial progress towards democratic political institutions. There are increasing international worries, however, that the same lack of transparency that may smooth the operation of the undemocratic political regime may also be leading to increasing difficulties in the management and financing of both domestic and international production and trading ventures. In other words, the difficulties of trying to combine open trade and a closed political system may be growing so as to make the current set of policies unsustainable. To restore balance while maintaining growth would seem to require gradual relaxation of restraints on freedom of speech, and provision of effectively democratic means for translating pubic opinion into public policy. Transparency of economic institutions and regulations, and the absence of corruption, so widely admired, and increasingly required, by investors and traders around the world, both facilitate and demand parallel changes in political life. If economic openness brings in investors, traders and tourists who then get enmeshed in crime and corruption, they are bound to recoil. Such a recoil will be faster and more costly to digest if there are hints of falling dominoes and mysterious contagion.

Education and Research

One common factor that underlies all successful transitions, whether economic, social or political, seems to be broad and better education. There is substantial evidence that economic growth in developing countries proceeds faster where educational attainments are higher, and where literacy is more pervasive. This seems only reasonable, as the greatest part of the productivity growth of the poorer countries relies on catching up to the levels of technological and organisational efficiency already in place elsewhere in the world. To search out and learn from the successes and failures of others is likely to be easier and more effective when education levels are higher and widely met. The estimates of high domestic productivity returns to research and development (Coe and Helpman, 1995) which frequently go hand in hand with tertiary education, combine with the prevalence of border effects to maintain the case for domestic research spending even in the presence of major research activities in other countries.

Social capital, taken to comprise the norms, networks and trust that underpin civil society, has long been found to depend heavily on education. Empirical research consistently shows that education levels are the most important and pervasive determinants of both trust in others and engagement in community activities. The implication of these results is that rising education levels are not only good for the individuals receiving the education, who thereby receive higher incomes and greater satisfaction from their other activities, but also for the societies in which they live.

The latter inference has recently been challenged by Nie, Junn and Stehlik-Barry (1996), who agree that trust levels are generally higher where education levels are higher, but present evidence to support their claim that the effects of education on participation (as measured by the US General Social Survey) apply only to relative education. They argue that those with relatively high levels of education are able to attain positions of leadership, and tend to participate more than those with lesser education. However, they argue, rising general levels of education do not lead to rising general levels of participation. Although the issue is not yet settled, subsequent research has shown that when education levels of one's peer group are appropriately defined the evidence remains strong that social engagement increases strongly with education levels regardless of relative education effects. For some types of activity, for example reading groups, participation increases with one's own education and with average education levels, while for other types of activity these own-education effects are partly offset by relative education effects. For all total measures of engagement, at least in the US data studied thus far, there remains a strong link from education to both trust and social en insignificant (Helliwell and Putnam, 1999).

Returning to democracy and political engagement, there is also strong evidence that the likelihood of a country supporting democratic rights and freedoms depends positively on education levels as well as on levels of per capita GDP. This should also come as no surprise, as those citizens with higher levels of education are more likely to take an informed interest in what their governments are doing, and to want an active say in the decisions being taken on their behalf.

There is also a further relation, not yet fully analysed in the literature, linking education and health status, with those who are better educated taking better care of their own health as well as taking effective action to obtain timely medical assistance where necessary. This linkage is likely to be general as well as relative, so that societies with higher average levels of education are likely to have higher average levels of health, which in turn are likely to feed back to provide a more productive economy and society.

All of the above roles of education provide evidence of social returns that augment the already well-documented private returns to education, suggesting a high policy priority for widely accessible high-quality education. There is evidence that the returns are high for both basic literacy and for higher education, and also some indication that equality of educational opportunities is likely to support a more sustainable and balanced growth path.

Inequality and Insecurity

Although inequality and insecurity are obviously not institutions, they do differ systematically among countries and over time. In addition, they have been found to be linked to several of the variables already mentioned. For example, several studies (for example, Persson and Tabellini, 1994) have presented evidence that economic growth is higher in countries where income is more equally distributed. There is also a persistent finding from several countries (Wilkinson, 1992; Ben-Shlomo *et al.*, 1996; Mustard, 1998) that several measures of health status are lower in regions or countries where there is greater inequality of income, even after account is taken of the fact that regions and individuals with higher levels of income have better health outcomes. The inequality effect may be partly because there is a diminishing payoff to income as a determinant of health (Gravelle, 1998), but there must be more at play than this. Finally, it has been suggested that greater inequality may also have negative effects on measures of social capital such as trust and participation.

Government and Commercial Institutions

The most important growth-supporting institutions provided by governments are those providing the rule of law, including criminal justice, commercial and civil laws, and a civil service that is free of corruption and capable of developing and administering the framework of laws and regulations required to support a modern society. Within such a framework, there is a real possibility that an enterprising civil population, supported by advice and finance from home and abroad, can develop the commercial ventures to employ and feed the people in such a way as to continually expand their options for contributing to an economically secure and environmentally, politically and socially secure future. Behind this broad picture lie many essential elements as I have discussed. Whether individual items are provided by governments, non-governmental agencies, or private investors matters less than the quality of their provision. As the pre-1989 experience in the USSR shows, a fully state-operated system is not likely to provide individuals with sufficient freedom and opportunities to develop and exploit their talents. On the other hand, post-1990 Russia has shown all too clearly that without some critical combination of social trust and public institutions, individual and commercial freedoms are of little use, with or without access to foreign expertise and capital. Indeed, in the absence of the required domestic laws and institutions, an open economy may be in more trouble than a closed one, since the absence of order may scare off many legitimate investors, leaving a vacuum to be filled by those venturers more willing and able to operate by stealth and corruption.

How Much Openness?

The discussion above suggests that openness to world markets has many dimensions and many complexities. In a world of Good Samaritans, nothing but good could flow from opening the doors to their help and advice. But that is not the world that exists, so domestic institutions have to be strong enough to attract and be enriched by good ideas from abroad, while not providing an attractive home for environmental, social or economic exploiters of human and natural resources. What is the evidence on this score? An important study by Sachs and Warner (1995) divided the nations of the world into two groups. One group included all countries that reached fairly modest degrees of four different measures of openness,[6] with all other countries considered to be closed. Among their group of open economies there was systematic evidence of convergence, with growth rates higher for those countries with initially lower levels of GDP per capita. Among the closed economies, by contrast, there was no such relation. Their conclusion was that developing countries wishing to raise their levels of GDP per capita towards those already achieved in the richer countries had to have sufficiently open economic and political systems to allow the lessons of foreign experience to be absorbed and applied.

Does this mean that national border effects are harmful, that national policies are bad if they deter any foreign investors, and that globalisation is inherently beneficial? No, it does not. First, the Sachs and Warner classification of open economies still admits of substantial domestic policies influencing the structure and pattern of openness.[7] More fundamentally, the evidence on national border effects presented earlier in this chapter offers a test of whether there is much to be gained from further increases in the degree of globalisation, at least among the industrial countries. The evidence shows that even among the industrial countries, merchandise trade intensities are ten times higher than those among the industrial countries, with border effects for financial and other service trade being even higher.

If raising the degree of international trade intensity to that already existing within national economies would lead to much by way of further productivity increases, then we would expect to find systematic evidence that smaller countries have lower levels of productivity and per capita incomes than larger countries. However, there is almost no evidence of scale effects of this sort. My conclusion from this evidence is that the degree of openness already existing among the industrial countries is great enough to permit the most advantageous international trading to take place, and to allow sufficiently free access to the best of foreign experiences and ideas. There are many developing countries with much lower degrees of openness, and many of these have no doubt much to gain from further increases in openness, especially if domestic capacities and institutions are already strong enough to glean the best and resist the worst of what is offered by the global economy.

CONCLUSION

The main message of this chapter is that there is much more scope and need for national policies than is popularly thought. This is especially true for policies of the sort needed to build institutions capable of supporting balanced and sustainable growth. This requires economic policy-makers to take a broader than usual perspective. The need for such an enlarged perspective, and for the need to take institution-building seriously, is for me the most striking lesson to be drawn from the experience of the 1990s.

NOTES

[1] Department of Economics, University of British Columbia. An earlier version of the paper was delivered at the meeting of the Canadian Association of Business Economists, Ottawa, March 26th, 1999 and the MIER National Outlook Conference, Kuala Lumpur, December 2–3, 1998. I am grateful for the CIDA support of the Queen's MIER project, and for SSHRC support of the underlying research. The Kuala Lumpur version of the paper is available as a Development Discussion Paper of the John Deutsch Centre at Queens University.

[2] Parts of this section, including Figure 1, are drawn from my paper, 'Canada's national economy: there's more to it than you think!' in Harvey Lazar and Ian McIntosh (eds) *The State of the Federation 1998/1999 – How Canadians Connect*, Kingston: Queens University.

[3] Despite its use in many early studies of international trade, the equation was considered suspect in that it could not easily be shown to be consistent with the dominant Heckscher-Ohlin model explaining net trade flows in terms of differential factor endowments. Anderson (1979) showed that the gravity model could be derived from expenditure share equations assuming commodities to be distinguished by place of production. Helpman (1984) and Bergstrand (1985) showed that the gravity model can also be derived from models of trade in differentiated products. Such trade must lie at the core of much of manufacturing trade, given the very large two-way flows of trade in even the most finely disaggregated industry data. Finally, Deardorff (1997) showed that a suitable modelling of transport costs produces the gravity equation as an estimation form even for the Heckscher-Ohlin model.

[4] However, this conclusion is heavily dependent on the nature of the data used to represent intra-provincial trading distances. Current research using analytical geography and census data to develop more firmly grounded measures of intra-provincial trade distances should show more clearly whether there are important differences between intra-provincial and inter-provincial trade densities.

[5] Tables 5 and 6 in Helliwell, Lee and Messinger (1998) show the forecast and actual post-FTA changes in Canada-US trade for each of 25 major sectors. Averaging across the sectors, Canadian exports were forecast, by the trade model used to support official pre-FTA estimates, to increase by 33 per cent, relative to GDP, but actually increased by more than 90 per cent. Imports were forecast to increase by 12 per cent, while actual growth, relative to GDP, from 1989 to 1996 was 46 per cent. These are simple averages of the sectoral results, which are larger than the figures for total trade because some of the smallest sectors, such as knitted products, have had the fastest post-FTA growth in two-way trade.

[6] These included a black market foreign exchange premium of less than 20 per cent, quotas covering less than 40 per cent of imports, absence of excessively distorting export marketing boards (a measure only applicable to African economies) and a non-socialist system. Since the countries of the USSR were not in the sample, the latter measure led to the exclusion of Angola, Benin, China, Congo, Ethiopia, Hungary, Mozambique, Nicaragua, Poland, Somalia, Zaire and Zimbabwe from the group of open economies.

[7] Among the Asian economies, Malaysia is recorded by Sachs and Warner as always open since independence in 1963, Singapore since independence in 1965, Taiwan open since 1963, Korea since 1968, Hong Kong and Thailand always open, and Indonesia since 1970.

REFERENCES

Almond, Gabriel A. and Sidney Verba (1963), *The Civic Culture: Political Attitudes and Democracy in Five Nations*, Princeton: Princeton University Press.

Anderson, James E. (1979), 'A Theoretical Foundation for the Gravity Equation', *American Economic Review* **69**, 106–16.

Ben-Shlomo, Y., I.R. White, and M.G. Marmot (1996), 'Does the Variation in Socioeconomic Characteristics of an Area Affect Mortality?', *British Medical Journal* **312**, 10013–4.

Bergstrand, Jeffrey H. (1985), 'The Gravity Equation in International Trade: Some Microeconomic Foundations and Empirical Evidence', *Review of Economics and Statistics* **67**, 474–81.

Coe, D.T. and E. Helpman (1995), 'International R&D Spillovers', *European Economic Review* **39**, 859–87.

Deardorff, Alan (1997), 'Does Gravity Work in a Frictionless World?', in Jeffrey A. Frankel (ed.), *The Regionalization of the World Economy*, Chicago: University of Chicago Press, pp. 7–28.

Engel, Charles, and J.H. Rogers (1996), 'How Wide is the Border?', *American Economic Review* **86**, 1112–25.

Feldstein, M., and C. Horioka (1980), 'Domestic Saving and International Capital Flows', *Economic Journal* **90**, 314–29.

Gravelle, H. (1998), 'How Much of the Relation Between Population Mortality and Unequal Distribution of Income Is a Statistical Artifact?', *British Medical Journal* **316**, 383–5.

Helliwell, John F. (1994), 'Empirical Linkages Between Democracy and Economic Growth', *British Journal of Political Science* **24**, 225–48.

Helliwell, John F. (1996a), 'Economic Growth and Social Capital in Asia', *NBER Working Paper No. 5470.*

Helliwell, John F. (1996b), 'How Much Do National Borders Matter For Quebec's Trade?', *Canadian Journal of Economics* **29**, 507–22.

Helliwell, John F. (1998), *How Much Do National Borders Matter?*, Washington DC: Brookings Institution.

Helliwell, John F. and Ross McKitrick (1998), 'Comparing Capital Mobility Across Provincial and National Borders', *NBER Working Paper No. 6624* (June).

Helliwell, John F., Frank C. Lee and Hans Messinger (1998), 'Effects of the Canada-US FTA on Interprovincial Trade', *Industry Canada working paper.*

Helliwell, John F. and Robert D. Putnam (1995), 'Economic Growth and Social Capital in Italy', *Eastern Economic Journal* **21**, 295–307.

Helliwell, John F. and Robert D. Putnam (1999), 'Education and Social Capital' *NBER Working Paper No. 7121.*

Helpman, E (1984), 'Increasing Returns, Imperfect Markets, and Trade Theory', in R. Jones and P. Kenen (eds), *Handbook of International Trade*, Amsterdam: North-Holland, Volume 1, 325–65.

Inglehart, Ronald (1990), *Culture Shift in Advanced Industrial Society*, Princeton: Princeton University Press.

Knack, Stephen, and Philip Keefer (1997), 'Does Social Capital have an Economic Payoff? A Country Investigation', *Quarterly Journal of Economics* **112**, 1251–88.

Marer, Paul, and Salvatore Zecchini (eds) (1992), *The Transition to a Market Economy: Volume 1- The Broad Issues*, Paris: OECD.

McCallum, John C.P. (1995), 'National Borders Matter: Canada-US Regional Trade Patterns', *American Economic Review* **85**, 615–23.

Mustard, C.A. (1998), *Income Inequality and Inequality in Health: Implications for Thinking About Well-Being*, Ottawa: Centre for the Study of Living Standards.

Nie, Norman H., Jane Junn and Kenneth Stehlik-Barry (1996), *Education and Democratic Citizenship in America*, Chicago: Chicago University Press.

Ohmae, Kenichi (1995), *The End of the Nation State: The Rise of Region Economies*, New York: The Free Press.

Persson, Torsten, and Guido Tabellini (1994), 'Is Inequality Harmful for Growth?' *American Economic Review* **84**, 600–621.

Putnam, Robert D. (1993), *Making Democracy Work: Civic Traditions in Modern Italy*, Princeton: Princeton University Press.

Putnam, Robert D. (1995), 'Tuning In, Tuning Out: The Strange Disappearance of Social Capital in America', *Political Science and Politics* 664–83.

Sachs, Jeffrey D. and Andrew Warner (1995), 'Economic Reform and the Process of Global Integration', *Brookings Papers on Economic Activity* **1**, 1–118.

Wei, Shang-Jin (1996), 'Intra-national Versus International Trade: How Stubborn Are Nations in Global Integration?', *NBER Working Paper 5531.*

Wilkinson, R.G. (1992), 'Income Distribution and Life Expectancy', *British Medical Journal* **304**, 165–8.

5. It's a Small World After All: The Global Economy in the Networked Age

Allan I. Mendelowitz

GLOBALISATION

Globalisation is the term used to describe the profound and rapid impact that events in one part of the world have on the social, political and economic institutions and lives of countries elsewhere in the world.

In earlier periods, despite the large volume of trade, investment flows, and patterns of migration, no one talked about 'globalisation'. In fact, globalisation only became a term of reference a decade ago. However, it has crept into our consciousness and proceeded to claim our attention across a whole host of venues. In finance, the events in one part of the world ripple through world financial markets and impose consequences on countries far away from the site of the economic earthquake. The financial crisis in the late 1990s in Thailand spread through Southeast Asia and then continued on to impact countries as far away as Russia and Brazil. Cultural events cut across national boundaries and continental divides. Ameliorating environmental degradation has taken on global proportions, as the debate has raged over how to respond to the pollution of the global commons. Countries have come together to negotiate worldwide treaties to protect endangered species and to ward off global warming by reducing greenhouse gas emissions. Even the principle of non-interference in the internal affairs of another country is being breached. In 1999, traditionally internal matters were deemed to have such far reaching global consequences that NATO waged a war in Yugoslavia over what in the past would have been viewed as purely a domestic matter.

Globalisation is a fact of life, but where did it come from and where will it take us? Globalisation happens when the barriers to deep interaction across borders fall. In the economic sphere, the post World War II era began with the formation of multilateral trade and finance institutions that were intended to promote greater economic interaction between countries. These institutions were created to promote economic growth and trade in the hope of avoiding a repeat of the economic crises following World War I and their role as a contributing cause of World War II. In the arena of international trade, the General Agreement on Tariffs and Trade (GATT) provided the forum in which the world's trading nations gathered together to negotiate reductions in barriers to trade. Through successive rounds of multilateral trade negotiations, tariff barriers have been significantly reduced and in some cases eliminated. When significant progress had been made on reducing tariff barriers, attention was turned to eliminating non-tariff barriers: protection of intellectual property; barriers to trade in services; discrimination in government procurement; trade related investment matters; etc. The reduction in government imposed barriers to trade has paid off spectacularly, with international trade in the post-war era growing more than twice as fast as worldwide Gross Domestic Product (GDP). Despite this growth in trade and the rise of the multinational enterprise, no one spoke of globalisation until recently.

The barriers to the type of deep economic, social, cultural and political interactions that are characterised as globalisation were only partly the result of government action. Other barriers that stood in the way of globalisation were naturally occurring – distance, language, and religious and cultural differences. The rise of globalisation can be traced to the changes in technology that have reduced and eliminated naturally occurring barriers. Certainly, the development of the jet transport is one such technology. And, most importantly from the perspective of this paper, is the development of ubiquitous, low-cost, modern digital telecommunications.

A simple progression from decades of my life – and I am not all that terribly old – illustrates the point. One type of event in human history always stands out in the minds of those who live through it – war. Those who experience it first hand remember it with an unrivalled intensity. Those who experience it second hand remember it in the ways in which the images of war are brought to them. The first war that I remember was the 1950s Korean conflict. The images of that war were black and white 'Movietone' newsreels shown at the local cinema. They appeared with a lag and lacked the power and punch that is now associated with war reporting. A little more than a decade later the war was Vietnam, and the pictures came from video tapes that were shown in living colour in virtually every home, every day on the network evening news broadcasts. During the 1991 Gulf War, CNN provided round-the-clock live TV broadcasts, from both sides, as the war unfolded. But, the coverage of the 1999 Kosovo war went beyond even that. The Internet provided multiple direct links to the unfolding events, in many cases without the intervention of news organisations. Instant news – and opinion – from everywhere and anyone, updated in real time. News broadcasts in the United States regularly showed Kosovo refugees who sought refuge in the United States huddled around a computer screen watching Internet broadcasts of news direct from the Balkans. And a staple on the radio news I listened to in my car as I commuted to and from work was the reading of e-mails exchanged between high school students in the United States and high school students in Kosovo.

As striking as this example is, it only begins to hint at the dramatic changes that the Internet and other networking technologies are having on every aspect and institution of social, political, and economic life. We are at the edge of a great transformation whose impact could be every bit as profound as the Industrial Revolution. The primary difference is that the changes are happening at a much faster pace than those of the Industrial Revolution.

THE NET CHANGES EVERYTHING

The Internet is the most prominent and visible of networking technologies. It is credited with holding extravagant promise for the entire globe. Is this believable? History is replete with exaggerated hype for new technologies that failed to achieve their promised potential. (Of course, there are also notable excesses on the other side as well – witness Charles H. Duel, the head of the US Office of Patents, who observed in 1899 that, 'everything that can be invented has been invented'.) In the case of the Internet, the hyperbolic prognostications may actually be understatement rather than exaggeration. An increasing body of research, as well as first hand observations, suggest that the Internet has the capacity to change nearly every aspect of social, political, and economic life. In the business world it is an enabling technology that makes possible new products and services and new ways of organising markets, connecting with customers, managing relations with suppliers, structuring the corporation, and designing business processes.

THE SIZE OF THE NET

A US Department of Commerce (1999) study included the compilation of a significant amount of data from various sources. Among the data were estimates of the growth of the Internet over the year May 1998–May 1999. The reported estimates included: an increase in the number of world-wide web users of 55 per cent; an increase in the number of Internet hosts of 46 per cent; an increase in the number of web servers of 128 per cent; and an increase in the number of new web addresses of 137 per cent. And, not unexpectedly, because other countries are starting from a smaller base, Internet use outside of the United States is growing faster than in the United States.

The inescapable conclusion that can be drawn from these data is that *the use of the web is exploding and no country can escape its impact.*

The report also included the estimate that 171 million people across the globe had access to the Internet in May of 1999. Out of that total, 97 million, or 57 per cent were located in the United States and Canada. This number represents about 37 per cent of the US population having access to the Internet, as compared to 8 to 10 per cent in other large developed countries such as France, Japan and Germany. Furthermore, the pace of change is unrelenting. Newspaper articles and magazine covers appear daily reporting the latest Internet innovation and advance. New Internet companies appear like mushrooms after a summer rainfall. And Internet millionaires and billionaires are created in large numbers at an age many of us still think of as not yet fully grown.

The observation that can be drawn from the data is that *the United States' lead in the use of the Internet means that researchers should look to the United States to gain insights into the impact of the Web and what is in store for other countries as the use of the Internet spreads.*

The data on e-commerce in the United States reveal that at the retail level the value of Internet based transactions is still small – in 1998 it was less than one per cent of all retail transactions – but growing so rapidly that the value is outstripping even the most optimistic recent projections. Business-to-business e-commerce is significantly larger and also growing rapidly.

The observation that can be drawn from these data is that *if a relatively small amount of web based business is able to create such visibility and have such an impact, the spread of the web will have a transforming impact on all commerce.*

COMPUTERS, NETWORKS AND THE PRODUCTIVITY PARADOX

The impact of investment in information technology on the performance of the US economy has been the subject of debate for some years. Some analysts concluded that despite the very large and sustained investment in information technology, there had been no measurable benefit in terms of US economic performance. Over a decade ago, Nobel Laureate and MIT economics professor Robert Solow observed in an oft-quoted remark that one could see the impact of the computer age everywhere but in the productivity statistics. This circumstance has been referred to as the 'productivity paradox'.

The situation began to change when the Internet became available to the general population in about 1992. Before that date the Internet was the domain of the Pentagon and a small community of academics. The statistics that are starting to appear for the 1990s now suggest a change is taking place. The United States in 1999 was in the midst of its longest ever sustained peacetime economic expansion which had the potential to become the longest economic expansion in its history. Unemployment had fallen to a 30-year low. Despite the length of the expansion and the very low rate of unemployment, and contrary to what was the pattern in past expansions, prices were not rising. Inflation in the United States was virtually non-existent. As Figure 5.1 shows, inflation was far lower during the last two years of the 1990s than it was during the comparable period of every post-war economic expansion of the past 40 years. Furthermore, the low level of inflation is not a statistical artifice: informed students of the US Consumer Price Index (CPI) consider the index to have an upward bias. Any errors in the index will tend to overstate the true level of inflation, not understate it.

Figure 5.1. Per Cent Change in Inflation During the Final Eight Quarters of Business Cycle Expansions

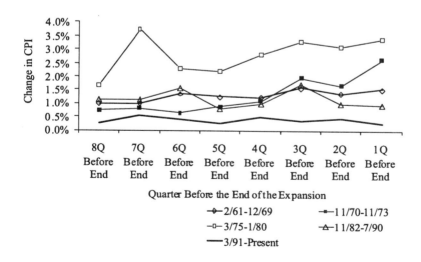

Sharply falling prices for information technology (IT) products make a direct contribution to the low inflation. The estimate is that falling prices in these industries brought down overall inflation by 0.7 per cent in 1996 and 1997 (*ibid.*) However, as will be discussed below, IT and networking technologies make an even more important contribution to lower inflation in terms of the role they play in lowering the cost structure of the entire economy and enhancing the efficiency with which goods and services are produced.

The data on inflation are accompanied by other data, which, when taken together, form the basis of an interesting story. While prices have been stable, real wages in the United States have been rising. Nevertheless, at the same time, corporate profits as a share of GDP have also been rising. Profits are the residual that is left after subtracting costs from revenues. If real wages are rising and prices are stable, profits can only increase over time if businesses are able to continually reduce their costs. Figure 5.2 shows a sharp increase in the 1990s in the share of US Gross Domestic Product (GDP) going to corporate profits. Such an increase is only possible in an environment of rising real wages and stable prices if costs are being reduced.

Figure 5.2. Ratio of Corporate Profits to GDP from 1973–97

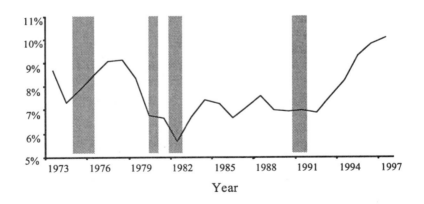

Note
GDP shown with inventory valuation and capital consumption adjustments, before tax, from quarterly data. Shaded bars represent periods of economic recession.

Source: Economic Report of the President, 1999; US Department of Commerce.

One indicator of how costs are being cut is the level of inventories the economy needs to build products and satisfy consumer demand. Figure 5.3 compares the inventory/sales ratio over the current economic expansion with other expansions of the past four decades.

Figure 5.3. Inventory/Sales Ratios Over the Course of Past and Current Business Cycle Expansions

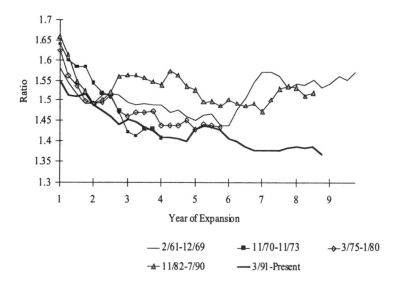

As can be clearly seen in the graph, the 1990s expansion took place with a steady decline in inventory levels. The importance of this graph cannot be understated. First, it gives an indication of how cost is being taken out of the economy. Inventories are an important component of the cost of doing business. Lower inventories directly lower the cost of production and distribution. Second, the data are important in terms of the sustainability of the expansion. Recessions do not just happen. There has to be something that triggers them. Sometimes they are made in Washington when the Federal Reserve raises interest rates in a deliberate attempt to attack actual or anticipated inflation. Sometimes they are the result of cutbacks in production that are prompted by undesired inventory build-up. The fact that US industry has been reducing the level of inventories at the same time that the US economy has been growing so strongly yields a double benefit. The lower cost structure of industry helps to keep inflation low and, consequently, makes it less likely that the Federal Reserve will tighten monetary policy and slow growth. And the falling inventory levels help to reduce the likelihood of an unintended inventory build-up that could also trigger an economic slowdown.

Despite the earlier scepticism embodied in the debate over the productivity paradox, there now does seem to be something different happening in the economy. The statistics mentioned above illustrate the starting point of this transformation. The hints contained in the macroeconomic data are reinforced by first hand observations at a small sample of firms with respect to how they are using networking technologies to transform their operations in ways that lower costs, reduce cycle times, and improve customer service.

A key reason why the investment in computers and information technology is having a different impact today than in the 1980s is that a very different technology is being deployed. When computers became available in the first decades after the Second World War, they represented a great advance. However, they did not transform how business was done. In the most fundamental sense, the advent of the computer in many cases heralded the transfer of paper-based processes onto computers. That change enabled larger quantities of information to be processed more quickly and accurately. However, it did not fundamentally change business processes.

Even the arrival of the personal computer (PC) was not a transforming change. It brought the power of a computer to the desktop and the home; however, it likewise did not transform business processes. In fact, Ken Olson, the founder of Digital Equipment Corporation observed in 1977 that, 'There is no reason anyone would want a computer in their home'.

What changed in the 1990s was the coming together of computers, low-cost digital communications, the opening of the Internet to commerce, and the easy-to-use graphical-interface web browser. It was the rise of the Internet as a universally accessible phenomenon that enabled computers to have a transforming impact that was not seen in earlier years.

Notwithstanding the interesting data discussed above, standard measures of economic activity are not good indices for capturing the full implications of the Internet and other networking technologies. The Internet creates significant changes in the quality of life, products, and relationships which traditional indices of economic output, productivity, and standard of living do not measure. For example, Gross Domestic Product per capita is becoming an increasingly imperfect indicator of social welfare. It fails to reflect all of the ways in which networking-based changes can raise real income and improve the quality of life. For example, take the case of a consumer making a lower-cost online purchase rather than going to a mall to make an equivalent higher-cost purchase. The lower-cost online purchase should be reflected in both GDP figures and price indices. However, what will be missed is:

- the benefit that the consumer gains from having more leisure time (i.e. the time saved that would have been spent going to the mall);
- the transportation costs saved by not driving to the mall (gasoline and wear and tear on the car); as well as
- the avoided negative externalities, such as the added urban congestion and air pollution associated with a trip to the mall.

Such changes are real and important, but they do not get counted.

Furthermore, it is impossible to foresee all of the cascading changes that will follow from a change that is as significant as the emergence of the Internet. For example, when the concept of 'just-in-time' (JIT) inventory first arrived in the United States its immediate appeal was its promise to lower inventory levels, thereby decreasing required levels of working capital and increasing profitability. However, when JIT was adopted, it became clear that it could only work with zero-defect parts, because each time a defective part entered the production line, the line was forced to shut down. In response, companies installed systems that assured defect-free components, and that, in turn, resulted in higher quality final products. Higher quality products meant lower re-work costs and warranty charges and more satisfied customers, all of which brought greater revenue and higher profits. In the end, a change undertaken to decrease working capital led to significant unanticipated improvements in efficiency and profitability. These are the kinds of transformations and unanticipated benefits that should be expected to flow from the availability and usage of networking technology.

MARKETS BECOME BORDERLESS AND TIMELESS

The World Wide Web is a borderless 7x24 world: access is available to anyone, from anywhere, at anytime. If you have Internet access, you suffer no limitation due to distance or location. The sharply plummeting price of telecommunications makes the exchange of information low cost and efficient. The boundary of the consumer's market-space is the World Wide Web. And, for businesses, the value chain can be managed from anywhere in the world with the rich and deep exchange of information available with digital networks.

For example, some types of service workers no longer need to be in close proximity to provide their professional services. In the United States, high technology companies seeking to convince the Congress to amend current immigration law to permit the temporary migration and employment of more high-technology workers, such as software engineers, have expended considerable political capital. Yet, digital networks make such efforts seem out of touch with current reality. Such workers can be employed effectively from anywhere they happen to live. Bangalore, India has become a world centre for software engineering and computer programming. A preponderance of Chief Information Officers with whom I have discussed this issue responded that they use programmers in India as an integral part of their programming teams. Another example from India involves the use of services provided by Indian physicians. Medical doctors in the United States typically dictate their patient evaluations into recording devices. Such recordings are now transmitted to India where they are transcribed by Indian physicians and transmitted back to the United States in real time. The cost is lower than it would be using US typists and the quality of the transcription is higher because the Indian physicians are far better able to understand the technical material that is being transcribed.

Furthermore, as advances proceed apace and new mark-up languages are adopted which support translation-on-the-fly, accessing the Web in a language other than English will be a far smaller impediment.

MARKETS ARE CHANGING

In the pre-Internet world the cost of acquiring price and availability information about markets was very high. Similarly, the cost to business of acquiring information about specific consumer preferences was also high. The Internet lowers the cost of acquiring information for all parties and changes the dynamics of price determination.

The 'Law of One Price' is moving from economic models to the real world. In economic models any product is sold to every consumer for the same price. This outcome results from the forces of competition interacting with consumers who are assumed to have perfect knowledge about all prices and alternatives. However, in the real world this is rarely the case. Imperfect information makes it possible for sellers to 'price discriminate', i.e. some buyers are charged more and some are charged less. However, networking technologies are now changing that by enhancing consumers' ability to find the lowest priced products. It is now possible to use an artificial agent, or 'Bot', to search the Web to find the lowest priced source for a specific good. While actual purchasing decisions may reflect considerations other than just the selling price (e.g. speed of order fulfilment, transaction costs for shipping and handling, reliability of the seller, etc.), Bots have the potential to make one of the fundamental constructs of economic models a reality – perfect information and its resulting impact on prices. The implication for companies is that they will increasingly become price takers. The power of the market to set prices will grow and the ability of firms to set prices administratively for the products that they sell will be further weakened. In such circumstances, higher prices for what are their core commodity products will only be sustainable when firms can differentiate their products in ways that consumers perceive add value.

In an economy where the Law of One Price exists and entry costs are low, 'Relationship, Relationship, Relationship' is the new business imperative. 'Location, location, location' is less important in a networked economy than the relationships built with consumers. In this economic environment, companies must find ways both to differentiate their 'product bundle' and to strengthen the relationship with their customers in order to justify higher margins and increase sales. Personal computers have become a commodity product sold in fiercely competitive markets with virtually perfect price and product information. Consequently, computer companies are searching for ways to differentiate their products in ways that consumers value. For example, Micron Technologies has bundled its computers with a year of free unlimited Internet-based computer and software training courses. Gateway Computer has bundled its computers with a year's free access to the Internet. In the highly competitive retail book market, Amazon.com creates 'virtual communities' where customers post on-line reviews of the books they read. That information enables the company to individualise its marketing by recommending new books to customers based on their revealed preferences. Realisation of the 'law of one price' appears to be driving companies to redefine their products in terms of bundled services or a total experience.

New types of intermediaries are supplanting traditional intermediaries in distribution systems. Online matchmaking and sales are supplanting traditional wholesalers, distributors and retailers. This supplanting of old intermediaries is taking place because Internet-based sales systems are able to create markets at substantial cost savings as compared to traditional markets. Savings on advertising, sales commissions, inventory, and excess production make the distribution segment of the economy more efficient. Internet based stock trading is replacing the stockbroker and his telephone. The monopoly that well known investment banks have held over initial public offerings (IPOs) because of their distribution systems is now threatened by direct distribution of new stock offerings over the Internet. Internet based business-to-business communities are bringing buyers and sellers together more efficiently than tradition trade shows and trade publications. And the Internet has become the auction venue of choice for selling one of a kind items and surplus products.

PRODUCTS ARE CHANGING

The products sold in today's marketplace are being replaced, changed, and complemented by the availability of networking technologies.   First, networking technologies present a new channel for supplying some existing products.   Second, networks allow for a variety of services to be added to existing products, both complementing and replacing current functions and services.   Third, mass customisation is permitting companies to respond to individual customer needs with distinct products and services.

A New Medium for Supplying Goods and Services

The Internet offers unparalleled opportunities to reduce the cost of production, sales, and distribution of products that can be converted from atoms to bits and bytes. Products like software, recorded music, and videos are all similar in one very important respect: the first copy of any one of these products is very expensive to make.   It can take many millions of dollars to write a computer program or make a movie. However, after the first copy has been made, all subsequent copies are very inexpensive.   No matter what a computer program cost to create, the marginal cost of making the second copy on a CD-ROM is only about US$0.10.   Once the program is written, the major costs are packaging, distribution, and marketing.

Such products are perfect for sale and distribution over the Internet. Music, software and videos can all be stored on Internet servers and downloaded on demand. Once the first copy is made, there is no need to incur production, inventory, or distribution costs because the consumer can be sold disembodied bits and bytes rather than a physical product. One of the new products introduced in 1999 was a 'Walkman' sized digital device that stores and plays music downloaded from the Internet. Two other new products in the same vein are digital books. These devices download from the Internet and store the text of books. These devices are about the size of regular books, and one even permits underlining and making margin notes on the digital pages of the books.

Adding Characteristics to Products and Enhancing Capabilities

Products are beginning to appear that use networking technologies to augment the attributes and capabilities of the products and, thereby, to differentiate them in the market.

For example, a General Electric subsidiary sells plastic to manufacturers who use it in their products. The plastic is stored in silos with sensors linked to an Internet connection. When the inventory of plastic drops to the point at which replenishment is needed, the sensor identifies the need and the silo automatically orders more inventory over the Internet. General Motors already offers an active safety and security monitoring system that combines sensors, a cell phone, and a Global Positioning System (GPS) receiver to provide a new range of services. If the system senses that the airbags have inflated, the system will automatically call to report the possibility of an accident and the car's location so that help can be dispatched, if needed. Several auto companies announced in 1999 that they would offer the option of an Internet-based radio for their cars. For a US$9.95 per monthly fee subscribers will have access to the same 100 stations anywhere in the country. One automaker is planning to offer vehicles that detect problems before they are apparent to the driver, and automatically alert their repair shop about the needed repairs. This application has almost boundless potential for many other products, such as household appliances, which could use networking technologies to provide this type of value-added service. And one home appliance maker has already demonstrated an Internet linked refrigerator that can monitor food consumption and may be able to order restocking over the Internet.

The Internet can also be used to upgrade and modify products after they are in customers' hands. Cisco Systems, a leading producer of Internet equipment sells products that consist of both hardware and software. Their products can be upgraded over time with new software. The company enhances the value of its product to its customers by providing software upgrades free if they are accessed over the Internet. This approach adds value for the customer while imposing minimal additional distribution costs on the seller.

Mass Customisation

The Internet allows consumers to interact directly with manufacturers and service providers, to input important preference information, and to access product data. This more robust data exchange transmitted automatically through the supply chain, enables unprecedented efficiency gains. Products will increasingly be 'mass customised' – tailored specifically for end users through direct consumer interfaces without the traditionally high costs of customisation achieved through human interaction with the consumer. The process is just beginning, but it should proceed rapidly. Already in the 1990s the leading build-to-order computer manufacturers provide Internet based ordering that gives the customer the ability to purchase a computer built exactly to the customer's specification. When a Dell customer does this, the automated system informs the company's suppliers as to what parts and components to ship to make the newly ordered computer. This capability should spread to many other products. For example, such Internet based sale of men's clothing would permit suits to be produced and sold with the combination of a jacket and pants that fit the actual purchaser rather than the statistical profile of the average purchaser.

CORPORATE STRUCTURES AND ALL BUSINESS PROCESSES ARE CHANGING

The level of competition in the US economy is much higher than it had been earlier in the post-war era. A number of factors have contributed to this circumstance:

* Substantial deregulation of major sectors of the US economy, including telecommunications, financial services, energy, civil aviation, and surface transportation;
* A significant increase in the internationalisation of the US economy with the share of US GDP that is exported and imported doubling over the past two decades;
* A significant overhang of excess capacity in the world in a number of major industrial sectors, making for very hungry competitors; and
* The very rapid rates of innovation in technology, business models and products do not permit a successful company to just rest on its laurels. The watchword for the US economy at the end of the twentieth century is: 'If you stop for lunch, you are lunch.'

A consequence of this high level of competitiveness is that producers have increasingly become price takers. That is, the United States economy has made the transition from a world of 'cost-plus' pricing to a world of Economics 101. The market sets the price and companies have to figure out how to get their costs down to a level that will permit them to make a profit. Were the competitive pressure less, it is likely that the appeal of new, more efficient ways of doing business would also be less. But, that is not an option. In this context the Internet is an enabling technology that permits the adoption of new more efficient ways of doing business.

Corporate Structure

Corporate structure is in flux. Earlier in the post-war era the vertically integrated company was considered to be the most efficient way to organise a business. The understanding of this organisational form is most closely associated with the work of Chandler (1962). The vertically integrated firm was dominant in its era because of its ability to manage and process information efficiently in the context of a complex production process. The structure survived as the efficient organisational solution as long as the costs of acquiring, managing, and processing information did not change. A company could succeed if it did a good job of vertically integrating the different functions in its value chain. This was true even if it was not best in class at doing the individual processes that made up the value chain.

The advent of networking technologies changed the equation. The Internet and other networking technologies dramatically lowered the cost of exchanging information within the firm and between firms. Or to put it another way, 'If it is cheaper to conduct transactions internally, the organisation grows, if the opposite, then it shrinks. The industrial era leveraged internal transactions, but networks make the value of central control and expensive bureaucracy lower' (Malone and Laubacher, 1998).

The ability to manage a supply chain efficiently outside the confines of a single company is giving rise to new organisational forms. Companies are increasingly focusing on their core competencies and outsourcing the rest. The force of competition means that every stage of the value chain needs to be done efficiently if a business is to succeed. The maxim for success is 'Do what you do best and outsource the rest'.

The most competitive companies are doing just that. Cisco Systems' core competency revolves around the design of new products and the managing of customer relations. It is about a US$10 billion dollar a year company with only about 500 production workers. Half of Cisco's products are produced and shipped to customers without Cisco ever seeing them or touching them. Product quality at supplier plants is monitored by Cisco using a network. The Federal Express Corporation is a large and successful world-wide express package delivery company. Federal Express had to develop a complex logistics management system in order to do its core business – the picking up, routing, tracking, delivering, billing and verifying of millions of packages a day. Once it had developed this capability it realised it had an asset that was of great value. It had developed the capability for managing supply and distribution chains far more efficiently than any manufacturing business. This capacity is its most valuable core competency and it initiated a whole new line of business taking over the integrated supply and distribution chains of manufacturing companies.

Business Processes

The availability of the Internet and other networking technologies has created great scope for corporations to improve the efficiency of just about every business process: new product development; production management;

customer relations; financial management, and human resources administration. Increasingly companies are relying on networked-based solutions because they are scalable, they reduce cycle time, and they improve quality and customer satisfaction.

Customer Relations

The types of jobs in the US economy in which productivity growth have historically been the poorest have been labour intensive service jobs. Networking technologies offer for the first time the potential for significant productivity improvement in this area. Some of the most labour intensive business functions have revolved around customer relations – taking orders, filling orders, and responding to requests for post-sale customer support. Companies like Cisco Systems and Federal Express have developed networked based solutions to reduce the labour content in these functions significantly. Federal Express developed an Internet based tracking system that permits any customer to determine the exact status of his or her package by going to a Federal Express website. Federal Express estimates that the company avoided building several new call centres to respond to customer queries and avoided hiring 2000 new employees. Cisco Systems has moved 80 per cent of its customer orders to an automated web-based system. Cycle time on orders was reduced, new order error rates were virtually eliminated, customer satisfaction rose, and Cisco avoided hiring an additional 700 employees. Cisco has also moved about 81 per cent of its customer technical support to an automated web-based system. The technical support offered through the website is the more routine and predictable type of assistance. Responding to the remaining 19 per cent of the technical support queries requires a staff of nine hundred highly trained software engineers. The company's customers are highly satisfied with the automated support. And the technical support staff is happy not to have to bother with routine and lower level types of questions. Their time is taken up with more challenging and interesting problems. And the company is pleased to have reduced the staffing levels required for customer support. The involvement of customers in such systems blurs the line between the customer and an employee; clearly the customer is a customer, but in the process of placing an order or accessing automated customer technical support the customer is performing functions that had previously been performed by employees.

Human Resource Management

Networked-based solutions offer broad scope for reducing the costs of managing employee relations and human resources (HR) functions. Leading-edge companies are moving employee training to the corporate Intranets. Employees can access the training from their desks at times that are most convenient for them. All employee manuals, newsletters, organisational communication, and benefits information are being placed on corporate Intranets. Companies are able to keep the information updated in real time and avoid the high costs of duplication, distribution, and storage required by paper-based systems used for these purposes. Interactive employee websites also allow employees to maintain their own information in the company's personnel systems. In the old way of doing things an employee who has a new home address would fill out a paper form and then give it to an HR employee who would input the information into the company's HR data system. With an interactive Intranet website the employee with the new address simply enters the information directly into the system obviating the need for the HR employee. The leading-edge companies have also adopted automated travel management systems. Employees use web-based systems to make travel arrangements, complete necessary documentation, and when the travel is over the automated system fills out the employee's travel voucher using the travel authorisation data and the employee's credit card charges. If all charges are within the boundaries of standard expense levels, the voucher is accepted and the employee receives an electronic funds reimbursement in 48 hours of his or her return from travel.

New Product Development

The availability of networks has enabled dramatic changes in new product development that are reducing costs, cutting cycle time for new product introduction, and better matching new products to consumer preferences.

Software companies routinely release development copies of their software to the public. The role of the public in this process is to use and test the new software to assess useability and to debug the programs. Programs with millions of lines of code are very difficult to de-bug fully. By providing beta versions to the public, the companies are able to enlist the input of hundreds of thousands of knowledgeable users to perfect the product. The Internet provides a real time mechanism for the software companies to stay in touch with their 'beta' testers. This mechanism can even be a source of revenue for the companies. Microsoft in 1999 charged customers US$59.95 for the privilege of receiving a copy of the final beta version of Windows 2000 and helping Microsoft to perfect its product.

In the automobile industry, which has used propriety networks for the past decade and a half, the networks have enabled the use of platform teams that cut across all departments from design to manufacturing, as well as in-house and outsourced service providers to dramatically shorten the cost and cycle time of new car design and introduction.

In the financial services sector, the Internet has enabled a significant shortening of the time and cost of syndicating large loans.   A loan syndication is a very paper intensive process.   Typically the legal documents are large and change daily.   Significant sums of money were being spent copying and distributing copies of documents to participating banks around the world.   This is being replaced now with an Internet-based system.   The lead bank in the syndicate maintains all of the documents on a website and participating banks access each iteration of the documents in real time via the Internet.

Impact on Employment

As all of these changes take place they are having a profound impact on the nature of employment.   The substitution of automated networked-based business processes for labour intensive services is dramatically changing the workplace: some jobs are disappearing, others are changing, and new ones are being created.

In a leading-edge-networked company the changes are dramatic.   Their current activities are a preview of what is in store for the rest of the world's economy as the changes spread.   Virtually all communication is via e-mail. Consequently, professionals type all of their own 'written' communications. Secretaries are no longer needed to type letters.   Virtually all of the documents are digital and retained in digital form.   Secretaries are no longer needed to file papers and documents.   Networked cross-functional teams carry out new product development efficiently.   Old rigid corporate offices and divisions are a thing of the past.   Order processing and customer technical support is highly automated on the Internet and fewer employees are needed for these tasks.   And, when the product is shipped, the billing is fully automated. The chief financial officer (CFO) has real time information on all aspects of the business using automated systems.   Even though the finance department operates with far fewer 'bean counters' than previously, the CFO is able to determine precisely the current financial condition of the company on any day of the year and at any time of the day.

This capsule of a networked company is taken from the best of the real world today.   And it represents the universal model of the future because of its superior efficiency.   Today there are three different types of companies:

- Companies born on the web;
- Established companies that are effectively using network technologies to improve the efficiency of their operations; and

- Companies that don't get it or can't get it.

The world of tomorrow will have only two types of companies: the first two categories. The companies that can't get it or don't get it will cease to exist because they will not be able to compete in a global marketplace with companies that are securing the greater level of efficiency enabled by networking technologies.

IN SUMMATION

Lest those in the cloistered confines of the University view all of this from the perspective only of disinterested researchers, be warned that academia will not escape the Internet earthquake.

Education in the past has been a bundle of products and services. A university degree represented:

- Content, i.e., substantive education;
- Cachet, i.e., the social and economic benefit of being educated at a university of distinction; and
- Social experience, i.e., the contacts and friendships formed over the university years.

The Internet is making it possible to separate out the different components of a university degree and acquire them separately. The borderless world of the Internet makes it possible for a student to attend a lecture anywhere in the world without having to travel to a far destination. There is nothing to stop a student in New Zealand from attending courses at Oxford without leaving home. The content can be acquired with or without the cachet of an Oxford degree. Furthermore, an economics student need not settle for a lecture from me, when he or she may take an entire course of study taught exclusively by Nobel Laureates. It is easy to do on the Internet because Internet solutions are perfectly scalable. There is no limit to the size of the Internet classroom. Furthermore, the nature of education will change. It has been known for some time that students remember much more of what they do, as compared to what they read or hear. The future of education is unlikely to be just talking heads broadcast over the Internet. The Internet offers the potential of a far more effective teaching tool through the use of multisensory, multimedia learning simulations.

Academia, business, government, and communities will all change with the spread of the Internet and the broadband communications capability that will allow it to realise its full potential. No one and no institution can escape the changes that are coming.   The networked era presents the fall of barriers that makes the progress of globalisation the unavoidable future for everyone.

REFERENCES

Chandler, Alfred (1962), *Strategy and Structure: Chapters in the History of the American Industrial Enterprise*, Cambridge: MIT Press.

Malone, Thomas W. and Robert J Laubacher. (1998), 'The Dawn of the E-Lance Economy', *Harvard Business Review* 145–152.

US Department of Commerce (1999), *The Emerging Digital Economy II*, Washington DC, June.

6. Globalisation and New Zealand: Living in the Real World

Roderick Deane

The pressures of globalisation on New Zealand today are unquestionably intense and different from the past, but in a sense they are part of a continuum from which we can learn much.

Many years ago, I did a doctoral dissertation, now sadly dated, on foreign investment and capital flows in New Zealand, a topic which at the time was hugely controversial. Subsequent to that, I had the fascinating experience of working in the Reserve Bank of New Zealand for a period and the International Monetary Fund during a series of domestic and international capital flow crises. I recall also sharing with Tim Groser, another contributor to this volume, an interesting period during which our Prime Minister of the time, Sir Robert Muldoon, was anxious to reform the international monetary system and Tim and I wrote his speeches, sitting behind him at various international conferences trying to minimise our own embarrassment. Today I work in New Zealand's largest corporation which is interconnected with the rest of the world in surprisingly diverse and stimulating ways, including operating in an international transit market in telephony calls which comprises one of our fastest growing revenue streams. For New Zealand, the Internet is the latest startling illustration of globalisation at work.

My most outstanding realisation of New Zealand's exposure to and vulnerability within the global economy was in June 1984, when a series of extensive interventions in the New Zealand economy by way of controls over wages, prices, interest rates, dividends, the exchange rate, and so on, culminated in both a huge fiscal deficit, which on the definition of the time ran up to 9 per cent of GDP, and an explosive balance of payments current account deficit.

Despite a series of warnings to Prime Minister Muldoon that any significant new event could trigger a severe foreign exchange crisis, he announced a snap election one evening, and the following morning the foreign exchange screens were blank. Panic emerged and no one was prepared to quote on foreign exchange rates. In the space of a few weeks, the Reserve Bank sold more foreign exchange than it had previously sold in a year.

Under instructions from the government, the exchange rate was not adjusted prior to the impending election, and instead the Reserve Bank funded the external crisis by way of heavy subsidies of the forward exchange market and extensive borrowing from offshore banks through credit lines which had been established with just such a contingency in mind.

The lessons which could be learned from that period included the following.

First, poor economic policies and extensive government interventions are typically inimical not only to economic growth but also to international competitiveness. Politicians and civil servants are not good at assessing and judging free market situations such that they can exercise controls over those markets of any sustainable kind.

Second, despite the existence of exchange controls at the time and also import licensing arrangements, numerous parties, both domestic and abroad, had incentives to engage in international capital market activity, typically placing bets against the inadequacy of government policies. While offshore speculators are often blamed in these circumstances, New Zealand experience at the time suggested that well informed small and large domestic parties were indeed the principal speculators, which was not surprising given the need for them to protect their own positions. The principal offshore involvement came from those banks that were willing to assist with the huge short term funding required to prop up the ailing foreign exchange market place. There was no question that domestic traders rather than offshore capitalists stimulated the crisis.

Third, the capital flows were not driven by a few large wealthy individuals or corporations, but rather by a multitude of organisations including, interestingly, several large government commercial organisations which attempted to take large scale forward exchange cover in order to exploit for themselves the subsidies which the government was unwisely pumping in to the forward exchange market. When I queried the Prime Minister about the wisdom of this, he indicated that the Reserve Bank could make its own decision on the matter, at which stage we declined applications for forward exchange cover from government trading entities.

Fourth, the participants in the market had a common objective of spreading their risk by protecting their return on their assets or minimising their liabilities. This behaviour was economically rational but attracted considerable political abuse, despite the fact that the economic solutions to the dilemma, at least in a short run sense, were obvious to all, i.e. an exchange rate adjustment.

Fifth, no matter how detailed the controls might be with respect to the exchange rate, tariffs, exchange controls, or import licensing, at the end of the day these only operate at the margin to inhibit market flows and do not prevent major crises. These controls may divert flows or distort capital arrangements, but if the crisis is of major proportions it will override bureaucrats' attempts to defeat it.

This New Zealand experience of the mid-1980s was in some ways a small-scale reproduction of the type of capital market volatility experienced more broadly in Asia in 1997-8. The Asian crisis arose in part from a failure of government policies, in some cases extensive market intervention, and domestic economic imbalances, with a large number of players essentially losing their nerve and acting in concert to protect their positions. An over extended banking system in a number of Asian countries was not immediately analogous to the New Zealand experience, although the New Zealand banking system was certainly distorted by the extensive controls which surrounded it at the time.

All of this says that in many ways there is little new in the concept of globalisation at a generalised level.

In terms of living with the effects of globalisation, Telecom New Zealand is an interesting case study. The company is easily the largest on the New Zealand stock exchange, with a market capitalisation which vastly exceeds that of the next largest company, and indeed comprises around one-third of the total market capitalisation of the top 40 companies on the New Zealand exchange. In terms of the US Business Week publications list of the top 1000 companies in the world, at the last count Telecom stood around number 620. Within Australasia, we rank within the top ten companies in terms of capitalisation.

Globalisation impacts on a company like Telecom with respect to its shareholding, its financing, the technology we utilise, and with respect to the marketplace in which we operate, whether it be the market for top level management, the wholesale market for international traffic, or the competitive arena for our products and services.

For example, on the financing side, until early 1998 two large American corporations owned between them 50 per cent of Telecom stock. When Ameritech decided to exit its 25 per cent holding in early 1998, the secondary public offering which Telecom helped to promote along with Ameritech, comprised one of the largest six such secondary offerings in the previous several years. When Bell Atlantic decided to issue exchangeable notes off its own balance sheet in favour of its holding of Telecom stock, the exchangeable note issue was the largest which had been launched in the world at that time.

Although these matters were almost unremarked in the New Zealand media, they were huge financial transactions by New Zealand standards and very large transactions by international standards. From a Telecom New Zealand perspective, they were exercised in a manner that turned out to be very successful. In an analogous way, the company itself borrows extensively offshore by way of issues in other marketplaces, such as a major capital notes issue in to the United States, and via a series of cross border lease financial deals.

The advantage of this internationalisation is not simply that Telecom is able to fund its operations with the lowest possible cost of capital, but rather that it can finance its operations at all in the sense that funding a corporation of this size in New Zealand today would be impossible if there was reliance solely on the domestic marketplace. Transactions of the scale just referred to are inevitably of an international character and ensure competitiveness for Telecom with respect to both its equity and its debt financing. Given the pace of globalisation in the telecommunications industry, where other huge international telecommunications companies are free to operate as they wish in New Zealand, and indeed do so, it is readily apparent that a New Zealand company such as Telecom needs to be able to access its capital at the lowest possible cost and in the most efficient available manner.

On the shareholding front, despite the initial privatisation of Telecom a decade ago and subsequent secondary offerings by way of sell downs by the major offshore shareholders, more than 70 per cent of our stock is held offshore. While this may be disappointing to some New Zealanders the truth of the matter is that New Zealanders have ample opportunity to buy shares in Telecom either on the New Zealand stock exchange, or on the Australian or New York stock exchanges. For one reason or another, they have not chosen to do so, presumably in part in deference to the need for New Zealanders to diversify their own investments given that this country is such a tiny proportion of total world trading and commercial activity. Since we are less than 1 per cent of total world stock exchange valuations, it is to be expected that New Zealanders would wish to have a substantial proportion of their investments abroad to diversify risk and to capture external growth opportunities.

Moreover, funds managers who invest in Telecom extensively have their own prudential limits in terms of the size of the investment stake they can take in any one company. If Telecom were restricted solely to shareholdings by domestic funds managers and domestic residents, those funds managers would in most cases exceed their prudential limits in terms of exposure to a single entity. This would be a problem not only for the funds managers but also for Telecom in the sense that it would at the end of the day contribute to a higher cost of capital and inhibit the growth of the company.

All of this makes it doubly important that the concerns of overseas investors are keenly appreciated by New Zealand governments. Foreign investors typically look for sound economic policies and less rather than more regulation in order to provide greater certainty with respect to trading market conditions. Threats of regulation to industries such as telecommunications will simply increase the cost of capital for companies such as Telecom, to say nothing of suppressing innovation and enterprise.

On the technology front, the freedom to access equipment, and new products and services, together with all the latest technology surrounding those, is another tremendous benefit of internationalisation, both to supplier and consumer alike. Rapid emulation of overseas experiences is a much more efficient and economical approach than attempting to develop or invent technologies such as an Internet protocol network, ATM, ISDN, ADSL, and so on here within New Zealand. We have neither the scale nor the expertise to do this other than in some niche market areas.

In terms of the marketplace more generally, a company such as Telecom has international exposure in a variety of ways. The largest single investment project in New Zealand at the present time would have to be the Southern Cross cable, in which Telecom has a 50 per cent equity stake, along with international partners Cable and Wireless - Optus and MCI Worldcom. The cost of this cable, which stretches from the United States to New Zealand to Australia and back to the US, via Hawaii and Fiji, will be of the order of NZ$2.3 billion. This project is dependent on international trading and data traffic and major international partnering arrangements with other big players.

In an analogous way, the principal competitors Telecom faces in the domestic market are typically owned by large international telecommunications companies such as British Telecom, Vodafone, Telstra, and so on. Internationally driven efficiency standards will drive further reductions in competitive prices in New Zealand to the great advantage of New Zealand consumers, but also in a way which means that Telecom New Zealand has to be free to pursue the best international practices in pricing, marketing, technology, funding, and management. Too many New Zealanders regard a company like Telecom as essentially a domestic company; yet, to survive, Telecom sits squarely on the world stage in terms of the demands that will be placed upon it to succeed commercially.

The implication of all this for a company like Telecom is that we are essentially integrated into the global economy, which helps to lower our systems costs, provides us with the latest technology, yields us the lowest cost of capital, and intensifies the competitive pressures upon us to the benefit of all New Zealanders. Despite this internationalisation of a company that some years ago appeared principally domestically oriented, national sovereignty remains strongly protected given the framework within which we must work, of New Zealand government economic policies, and New Zealand laws and regulations.

It is interesting to observe that globalisation can in fact impose higher standards than New Zealand might choose to adopt, as illustrated by our need to comply not only with New Zealand standard accounting requirements but also with the listing requirements of the New York stock exchange in order to be listed on Wall Street and to comply with US GAAP (Generally Accepted Accounting Principles). And yet, as a NZ based company, Telecom is also subject to New Zealand disclosure regulations - totally uncoordinated with US GAAP disclosure provisions - which require us to provide a third set of accounts, in addition to those required under New Zealand accounting standards and United States accounting standards. The additional cost imposed by these requirements is substantial (and probably totally unnecessary!).

Free capital flows also impose their own sets of constraints, but these can be beneficial to New Zealanders in the sense that if we spend substantially more than we earn as a nation, and thus incur external current account deficits, financing those deficits by means of international capital flows imposes a set of disciplines upon governments and government policies which are more likely to be beneficial than detrimental to the country. Capital controls if they were to exist simply attempt to shield governments from the disapproval of their citizens, as illustrated by those countries where governments had pursued their own excesses and their leaders subsequently complained that capital liberalisation had gone too far because it imposed disciplines on those excesses. Parties such as George Soros, benefited not so much from skills in international capital speculation but rather from predicting government ineptness and the outcome of that ineptness.

One of the more intriguing issues facing the New Zealand corporate world is why a series of major New Zealand companies have too often not been successful with respect to their offshore investments. Companies such as Fletcher Challenge, Carter Holt Harvey, Brierleys, and indeed Telecom, have recorded their failures abroad and in some cases overseas excursions have written off more shareholder value than they have created. This presumably reflects a lack of sufficient global experience and global exposure and argues the case for more such experiences and exposure rather than less. Beyond that, New Zealand still remains too commodity dependent with respect to some of its larger corporates and we have not driven powerfully enough into the value-added products and services.

This brief account of some of the lessons from the impact of international capital flows on New Zealand during a time of crisis in the 1980s, and the experience of our largest corporate, Telecom, in adapting to a more open and vigorous global economy, suggests that it is the strength and vigour of our own economic policies and our own skill in managing our corporate affairs which really matter most in terms of our success as a nation.

Strong monetary and fiscal policies, open and competitive markets, minimal regulatory interventions by government, and a strong sense of vision and commitment as to where we want to head as a nation, are the critical underlying government policy issues.

To that list must be added the need for New Zealand corporates to accept that increasingly their success will be dependent on their ability to survive in a world which is much broader and more integrated than that of New Zealand alone. Past international excursions have been uneven in success, and imply the need for considerable strengthening of our corporate management, much more discipline around the way in which we build economic value within our enterprises, and a greater determination and skill at being internationally competitive.

At a government policy level, in some ways over recent times we have stepped backwards rather than forwards. This is illustrated by the fact that government expenditure has typically been rising faster than private sector activity, that regulations have been extended in a number of arenas, that critical issues such as the monopoly producer boards have not yet been resolved, and that property rights interventions of a sort not seen in New Zealand for many years have invoked a sense of nervousness amongst both domestic and overseas investors. All of this is reflected in the relatively low corporate valuations seen in New Zealand today. It has also resulted in reductions in the previous gains we had made in terms of our international competitiveness, as illustrated by the Geneva based World Economic Forum's 1998 report which shows that in the latest report we rank at number 13, compared with number five one year prior to that and number three two years prior to that. Our rate of economic growth relative to other countries such as Australia and the United States over the past couple of years has been unsatisfactory.

One cannot escape the feeling that we are not really grasping the exciting opportunities we face as a nation. Globalisation of many activities within New Zealand is inevitable. The trick is whether we can accept that and grasp some portion of those opportunities ourselves in order to restore our international competitiveness and resume the sort of vigorous economic growth that we were experiencing in the early to mid-1990s. The remedies lie in our own hands. Can we take up the challenges?

7. Competition Policies: Multi-national Approaches

Kerrin M Vautier

THE INTERNATIONALISATION OF 'COMPETITION POLICY'

Background

Cross-border approaches to the promotion of competition are being developed at the bilateral, regional and multilateral levels: competition is the subject of bilateral cooperation agreements, competition policies feature in Regional Trading Arrangements (RTAs) and WTO trade rules contain elements of competition law. This array of cross-border initiatives to promote competition says a lot about the complexity of competition issues in globalising markets. Business is increasingly conducted in trans-national markets which are being affected by rapid changes in technology and different forms of business organisation.

There are many challenges for international discussions in the 'competition policy' area. Sovereign powers in national jurisdictions have a diminishing ability to regulate business or markets. The economic and institutional circumstances of trading nations are diverse. A unifying competition culture does not yet exist. But, globally, important policy developments have been affecting competition in a positive way. During the last decade or so there has been a major shift towards more market-oriented policies, in both developed and developing economies, including within APEC. Emphasis has been on lowering border barriers in order to free international trade and foreign direct investment and on a wider liberalisation agenda involving industry deregulation, corporatisation and privatisation. Promoting competition is increasingly accepted as the preferred means for organising economic activity efficiently. And there is growing awareness that efficiently-functioning markets are essential for our shared goals of growth, employment, and development.

In those countries with a recent history of heavy regulation, deregulation has been seen as an important instrument for improving the efficiency of markets. This has raised some new competition issues relating to business conduct in privatised network industries and natural monopolies. Other countries with lighter regulation (financial services in East Asia, for example) are finding it necessary to increase prudential and governance controls in response to market failures.

Now one can properly ask: to what extent does the freer and more efficient movement of goods/services/investment need to be accompanied by inter-government measures to 'regulate' business conduct? This question relating to the risk of anti-competitive business conduct in trans-national markets is not new, as we shall see. In fact, so much prominence has been given to the risks of anti-competitive business conduct, as border barriers fall, that competition law (historically a matter of national policy) is often seen in international circles as synonymous with 'competition policy'. And, as markets enlarge, there is certainly an interest in the alternative ways of dealing with the risks posed by powerful or colluding or merging firms.

The achievements of RTAs in this regard are noteworthy but limited. Both bilateral and multilateral approaches have severe limitations and there is considerable nervousness about acceding to multilateral disciplines on competition, especially since there is no consensus on whether or not each economy should have a general competition/anti-trust law.

SOME KEY ISSUES

Scope

It is problematic that the term 'competition policy', which is becoming firmly established in the lexicon of international organisations, is open to very different interpretations. These depend in part on historical associations, in particular on a country's stage of economic development, and in part on where policy-makers/advisers wish to focus their international discussions given the complexity of the area and its potential threat to a range of established policy positions.

To focus on business conduct and competition law alone yields a very narrow interpretation of the scope and role of policy that is explicitly competition-related. The United States is the main proponent of this stance. It is a strong advocate of national anti-trust laws and of bilateral cooperation to assist with enforcement. And it considers that multilateral competition disciplines would risk dilution of its own anti-trust law.

Concerns about 'colonisation through harmonisation' are raised in this context especially given the present lack of conviction (in developed as well as developing nations) that a general competition law is necessary for all economies.

Limiting 'competition policy' to legal remedies for anti-competitive business conduct/transactions, risks undue policy compartmentalisation. The main consequence is that government actions and transactions are not explicitly accommodated within a 'competition policy' framework. And yet governments are mainly responsible for distorting the competitive process and for interfering with the efficient functioning of globalising markets. Take government procurement, product standards and antidumping, for example. Why should these remain in separate policy compartments not subject to competition scanning? Since most antidumping actions are taken by developed countries (notably the US and EU – see WTO, 1997 Table V.4) these are of particular concern to developing economies as they aim for growth and development via exports.

Fortunately, a broader scoping of 'competition policy' has started to emerge in international discussions, particularly in APEC and the special WTO Working Group. This is consistent with the major shift in domestic policy orientation referred to earlier. Competition-promoting policies are seen to include deregulation, regulatory reform, and mutually reinforcing trade policies. But inclusion of trade and regulatory policies is not a sufficient basis for promoting competition in globalising markets. A competition dimension needs to be reflected in all policy-making (irrespective of traditional policy labels) that impacts on competition and efficiency in these markets. The purpose of a more seamless approach to national policies – which treats competition as a cross-cutting policy issue – is to factor this dimension not only into trade and regulatory policies but also into foreign direct investment, intellectual property and occupational regulation.

Thus, competition law is a subset of a range of policies relevant to the promotion or defence of competition in both national and trans-national markets. It can be seen as a safeguard, in the event that opportunities remain for businesses to undermine the competition-promoting policies of governments.

'Beyond the border' policies are relevant to what has been called 'deep integration' in contrast to 'at the border' tariff and non-tariff measures that are associated with 'shallow integration'. Removing all border barriers to trade in goods and services does not assure non-discriminatory access by foreign supplies – that is, if policies and regulations inside the borders discriminate against foreign supplies in such a way as to undermine the competitive process. So there is really a natural progression from the removal of border barriers to the removal of other barriers to competition within the border that directly or indirectly discriminate against supplies from other countries.

Having made the distinction between 'at the border' and 'beyond/within the border', it is noted that it is not particularly robust in respect of competition policies. Promoting effective competition needs to address entry conditions affecting access into a country; impacts of domestic policies on conditions facing business within that country; and cross-border spillovers of government or business actions that negatively impact on the competitive process.

Objectives

The objectives of so-called 'competition policy' become very important here. Looking at individual economies, the objectives of so-called competition policy range from efficiency/welfare to diffuse and sometimes conflicting aims. In large part this reflects the difference between what can be termed a 'market conditions' approach and a 'market outcomes' approach.

Trade related issue?

At an international level, discussions on 'competition policy' have been encouraged by the perception that this is a 'trade-related' issue. Is it? It might seem counter-intuitive to suggest not. Trade and competition can be mutually reinforcing in contestable markets. In that sense they are related. Some competition issues are very much trade-related, e.g. antidumping and export cartels. In that sense there is an interface. But there is an important distinction between a *trade* objective that favours *trade maximisation,* and a *competition* objective that favours *welfare maximisation.* For a start, there is a *trade-effects* motivation for competition law, most apparent in the EU. In other words, competition law is seen as a tool to ensure that business conduct does not adversely affect international trade.

A trade-related rationale for 'competition law/policy' follows the trade policy priority of market (country) access, an objective that drives negotiated trade concessions in the WTO. At the multilateral level, there are concerns that existing or new private practices might nullify or impair the benefits of negotiated trade concessions[1]. So competition law is seen as a support mechanism for 'market access' and trade.

However, 'competition policy' is not simply or even primarily a trade-related issue. The role of international competition policies is not to maximise the benefits of free trade, or to combat actions that might nullify or impair negotiated trade concessions. Competition in markets is desirable because of its contribution to efficiency and welfare. Free trade and competitive behaviour are two basic conditions for efficient resource allocations. It is the link between competition and efficiency that has been driving the convergence of more market-oriented domestic policies.   The same link is relevant to any multi-national approaches to promoting competition, the appropriate focus of which is competition from all modes of domestic and foreign supply.   The internationalisation of 'competition policy' should drive off *competition* and *market* concerns, rather than *trade-related* and *country* concerns. The economic rather than the legalistic idea is that welfare will be maximised when there is less focus on national boundaries, and more focus on minimal barriers to resource allocations.

The distinction between *welfare* and *trade* maximisation is most important in international trade disputes. The aim of maximising a country's international trade, or the interests of individual exporters, is potentially distortionary to the competitive process. First, not all measures to increase trade (export subsidies for example) are compatible with well-functioning markets. Secondly, not all perceived impediments to trade (for example, a particular distribution arrangement in the importing country) represent a competition distortion.

In theory, trade and competition policies share the same ultimate aim of promoting efficient production and consumption in the world economy. However, in practice, we cannot be so sure.

Fair markets?
We have all heard claims that competition should be fair as well as efficient. But the notion of fairness in competition, as with fairness in trade, is typically linked with distributive policy to promote the wellbeing of particular competitors or traders, as distinct from promoting conditions conducive to an efficient process of competition and trade.

In a paper given to PAFTAD (Vautier and Lloyd, forthcoming), it was argued that the key meaning of *fairness* in the context of so-called competition policy is *competitive neutrality* coupled with transparency and accountability in policy formation and application.   It was also argued that merit-based competition contributes more to fairness than do market positions secured by special government-endowed privileges, protections and shelters, with their discriminatory impacts both within and between economies.   In the sense of more open, transparent, competitive, and well-functioning markets, no contradiction is seen in the call for fair and efficient markets.

MULTI-NATIONAL APPROACHES

The Choice of Level of Action

Not surprisingly, as markets enlarge beyond country borders there is a general case in principle for some form of cooperative action to address cross-border competition problems caused by governments or businesses. The following approaches[2] can be distinguished: bilateral, regional, non-binding multilateral (sometimes called plurilateral), and binding multilateral.

Centralised vs decentralised approach

The choice of multi-national approach is of course affected by preferences for centralised vs decentralised solutions to cross-border competition problems. While both are forms of concerted action, they differ fundamentally in respect of institutional arrangements, powers of enforcement, and maximisation objectives. The most centralised solution would involve a supra-national authority with enforcement capability in relation to global competition rules aimed at global welfare maximisation. Such an authority has had its proponents. The least centralised solution relies on national regimes, supplemented by some level of inter-government cooperation on a voluntary basis. Several options lie in between.

Bilateral level

Here we have two-party cooperation agreements or mutual legal assistance treaties. These are usually between the governments of two countries but can be between an RTA and an outside government – as with the 1991 and 1998 competition cooperation agreements between the European Community and United States. Most involve the United States.

But these voluntary cooperation agreements are presently extremely limited in terms of country coverage and the scope for information exchange and enforcement. National autonomy limits information exchange and the ability to take enforcement actions at the request of another country. There is positive comity but no obligation to act. Bilaterals do not exclude extra-territorial action. Hence the continued threat of extra-territorial action undermines the cooperative spirit and intent of these agreements.

Regional level

Regional agreements involve members of an RTA pursuant to GATT/WTO rules[3]. The chapter returns to these.

Non-binding multilateral

There are several non-binding multilateral instruments that bear on competition, including:

- The GATT 1960 Decision on Arrangements for Consultations on Restrictive Business Practices. The focus here is on the effects of the business practices on international trade, i.e. the focus is not on competition and efficiency;
- The UN (1980) Set of Multilaterally Agreed Equitable Principles and Rules for the Control of Restrictive Business Practices. These cover a comprehensive list of practices that enterprises should refrain from if they restrain competition. The UN Set, as it is called, has been a useful form of competition advocacy. But the primary objective is the trade and development of developing countries;
- The OECD (1967–1995) Recommendations for bilateral cooperation on anti-competitive practices in international trade. Cooperation includes notification of investigations, information exchange, and (voluntary) coordination of action. These Recommendations appear to have played an important part in the development of bilateral agreements on competition law and enforcement, including in respect of positive comity;
- The OECD (1976) Guidelines for Multinational Enterprises. These Guidelines were aimed at anti-competitive conduct by multinational enterprises, such as abuse of a dominant position and cartels;
- The OECD (1998) Recommendations on Effective Action against Hard Core Cartels[4] (domestic and international). The OECD, in generally focusing on the 'new dimensions of market access', has also taken a trade-related approach to competition issues.

Basically, these non-binding agreements are codes of good behaviour, either for governments (as in the case of the OECD Recommendations), or for enterprises (as in the case of the OECD Guidelines and the UN Set). However, they are not generally regarded as having substantially modified market behaviour.

Binding multilateral

Historically, there have been no substantive multilateral rules explicitly relating to competition. Essentially, both export and import cartels lie outside the ambit of binding WTO rules. And, with only a few exceptions, private business conduct is not covered by international trade law.

The specific WTO provisions that do relate to enterprise conduct deal with:

- Dumping and subsidised trade (export subsidies, subsidies and countervailing duties);
- Enterprises with state ownership, import monopolies, or exclusive or special trading privileges;
- Private monopolies engaged in services, and specifically telecommunications.

The concern is with *trade effects*.

In the GATT, General Agreement on Trade in Services (GATS) and Trade-Related Intellectual Property issues (TRIPs), there are no obligations on WTO members to take enforcement actions on the basis of national competition law/regulation. In any case, most members do not presently have a comprehensive competition law. The inter-government consultation procedures, which form the basis of enforcement provisions, have only been invoked on three occasions, each involving the US/Japan consumer photographic film and paper dispute (better known as the Kodak/Fuji dispute).

Regional Trading Arrangements

Regional Trading Arrangements are conceived as trade liberalising mechanisms. It is therefore a challenge to take a regional view of competition issues.

The longest-standing regional agreement on competition is contained in the 1957 Treaty of Rome, now relevant to 33 countries[5]. Since 1990, six other RTAs[6] involving a further 15 countries have incorporated some agreement relating to competition:

- CER (1990);
- NAFTA (1992);
- The Andean Group (Bolivia, Colombia, Ecuador, Peru and Venezuela) (1991);
- Group of Three (Mexico, Colombia and Venezuela) (1994);
- MERCOSUR (Argentina, Brazil, Paraguay and Uruguay) (1996); and the
- Canada-Chile Free Trade Agreement (1996).

There are three categories of response to competition issues:

i the development of national competition policies and the potential for convergence between them;
ii approaches to competition problems that cross national borders but reside within a defined regional area;

iii approaches to intra-regional competition problems sourced from outside a defined regional area.

Elements of one or more of these categories are present in the RTAs mentioned. But there is considerable variation in both the provisions and institutional arrangements. The EU has adopted the broadest approach with a range of policies to promote intra-area competition, including region-wide competition rules and a powerful supra-national authority. CER has also taken a broad approach to the promotion of competition, including comprehensive competition law in each country. Its limited cross-border competition provisions are oriented towards efficiency, not trade and are enforceable through national statutes and institutions. Canada-Chile and the Group of Three can be grouped with NAFTA, given the similarity of the provisions in their agreements (which are much narrower than in either the EU or CER and relate solely to monopolies and State Trading Enterprises). MERCOSUR and the Andean Community have some institutional arrangements in place to support a strong trade-related regional approach, but these have yet to operate.

In the seven RTAs there are important differences in the treatment of antidumping, subsidies and countervailing duties, cartels and mergers – all matters of significance to the competitive process. For example:

- Three of the RTAs have eliminated the intra-area antidumping remedy.
- The EU has endeavoured to limit state aids that distort intra-regional trade, and countervailing duties are prohibited.
- CER has retained the countervailing duty remedy notwithstanding its prohibition and elimination of production and trade-distorting subsidies.
- The EU prohibits cartels including export cartels among non-EU exporters to the EU but excluding export cartels involving EU producers.
- CER's trans-Tasman competition provisions contain no provision relating to cartels.
- The competition law provisions of the NAFTA, Canada-Chile and Group of Three RTAs relate solely to monopolies and state trading enterprises.
- Of the seven RTAs, only the EU has introduced region-wide merger regulations and procedures.

Overall, a contribution to competition advocacy and policy convergence has been achieved. Much obviously depends on the competition culture within an RTA which explains why the MERCOSUR and ANDEAN protocols are not yet effective. Much has also depended on US influence. The US is consistent in its resistance to both regional level and multilateral level competition law and enforcement. And NAFTA did not succeed in bringing antidumping into its (very limited) 'Competition Policy' provisions.

APEC

The APEC Model

The APEC model is different. It is neither a formal RTA nor a negotiating rule-making alliance. Its *modus operandi* are geared to stimulating individual economies – developed and developing, large and small – to think about how their policy actions can contribute to the APEC vision of liberalisation and economic and social development. It has the potential to add value through cooperative endeavour and by setting the scene for region-wide strategy and economy-based policy, with the aid of guiding principles.

The Competition Policy Area

Competition Policy was one of the 15 policy areas nominated in the 1995 Osaka Action Agenda for inclusion in APEC's Collective and Individual Action Plans. Its stated objective links enhancement of the competitive environment in the Region with the efficient operation of markets and consumer benefits. There is also a logical link between this objective and the stated collective action to contribute to the use of trade and competition laws, policies and measures that promote free and open trade, investment and competition. There appears to be no intention here that a *trade* objective trump a *competition* objective.

Policy and enforcement review, transparency, technical assistance, and cooperation arrangements are all mentioned in the overall guidelines for the Individual Action Plans for APEC economies. Information exchanges, dialogue and building understanding are key collective actions. APEC has made no commitment to harmonisation of competition or regulatory policies/laws, but cooperation for convergence in policy direction is certainly implied.

Individual Action Plans (IAPs)

The Individual Action Plans reflect a range of views as to what is encompassed by 'Competition Policy'. (This is the scoping issue referred to earlier.) This is not surprising given the different stages of economic development and market orientation. A lack of consensus on objectives is also evident. Diverse objectives tend to spill over into perceptions of the role of 'Competition Policy' in relation to APEC's goals.

When the Competition and Deregulation policy areas are looked at together, there is a better sense of an economy's competition agenda. This is despite the Deregulation objective being cast in *trade and investment* terms not in *competition* terms. However, a review of the 1998 IAPs suggests that there is now less emphasis on trade and market access and somewhat more on how deregulation can improve competition and efficiency in the domestic economy (and competitiveness).

Competition Law

Even where economies share the same objectives, their preferred means for pursuing them can be quite different. Take competition law, which is a centrepiece for some but not an option for others. This is not a developed vs developing economy issue. Resistance to having a general competition law arises for two main reasons. First, Hong Kong and Singapore see free trade and open and deregulated domestic economies as a sufficient basis for competition within them. Second, developing economies consider that sequencing is a problem. They are not sure that competition law should be accorded priority relative to other measures to liberalise and deregulate their economies. There is also the question of institutional and technical capability to introduce and enforce such law. Neither of the two arguments is resolved.

Consensus Building

Initially, APEC's Competition Workshops tended to equate the 'Competition Policy' area with competition law. But a consensus has been building over several years that a much more comprehensive approach to competition issues is appropriate. Problems are seen with fragmenting policy discussions into traditional compartments and the complementarity between competition, regulatory and trade policies is increasingly cited.

Non-binding Competition Principles

So, where to from here? The answer lies in APEC's Collective Action Plan mandate to consider developing non-binding principles on competition policy and/or laws in APEC. In fact, progress in this regard became central to one of the themes for APEC 1999, *viz* 'strengthening the functioning of markets'. One of the specific deliverables for 1999 was 'developing a framework of non-binding competition and regulatory principles for endorsement by APEC Leaders'.

The PECC Competition Principles

PECC (the Pacific Economic Cooperation Council) has endorsed and released a set of principles for guiding the development of a competition-driven policy framework for APEC economies (PECC, 1999). PECC advocates these for endorsement by APEC Ministers and Leaders. It sees the Principles as a necessary response to APEC's long-term goals; as part of a coherent response to the Asian crisis; as a basis for greater coherence in IAPs; and as a reference point for Action Plan reviews.

PECC embarked on the *principles* approach in response to the complexity of the issues and the diversity within the Region. The purpose of the Competition Principles is to promote/defend competition in all goods and services markets and to create/maintain those conditions that will enable and encourage an efficient competitive process to work. The standard for the Principles is competition on the basis of economic merit. The coverage of the Principles is that range of government and private actions that impact on market conditions (including trade remedies, regulations, product standards and government procurement). The rationale for the Principles is to effect a broad shift in emphasis from policies that unduly favour producers, to policies that are more inclusive of the interests of consumers/customers.

The overall focus is thus on:

- principles (as distinct from rules);
- strengthening market conditions for creating opportunities (as distinct from trying to manage market outcomes);
- framework building (as distinct from policy prescriptions for individual economies).

This all fits with a very diverse group of economies at different stages of development. In fact, the Principles themselves explicitly recognise special implementation issues and the need for transitional arrangements.

The core principles

The core elements that anchor the PECC Competition Principles are:

- *comprehensiveness* – that is, the issue of scope and of building a competition dimension into all relevant policy-making;
- *transparency* – that is, no surprises about particular rules and how they are applied;
- *accountability* – that is, for policy choices and trade-offs;

* *non-discrimination* – that is, competitive neutrality as between the different modes of supply, such neutrality being a feature of internationally contestable markets.

Principles and disputes

These core principles, and the key requirements for upholding them in practice, should be helpful in those trans-national disputes that are seen in trade-related terms, i.e. disputes over access for and fairness in trade. To illustrate: Is opposition to parallel importing just a trade access issue, or does it have a competition dimension which also needs to be taken into account? Is antidumping just a fairness issue, or should adjudication have a competition dimension? Are export cartels a legitimate device for maximising a country's trade, or should competition criteria also apply? The proposition is that where there is an international conflict between competition and trade, it should be resolved in favour of protecting the competitive process rather than protecting particular trade flows or exporters or producers.

The APEC principles?

The APEC Competition and Deregulation Workshop, held in Christchurch, NZ at the end of April 1999, agreed that the PECC Principles:

* provided the foundation for consensus-building on a competition and regulatory reform-driven framework for APEC;
* provided a reference point for developing, in the short term, a set of core principles together with related actions, and
* were an important reference document for integrating the Principles into Individual Action Plans, which process could inform the further development of 'the APEC principles'.

The ball is now in the APEC court. It is hoped that as economic integration proceeds the PECC Competition Principles come to be seen as a solid bridge for crossing between international and domestic issues that affect the efficient functioning of enlarging markets.

THE WTO

The WTO and APEC models are very different. But a collective action for APEC is to continue to respond positively to the WTO's Trade and Competition Working Group to ensure information-sharing. APEC could take a leadership role on Competition Principles.

The WTO Working Group

A WTO Working Group to study issues relating to the interaction between trade and competition policy, including anti-competitive business practices, was established at the first WTO Ministerial Conference in December 1996.

Members suggested a number of issues for study in the Group's first two-year work programme:

- the relationship between the objectives, principles, concepts, scope and instruments of trade and competition policy;
- the relationship of trade and competition policy to development and economic growth;
- stocktaking and analysis of existing instruments, standards and activities regarding trade and competition policy, including experiences with their application, specifically:
  - national competition policies, laws and instruments as they relate to trade
  - existing WTO provisions
  - bilateral, regional, plurilateral and multilateral agreements and initiatives;
- the interaction between trade and competition policy:
  - the impact of anti-competitive practices (of enterprises and associations) on international trade
  - the impact on competition and international trade of
    state monopolies
    exclusive rights, and
    regulatory policies
  - the impact of trade policy on competition
  - the relationship between competition policy and the trade-related aspects of intellectual property rights investment.

After two years of deliberations this Working Group obtained a mandate from the General Council for continuing its education work during 1999 with a focus on:

- the relevance of fundamental WTO principles of national treatment, transparency, and most-favoured-nation treatment to competition policy and vice versa;
- approaches to promoting cooperation and communication among Members, including in the field of technical cooperation; and

- the contribution of competition policy to achieving the objectives of the WTO, including the promotion of international trade.

While avoiding specifics, the Working Group's recommendations, accepted by the General Council, covered three important elements: the relevance of general principles, international cooperation, and the link between competition policy and WTO objectives.

Competition Principles

The PECC Competition Principles are relevant to each of these topics. What is important however, is that the integrity of *competition* principles does not get muddied by the *trade* maximisation objectives of individual economies nor by specific concerns about *trade* nullification and impairment for which WTO remedies exist (Vautier, 1999). The issue for markets is competition, from all modes of supply, with an eye on efficiency and welfare enhancement.

WTO Objectives and Principles

It was earlier suggested that we could not simply assume that trade and competition policies shared the same objectives. And it is clear that competition policies, particularly insofar as these relate to business conduct, do not fold easily into the existing multilateral trade negotiating framework of the WTO. Difficulties relating to objectives, substantive provisions, the analytical framework and enforcement are all relevant.

Submissions to the WTO Working Group (on the Interaction between Trade and Competition Policy) show that the three major influences on the debate – the EU, US and Japan – have fundamentally different perspectives on the WTO's role in relation to 'competition policy' and how it interacts or should interact with trade. These different views of the three major players reinforce the problem of choice amongst the different levels of action.

The EU considers there should be international competition disciplines in the WTO and instruments to deal with anti-competitive practices with a significant international dimension, and that there should be a commitment by WTO members to adopt effective domestic competition policies, including but not confined to competition law. The US appears to be against any multilateral competition disciplines. Undoubtedly, it sees the risk of anti-trust dilution through negotiation. It considers that the focus of the Working Group should be on the role of competition policy in enhancing trade liberalisation and that implementation should be via domestic competition laws and bilateral agreements. Japan considers the WTO should introduce a pro-competition dimension into its trade measures, notably antidumping and safeguard measures, and it favours the voluntary adoption by WTO members of competition law and enforcement regimes.

There are clearly underlying tensions arising from attitudes to extra-territoriality as well as on where antidumping fits into international discussions on competition issues. Contrary to Japan's desire to have pro-competition thinking apply to trade measures, the US maintains that antidumping is not covered by the 'competition policy' compartment.

The WTO has no formal objective relating to the promotion of competition. Its framework is essentially international trade and government measures. It has promulgated some specific competition rules. But principles are applied selectively (see Vautier, Lloyd and Tsai, forthcoming): *non-discrimination* in GATT 1994 is restricted to Most Favoured Nation Treatment (MFN) but there are exceptions; the plurilateral nature of the GATS limits application of the *national treatment* principle; *comprehensiveness* is not demonstrated by the WTO's competition provisions. For example, these apply differentially to services and not at all to goods and the coverage of business conduct is very limited.

CONCLUDING REMARKS

Given its constitution, the WTO cannot take a comprehensive approach to competition-related policies. However, if the Europeans and others are to talk credibly about any sort of multilateral competition framework, then the way the WTO treats trade instruments, notably antidumping and cartels, must be part of that framework. In other words, comprehensiveness should be pushed as far as it can at each level. Competition principles could guide the formulation of all those multilateral rules and regulations that 'intervene' in markets. It is difficult to avoid the conclusion that the primary competition policy for the WTO is to liberalise trade and investment and to ensure that its trade rules and disciplines are designed, applied and enforced in a pro-competitive manner.

Undoubtedly, individual countries will have to take more responsibility for addressing those government and business actions that prevent and distort competition. Unilateralism must underpin multi-national approaches; they are complementary tracks: 'positive unilateralism consistent with a multi-national approach' (see Lloyd and Vautier, 1999, Chapter 12). Diversity of circumstances is not a barrier to accepting competition principles, although these need to be accompanied by practical capacity-building in developing economies.

Overall, *comprehensiveness*, *non-discrimination*, *competitive neutrality*, *transparency* and *accountability* are the core ingredients for coherence and credibility and progress on welfare-enhancing competition policies in globalising markets.

NOTES

[1] This led to the WTO Working Group being established to study the interaction between trade and competition policy.

[2] While extra-territorial application of national laws (used extensively by the US) is an option, it is not popular and itself gives rise to inter-government conflict.

[3] So, CER is included even though it has only two member States.

[4] The OECD defines 'hard core' cartel (regarded as the single most harmful form of anti-competitive conduct) as: An anticompetitive agreement . . . concerted practice, or . . . arrangement by competitors to fix prices, make rigged bids (collusive tenders), establish output restrictions or quotas, or share or divide markets by allocating customers, suppliers, territories, or lines of commerce.

[5] At the regional level, the centralised vs. decentralised choice applies most explicitly in the EU with its debate on the subsidiarity principle. In areas which do not fall within the Community's 'exclusive competence', the division of responsibilities between the national and EU levels is determined in accordance with principles set out in the Maastricht Treaty.

[6] An analysis of the competition sections of each of these regional agreements, and of the Competition Policy negotiating area of the 34-member Free Trade Area of the Americas can be found in Part III of Lloyd and Vautier (1999).

REFERENCES

Lloyd, P.J. and Kerrin M. Vautier (1999), *Promoting Competition in Global Markets: A Multi-National Approach*, Cheltenham, UK and Northampton, MA, USA: Edward Elgar.

PECC (1999), *PECC Principles for Guiding the Development of a Competition-Driven Policy Framework for APEC Economies*, June, PECC.

Vautier, Kerrin M. (1999), 'The PECC Competition Principles', Paper to the PECC Trade Policy Forum, June, Auckland.

Vautier, Kerrin M. and P.J. Lloyd (forthcoming), 'The Competition and Deregulation Policy Areas in APEC', in Yamazawa, I. (ed.), *APEC: The Challenges and Tasks for the 21st Century*, Japan: PAFTAD.

Vautier, Kerrin M., P.J. Lloyd and Ing-Wen Tsai (forthcoming), 'Competition Policy in the WTO: The Role of Multilateral Rules' in Pangestu, M. and W. Martin (eds) *East Asia and Options for the WTO 2000 Negotiations*, PECC/World Bank.

WTO (1997), *Annual Report 1997, Volume 1*, Geneva: World Trade Organisation.

8.   Link Issues and the New Round

David Robertson

It is some years now since the Marrakesh Declaration sealed the Uruguay Round final act and established the World Trade Organisation (WTO). Notwithstanding the many doubts and uncertainties that plagued the decade of preparations for, and negotiation of the Uruguay Round, once the final act was agreed it was acclaimed a triumph.   The enthusiasm was transmitted to the public as a major new institution in the global economy, with little reference to either shortcomings in WTO agreements or their trade focus.

The 'link issues' are largely spin-offs from the Uruguay Round negotiations, because agreements could not be reached or because the topics were raised too late for proper consideration.   Subsequently several of these topics were included in official proposals to expand the scope of the WTO. These suggestions have been approached by establishing review processes within the WTO. This has resulted in an 'agenda' of trade-linked subjects:

1. Trade and government procurement
2. Trade and investment
3. Trade and competition
4. Regionalism (trade and economic integration)
5. Trade and development
6. Trade and environment
7. Trade and labour standards.

These 'link issues' are evidence of an unacknowledged theme within the Uruguay Round, which has carried over into the WTO work programme. The traditional design of the GATT was to reduce barriers to international trade using negotiated reciprocal reductions in tariffs, with all other trade barriers outlawed (i.e. 'negative' or shallow integration).   The Uruguay Round negotiations, however, contained strong elements of policy harmonisation (i.e. 'positive' or deep integration).   The agreements on trade-related intellectual property issues (TRIPs), technical barriers to trade (TBT-SPS) and the enforcement embodied in the understanding on dispute settlement contain aspects of harmonisation.   This unheralded theme is continued by the 'link issues' which to be effective require harmonisation of national policies. (Harmonisation is also evident in OECD reports; e.g. the multilateral agreements on investment (MAI) and the 1997 report of the high-level advisory group on the environment.)

Absence of discussions on this harmonisation process arouses suspicions. Is it simple acceptance of globalisation and the surrender of sovereignty present in regional economic integration (e.g. EU, NAFTA)? Is it another consequence of trans-frontier activities, not only by business but by special interest groups (NGOs) seeking international solutions to by-pass national policies perceived as unsatisfactory (e.g. environmental and social strategies)? Or, is it implicit acceptance by major players that they can fashion other nations' policies to suit their own standards to facilitate their commercial expansion (e.g. biosafety)? We shall return to these questions later.

The status of 'link issues' in the WTO work programme differ.

- 1, 2 and 3 are under review in WTO working groups, preparing the ground for negotiations (although negotiations have not been formally accepted by ministers).
- 4, 5 and 6 are being considered by established committees in the WTO which meet at Council level; progress in all these has been slow, suggesting either major disagreements or reluctance to seek outcomes.
- 7 was formally rejected as a WTO issue at the Singapore ministerial meeting, but it is still being pursued by US authorities and some EU governments.

The high-profile of the Uruguay Round negotiations and the razzmatazz surrounding the Marrakesh ministerial meeting made the WTO a new target for campaigns by special interest groups, such as environmental lobbies and human rights groups. The understanding on dispute settlement was interpreted as granting decisiveness and enforcement powers to WTO processes that were not provided in other international treaties or agencies. This encouraged NGOs to become interested in trade policy as an instrument to bring their concerns into the public eye.

This brought environmental protection and labour standards on to the 'trade-linked' agenda in the closing stages of the Uruguay Round. Where WTO decisions have not met the interests of these special interest groups – for example, the decision on dolphin-tuna which failed to support the views of US 'green' groups and the first WTO ministerial meeting's decision to exclude 'core labour standards' from WTO processes – the institution has become a target for propaganda and invective, without much regard for the trade focus of WTO agreements. These efforts have placed the WTO at the centre of the diplomatic stage, in contrast with the GATT's low profile.

'Civil society' (so-called) seeks new environmental and social governance using 'stakeholder' meetings that bypass inter-governmental processes, such as the WTO Council.

A 'BUILT-IN' AGENDA

The nature of some WTO agreements left important matters to be settled later. For example, the General Agreement on Trade in Services (GATS) is only a skeleton that is being fleshed out by sectoral negotiations since the WTO was established. Similarly, the Agreement on trade-related investment measures (TRIMs) left many questions to be resolved. Several other WTO agreements contained conditions for reviews within five years; TRIPs, agriculture, and reassessment of WTO rules, including dispute settlement, technical barriers to trade (including SPS) and 'trade remedies'. This 'built-in' agenda provides the basis for the new round of WTO negotiations to begin in 2000. The prospect of success with this agenda would be enhanced by including industrial tariffs, the traditional core of GATT negotiations. Most supporters of the new round want a comprehensive agenda.

There is little scope to include the major 'link issues' in the negotiations though, if the process is to be completed within three or four years, as proposed. However, each of the link issues has its proponents among the major players. US official statements have called for the environment and labour standards to be included and they also want an agreement on government procurement (a plurilateral agreement in the WTO) to be included in the 'single undertaking'. The EU wants to include investment rules and competition policy. Japan wants to discuss trade and investment. Many developing countries, on the other hand, want to renegotiate obligations and to review the distribution of benefits from the Uruguay Round before opening a new round of negotiations.

Enthusiasm for the new WTO round wavered in 1999 with dissension over the election of a new Director General, faltering economic conditions in East Asia and elsewhere, the threat of protectionism in the US Congress (blocking 'fast-track' authority) and developing countries' scepticism about commencing another major new round of trade liberalisation. Economic uncertainties and growing apprehensions about globalisation add to the difficulties of getting support for opening a new round. In mid-1999 the WTO had 132 members, so achieving consensus to begin negotiations required strong leadership and a promise of widespread benefits. With several dispute settlements creating tensions among major players (for example US-EU over bananas and beef hormones), tensions between the Appellate Body and the WTO Council over aspects of the turtle-shrimp decision (1998) and the threat of disruptions from NGOs at meetings in Seattle, the circumstances for a major round were not auspicious.   The 'trade-linked' issues are complex and controversial and extend beyond trade policy, which made them unlikely to be included on the agenda.

THE 'LINK' ISSUES

The 'link issues' are evidence of the growing complexity of trade negotiations. Ostensibly, they arise because governments want to extend GATT/WTO success into policy areas that can substitute for trade measures (government procurement, investment and competition policies), which could frustrate benefits expected from agreed trade liberalisation. But, as mentioned above, there are also 'positive' reasons for pursuing such harmonisation, which extend beyond trade alone.

This chapter will review progress in the seven trade-linked issues, leaving the two controversial topics of environment and labour standards to the end.

Trade and Government Procurement

An agreement on government procurement (AGP) was included in the Marrakesh Declaration as a plurilateral agreement (with fourteen signatures). This was an elaboration of the Tokyo Round code, but attracted few new members. It was not part of the 'single undertaking', but EU and US authorities – despite differences – are now committed to 'multilateralising' the agreement by incorporating it into the WTO at the next trade round. At the Singapore ministerial meeting a study of transparency in government procurement practices was added to the work programme in an attempt to expand the effectiveness of the AGP. This complemented the AGP working group established in 1997 to review the existing agreement.

With the share of government expenditure in GDP rising in most countries over the past generation, it is perhaps surprising that opportunities for trade (and efficiency gains) in government purchases were not given more emphasis in the Uruguay Round negotiations. Purchases by governments and state-owned enterprises for their own use were excluded from GATT (1947). Yet in most OECD countries, government expenditure amounts to 40 to 50 per cent of gross domestic expenditure and foreign competition is almost nil. Even if only a quarter of present government expenditures are 'marketable' outlays, this still opens up major opportunities for efficiency gains by removing domestic preferences.

The GATS provides for non-discrimination in trade in all services, and a framework for the negotiation of market access and national treatment. Even so, Article XIII exempts laws, regulations and requirements on government procurement, although it does call for multilateral negotiations. It is the US intention to incorporate the AGP into the agenda for the round. Transparency will be the major stumbling block among OECD countries. It is difficult to establish the basis for government procurement decisions, which depend on administrative structures (e.g. federal/state relations, centralised control, etc.) 'Subsidiarity', has been a persistent problem in recent OECD and WTO negotiations on several topics. Many developing countries oppose including the AGP in the 'single undertaking', because government procurement plays a part in their development strategies.

Trade and Investment

International investment was a controversial topic during the Uruguay Round negotiations, and it has remained so. The TRIMs agreement did little more than reaffirm existing GATT commitments by outlawing performance requirements and trade balancing. Although investment rules could not be agreed in the Uruguay Round, early in the 1990s barriers to foreign investment were tumbling in developed and developing countries as the result of unilateral deregulation and bilateral or regional investment treaties. Investment flows expanded strongly after 1990, with developing countries participating increasingly as recipients and investors (UNCTAD, 1998); almost one-third of outward foreign direct investment (FDI) goes to developing countries. The WTO (1996) study indicated that foreign investment flows were growing faster than trade.

Formal and informal arrangements to facilitate international investment flows were spontaneous reactions to increasing international economic integration, stimulated by the Uruguay Round agreements, financial deregulation, economic reforms and advancing technology and communications. National authorities were already disregarding many of their policy impediments to trade and investment to facilitate global business. But bilateral treaties and regional agreements were creating a web around international commerce. A single set of multilateral rules on investment would be better.

The WTO working group on the relationship between trade and investment has shown wide acceptance that foreign investment contributes to economic development and is complementary with trade. Some developing countries, however, identify problems from derestricting foreign investment flows. One argument is that competitiveness is increasingly based on technology, which puts developing economies at a disadvantage and could hinder their industrialisation strategies. Some developing countries also argue there could be negative effects on the balance of payments, by frustrating import substitution strategies and sectoral development. These familiar arguments were not supported by any new evidence. This opposition to investment liberalisation was blamed on alleged anti-competitive behaviour by multinational enterprises, their monopoly over technology and high costs of technology transfers. Such restrictive business practices were raised also in the working group on competition policy.

Many non-OECD countries have overseas investors too, and their governments also support this proposal. However, others continue to pursue special interests, including development strategies and investment incentives to compensate investors for perceived country risks correcting market failures, etc. Special attention was drawn to preservation of the rights of developing countries to 'differential and more favourable' treatment under GATT Part IV.

The strength of aggregate investment flows to non-OECD countries suggests that there is a divergence between actual investment developments since 1990 and officials' perceptions as revealed in the working group. These differences have prevented a consensus to open negotiations in the WTO on a multilateral investment agreement. The experiences of Latin American and East Asian countries show strong FDI inflows, notwithstanding the recent financial roller-coaster. The overall growth in investment flows to non-OECD countries illustrates the contribution private sector investment decisions are making to economic growth and development. Most OECD countries are keen to proceed towards such an investment agreement, even after the collapse of the MAI (Henderson, 1999). Discussions in the WTO working group and the OECD have also revealed wide differences about the content of such an agreement, and the range of exemptions to be allowed.

With a complex web of agreements being reached on investment, stretching from over 1500 bilateral treaties through major regional integration agreements (NAFTA, EU) to non-binding guidelines (World Bank, APEC), there is a strong case for seeking a multilateral framework of investment rules. Most OECD governments and many governments from middle-income countries recognise the mutual benefits and wealth-creating aspects of foreign direct investment flows. Unilateral liberalisation is advancing the principles written into recent multilateral investment agreements – transparency, non-discrimination (with minimum exceptions), national treatment and market access. By bringing investment policies in line with the trading system, governments would remove biases from corporate choices about how to service markets. With all means of market access open, corporate decisions will be more economically efficient.

The WTO's credentials for undertaking negotiations on investment matters go beyond the TRIMs agreement. The Uruguay Round agreement on subsidies requires modification of investment incentive programmes. The

GATS contains provisions relating to investment in service industries which are absent from the GATT (1994). And TRIPs is also relevant because property rights are important 'owned assets' of multinational enterprises. If negotiations on trade and investment begin in the WTO, differences between national treatment of 'like' products (GATT 1994, article III) and 'commercial presence' for service enterprises in the GATS, will have to be reconciled. Coordinating all these components into an agreement on trade and investment will be difficult. An opportunity for negotiations is provided by the TRIMs agreement (article 9) which requires a review and an assessment of provisions on investment policy and competition policy.

On the other hand, unilateral liberalisation of national investment policies under pressures from market forces has been remarkably successful. There is a danger that formal negotiations may cause governments to adopt national positions against unilateralism as they seek reciprocity. Competition for investment inflows should promote continuing liberalisation, in which case any multilateral rules will be struggling to keep up with market-driven liberalisation (Robertson, 1996). The Uruguay Round final act contained important investment-related provisions. Preparing the ground for multilateral negotiations on investment, however, will require continuing analysis of contentious issues. The WTO is a negotiating body, not equipped to provide an analytical foundation to consolidate its wide range of agreements into a comprehensive investment agreement.

Trade and Competition Policy

Competition policy was introduced to the trade agenda in the closing stages of the Uruguay Round as differences among domestic competition policies were recognised as impediments to market access, as border protection was progressively lowered by multilateral liberalisation. Differences in national competition policies were alleged to be a source of distortions in trade and investment flows in 'globalised' markets. The only mention of competition policy in the Uruguay Round final act, however, was in the TRIMs agreement (Article 9). At the Singapore ministerial, a working group on the interaction between trade and competition policy was established, in parallel with the working group on the relationship between trade and investment.

The strong expansion in offshore production in the 1990s (UNCTAD, 1998) suggests that businesses have few problems adjusting to compete in different markets and to overcome border and domestic impediments. In many cases, governments' regulations or procedures are relaxed informally, or bypassed, to allow foreign investment to occur.

Competition (anti-trust) policy refers to the removal of controls and private restrictive business practices that prevent the efficient functioning of markets. It revolves around 'contestability'. The aim is to remove – or at least prevent increases in – barriers to entry or exit in specific domestic markets. This allows scope for potential new entrants (national or foreign) to constrain the behaviour of existing producers. Competition rules vary widely. They are applied through legal systems (in the United States) or by administrative processes (in the EU and Japan).

Applying competition rules requires major trade-offs among social objectives. Political considerations come into play. Some firms stand to gain by restricting entry to a market, and anti-competitive practices (collusion or exclusive dealing) are as effective as import barriers for achieving this. Government policies of all kinds are important incentives for 'rent-seeking'. In the same way that an import tariff by raising product prices transfers income towards domestic producers of the protected good, domestic lobbying to restrict entry to an industry transfers income towards existing producers. Political institutions and government structures determine the way lobbying works, and political forces help to frame competition laws and their application.

Most work on international competition rules relates to countries with established competition policies, which means that many will not participate. Among the advantages of using the WTO to draw up rules on competition are its comprehensive membership, its dispute settlement procedures and its continuous machinery for consultation. On the other hand, the WTO is an inter-governmental agency that does not deal directly with business practices.

The WTO working group on trade and competition policy has revealed very different views on competition policy. Major reconciliation is necessary before any negotiation of a multilateral framework of competition rules could be considered. Trade policy and competition policy are complementary in their effects, but they operate in different ways. Trade policy is a government policy using border measures, which tends to focus on producer interests and hence is amenable to capture. Competition policy, on the other hand, is concerned with the behaviour and efficiency of business within a country and the welfare of consumers. In consequence, competition policy (usually in the form of laws) is about business behaviour and conditions of market access, whereas trade liberalisation is about removing government measures that permit anti-competitive practices.

In the working group's deliberations, some representatives suggested that trade liberalisation should come first, followed later by competition policy. Developing countries argue that industrial development requires industry targeting and that both liberalisation and competition policy should be introduced later. This demonstrates how national governments perceive competition policy differently, depending on their circumstances. The dynamic Asian economies (NIEs) see problems of competition in terms of their restricted access to OECD markets caused by contingent protection, especially antidumping and voluntary export restraints. Some developing countries regard restrictive business practices by multinational enterprises as the major problem, especially issues relating to transfer pricing and monopoly pricing. OECD reviews, however, give emphasis to differences in domestic competition policies (laws and their enforcement) and the employment of government regulations to restrict trade. These different perceptions show a mixture of government measures and private anti-competitive practices as impediments to competition in markets.

The WTO working group on competition policy has stumbled in its consultations over antidumping. Antidumping rules protect producers from 'unfair trade', whereas competition policy seeks to enforce contestability. The two are in conflict. Antidumping is used as a strategic tool to restrain competition in a national market. Even the threat of antidumping action can cause foreign competitors to react, by withdrawing from a market or agreeing to price undertakings.

Antidumping was facilitated by the Uruguay Round agreement to allow constructed methods to determine dumping margins. Minor amendments to prevent circumvention strengthened further the effectiveness of antidumping; despite determined efforts by Japan, Korea and Singapore. Access to WTO dispute settlement procedures remains severely limited in antidumping cases.

The WTO working group on competition policy has been unable to get agreement on how to reconcile ready access to antidumping actions with proposals for a framework for negotiations on competition policy. Increasingly middle-income countries are adopting antidumping legislation; 60 countries have notified WTO of new antidumping legislation since 1994. Traditional users have continued to use antidumping. After the Singapore Ministerial communiqué was released, the US and EU authorities issued a joint statement expressing opposition to including antidumping in discussion on competition policy.

The significance of remaining border measures and antidumping actions are major complications before the WTO working group on competition policies.

Regionalism (Trade and Economic Integration)

During the Uruguay Round negotiations, whenever the process became bogged down, regional trade agreements (RTA) were put forward as an alternative approach to trade liberalisation. In reality, the reasons for intensifying and extending EU integration and for US adoption of NAFTA were political and had little if anything to do with the GATT negotiations in

Geneva. They did, however, cause small, unaligned countries to be concerned about their economic prospects in a globalising world economy. Many developing and transitional economies sought associations with the major players (EU and NAFTA) and formal trade agreements with their neighbours. Even then, there was often a political motive; namely to 'lock-in' domestic economic reforms using regional treaties or to prevent domestic protectionists from reversing liberalisation.

More then 100 regional trade agreements are now operating out of the 180 that have been notified to GATT/WTO since 1947. In addition, other such agreements are in force that have not been notified under article XXIV because they involve developing country members and are covered by the Enabling Clause and GATT Part IV (e.g. ASEAN free trade area). More than half of the RTAs operating under article XXIV were notified since the Uruguay Round was completed in 1994. All WTO members are now parties to RTAs, except Japan and Korea.

Regional trade agreements come in many forms and a major concern is whether they are all consistent with GATT article XXIV on customs unions and free trade areas, especially non-reciprocal preferential agreements such as the Lomé Convention. Minor revisions were made to article XXIV in the Uruguay Round, such as defining the transition period for elimination of tariffs among members of an RTA and establishing rules for averaging tariffs in a customs union.

All preferential arrangements, including RTAs, conflict with the fundamental GATT principle of non-discrimination, and serious doubts exist about their effect on the multilateral trading system. In its 1998 Annual Report, the WTO stated, 'There is still a risk that the spread of regional agreements may lead to discrimination becoming the rule rather than the exception . . .', making it '. . . important to reaffirm both MFN and the national treatment principles'. RTAs adopt subtle and hidden measures to protect their market gains and discriminate against outsiders, especially using antidumping, industrial standards and environmental regulations. This highlights the importance of strict disciplines in the GATT (Sampson, 1996).

Free trade areas are inherently trade and investment diverting, and create interest groups opposing multilateral liberalisation. Free trade areas preserve national tariffs and other trade barriers, which require 'rules of origin' to prevent trade deflection (Bhagwati and Krueger, 1995). Customs unions, on the other hand, avoid new preferences because they require a common external trade policy, which tends to be the average of pre-existing tariffs, and creates a single internal market. Free trade areas become even more complicated when they are extended to new members, such as in 'hub and spoke' arrangements (Wonnacott, 1996).

In December 1995, the WTO General Council recognised the threat posed by the proliferation of RTAs and established a committee on regional trade agreements. The intention was to follow a consistent system of review for all RTAs notified to assess compliance with article XXIV, rather than to establish separate working parties after each notification. (Over 80 working parties have reported on the conformity of RTAs since the 1950s; few have been declared to be in conformity, yet none were found not to conform!) This new committee represents belated recognition that article XXIV leaves many questions open.

RTAs cover much more than border measures affecting merchandise trade: differences in regulations affecting market access, trade in services, investment and competition policies, etc. are becoming important. Moreover, new preference arrangements and limited bilateral RTAs (that is, not including 'substantially all trade') are blurring the boundaries of article XXIV conditions. The new 'hub and spoke' families of agreements raise serious questions for the new committee to consider.

The proliferation of preferential arrangements around 'hubs' has made rules of origin important for investment and location decisions. These rules determine eligibility for preferential treatment and the local content component in some investment decisions. The EU has 14 sets of rules of origin applied with respect to its different preferential trade agreements. The US has six sets of rules which play an important role in NAFTA. Assessments of RTAs identify rules of origin as a major instrument of protection against non-members, and an instrument on the WTO committee's work programme.

The Committee on RTAs is charged to examine the implications of RTAs for the WTO. So far there has been little enthusiasm for this systemic review, probably because all the major players are deeply involved in RTAs. A legal review of article XXIV provisions has produced little. The Secretariat is now compiling a list of non-tariff instruments used by RTAs, but without identifying which RTAs employ each instrument. The main players appear to be avoiding any attempt to show RTAs in a bad light, despite widespread concerns about the effects of discrimination on the multilateral trading system.

Trade and Development

Trade and development was recognised as an area for special effort early in the GATT's life and special exemptions from GATT rules were introduced up to and including the Uruguay Round. Although membership of the WTO requires acceptance of the Uruguay Round final act as 'a single undertaking', many constituent agreements maintain special treatment for developing countries.

At the Singapore ministerial meeting, the need for special technical assistance for developing countries was acknowledged. For least developed countries a Plan of Action was adopted to promote development. A high-level meeting on development was organised by the WTO and UNCTAD in October 1997, which examined ways to enhance economic development through trade initiatives. Specific discussions were held on 'building the capacity of developing countries to trade' and 'encouraging investment in developing countries'. Another high-level meeting was held in March 1999. The Plan of Action and recommendations from these meetings are coordinated by the Committee on Trade and Development, supplemented by the sub-committee on Least Developed Countries.

The Singapore ministerial meeting also asked the WTO Council for trade in goods to explore and analyse ways to simplify trade administration to facilitate trade of developing countries, including training for trade and customs officials, improving recording systems, etc. Several Uruguay Round agreements provide assistance to trade; pre-shipment inspection, import licensing procedures, customs valuation, etc. Technical assistance to streamline trade and customs procedures, and to improve goods' handling have been shown to promote trade flows within South-East Asia, according to APEC agreements on trade facilitation. However, infrastructure bottlenecks in harbour facilities, transport networks, storage, telecommunications and legal-institutions require major investments. In May 1998, OECD ministers approved work on a proposal to untie official development assistance for least developed countries, and called for greater policy coherence on development by national governments and among international agencies (OECD (1998)).

Non-OECD merchandise trade has expanded roughly at the same rate as the value of total world trade in the 1990s (WTO Annual Report 1998). The distribution of this growth, however, shows Asian and Latin American exports (and imports) increasing faster than the world average and the OECD region. Sub-Saharan Africa and the Middle East lagged well behind; their shares fell by around one quarter between 1990 and 1997 (partly reflecting falling oil prices).

Least developed countries (39 of the WTO economies) lag far behind in trade expansion and account for only 0.4 per cent of world export volume. The marginalisation of least developed countries from WTO activities and their lack of administrative resources to evaluate its many agreements and rules, represent a major weakness in the WTO system as it moves towards a new round of trade negotiations. OECD Ministers acknowledged the need for a 'partnership strategy' to help developing countries at the OECD Ministerial Meeting, June 1999.

Trade and development will remain on the WTO agenda indefinitely. It is the only 'link issue' that is certain to be raised in the new round. Many developing countries are vulnerable in any review of the implementation of Uruguay Round agreements. Although developing countries were granted special and differential treatment in the implementation schedules, these extended adjustment periods are coming to an end. The issue of 'differential and more favourable' treatment (embodied in the Tokyo Round Enabling Clause) is coming into question. Least developed countries still have some time to meet commitments in the TRIPs, TRIMs and agricultural agreements, but these dispensations will run out during or soon after the next round.

Since the Uruguay Round negotiations began many developing countries have become integrated into the international economic system with significant benefits to their economies. They participated actively and influenced Uruguay Round outcomes (ATC, agriculture, tropical produce, TRIMs). The adoption of the WTO as 'a single undertaking' was significant, because this commitment required their full acceptance of the WTO package. At the same time, it creates justifiable concerns among developing countries. These grievances will be addressed in the various mandated reviews, but they would be more effectively dealt with in a new round of multilateral trade negotiations, where opportunities for trade-offs and reciprocity are greater.

Some OECD countries want to turn the new round into 'a development round', which would undoubtedly be well received by least developed countries, but to be effective this would have to go beyond purely trade interests covered by the WTO to cover financial and social aspects of economic development. On the other hand, the confusion over appointing the new Director General in 1999 created tensions between developing countries and the OECD authorities that increased suspicions about reviews of Uruguay Round obligations. Just how 'development' will be addressed in an atmosphere of growing suspicion remains to be seen.

ENTER 'CIVIL SOCIETY'

The five 'link' issues examined above do not offer foundations for agreements in a new round of negotiations. Differences among WTO members prevent accords even on the subjects for negotiation in the working groups on government procurement, investment and competition policy. Similarly, the WTO committees on trade and development and regional trade agreements have made little progress towards consensus on new rules or procedures. Commitments to take positive actions seem absent.

The other two trade-linked issues pose different problems. In effect, trade and environment and trade and labour standards have been resolved in the WTO context, but not to the satisfaction of some OECD governments or of vociferous NGOs which seek to exert political influence outside the parliamentary process.

The Marrakesh Declaration carried a separate decision on trade and environment that formalised an agenda for the committee on trade and environment (CTE). The committee's first report was submitted to ministers at Singapore (December 1996) and the CTE was directed to continue its work with particular reference to improving analytical understanding of the links between trade and the environment.

The CTE discussions gradually divided into two main themes; market access and links between international environment issues and the trade agenda. The many differences among member countries in the CTE appeared to have exhausted official discussions by the beginning of 1998. NGOs continued to attack the WTO and kept CTE work in the public eye, but officials had reached a stand-off. WTO jurisdiction over global environmental issues is limited to the effects of trade measures on the environment and the effects of environmental policies on trade and development. This is much narrower than the idea of global governance entertained by environmental NGOs. Continuing efforts to amend WTO articles are intended to ease present trade disciplines, to make exceptions on environmental grounds easier to obtain (especially GATT article XX). The alternative is to bring trade measures within multilateral environmental treaties (MEAs), and to bypass present WTO obligations. (Potential conflicts between trade measures available in MEAs and WTO obligations have been a cause for concern, but there have been no cases to 1999.)

There is reason to be concerned about trade measures being used as a lever to achieve social or environmental objectives. The analytical case against using trade measures to correct environmental damage is that they do not act directly on 'an externality' – a wedge between private and social costs. The policy objective should be to internalise the externality. Imposing trade restrictions will not prevent environmental degradation and could aggravate it. Trade measures are a second best solution leading to uncertain results (Robertson (1994)).

The attempt to link labour standards with trade policy made by the United States, with some European support at Marrakesh, presented a threat to the signing of the Uruguay Round final act. Introducing labour standards to the trade agenda has always been strongly opposed by developing countries.

The issue was raised again at the Singapore ministerial meeting, with the same result. The Singapore communiqué supported 'internationally recognised core labour standards' and identified the International Labor Organisation (ILO) as the organisation responsible for these standards. It rejected the use of labour standards to support protectionist measures and acknowledged that 'comparative advantage of countries, particularly low-wage developing countries, must in no way be put in question'. In case any doubts should remain, the chairman of the Singapore meeting made a statement that labour standards were not on the WTO agenda, that no new work would be commenced, and that the WTO had no competence in the matter. The focus of attention shifted to the ILO. In June 1998, the ILO produced a new *Declaration on Fundamental Principles and Rights to Work*, which obliges ILO members to respect, to promote and to realise the principles of seven ILO Conventions that define core labour standards.

Despite the CTE stand-off and the Singapore ministerial decision on labour standards, both these 'link' issues remain prominent on the political agenda. US President Clinton's address at the GATT/WTO 50th anniversary in Geneva (May 1998) was a call to enlarge the WTO remit to include environmental protection, consumer protection and labour standards, in order to make the trading system more open. He concluded, 'we must modernise the WTO by opening its doors to the scrutiny and participation of the public'. Clinton repeated this proposal in his 'State of the Union' address in January 1999. Similar statements have been made by European leaders. This ambitious agenda seems to bear no resemblance to the real life of the WTO, or the resources available to it!

WTO and Civil Society

The term 'civil society' has been adopted to denote non-market links that provide community support 'social capital' (Helliwell, 1998). This term, however, has also been 'pirated' by NGOs and single issue lobby groups. These groups are using the WTO as a weapon to substantiate what they choose to call 'post-sovereign governance' which seeks to bypass elected national governments and use inter-governmental agencies (such as the WTO and OECD) to pursue 'global social and ecological objectives' (Scholte, O'Brien and Williams, 1999). Such groups' declared goal is, 'to construct new, effective and democratic governance beyond the nation state'. Such remarks might not need comment if governments, including some from European countries as well as the United States and Canada, were not supporting increased roles for NGOs, without discrimination. These self-appointed groups, however, describe the WTO as promoting 'supra-state governance' through 'transworld regulation of trade and a permanent institutional framework' which has 'autonomy from governments.' In these terms, the WTO is attractive to 'a broad collectivity of non-governmental, non-commercial, more or less formal organisations . . . pursuing objectives that relate to reinforcing or altering existing rules, norms and deeper social structures'. Note, there is no mention of transparency or 'governance' of such organisations. Moreover, the NGOs seek access to WTO meetings to redress undesirable 'labour conditions, development problems, environmental damage, consumer protection and gender irregularities'. Hardly a trade agenda! By supporting this construct of civil society, the prospects for OECD governments to promote trade liberalisation are gravely weakened, as the collapse of the MAI negotiations demonstrated when NGOs for environmental, cultural and labour equity reasons conducted a coordinated media and Internet campaign supported by well-publicised demonstrations. The threat that NGOs pose to a new round is real.

The public profile of NGOs was raised by the failure of the MAI negotiations, and augmented by criticism of globalism by many of the same groups that make up civil society. New issues are being added to the list of government failures that also raise the profile of NGOs – genetically modified plants and foods, blunders in food safety and health regulations (BSE in the UK, dioxin in Belgium, etc.), ecological damage from warfare, etc. Public surveys show that advice from scientists, officials and economists is rejected in favour of opinions from media personalities and green groups! Public opinion favours these new, ill-defined, single issue NGOs, and governments seem to be building their reputations by default.

Even within the WTO, NGOs are regarded as 'intellectual competitors' to governments in the search for informed decisions. One major problem for the WTO, if NGOs are allowed a larger participation in WTO processes, will be to establish standards to assess their reliability, especially when providing information to such groups. Already the Uruguay Round final act provides for NGOs to contribute to WTO deliberations (WTO Article V). Even so, the WTO is a legally binding inter-governmental treaty and a negotiating forum, which at present prevents direct NGO participation in its affairs. WTO members remain divided over NGO attendance at WTO meetings, with developing countries strongly opposed. After the Geneva ministerial meeting (May 1998), the Director General instituted regular briefings for NGOs by WTO staff, and increased de-classification of documents. But dialogue with the WTO Secretariat is not sufficient for NGOs, who want to be included in formal working sessions.

The most significant advance made into WTO processes by the NGOs occurred in November 1998 when the WTO Appellate Body made a ruling in the *shrimp-turtle case* (brought by US authorities against Thailand, Malaysia, etc.) (Marceau and Pedersen, 1999). The Appellate Body accepted two *amicus* briefs from US 'green' NGOs that the dispute panel had rejected. These briefs contained not only information but also legal and political arguments, and they were not solicited by the dispute panel. The Appellate Body decided panels were obliged to take into consideration submissions by parties and authorised to take submissions from NGOs. Once the Appellate Body report on *shrimp-turtle* was accepted by the Dispute Settlement Board in November, 1998, NGOs were entitled to make submissions to any dispute panel – and they will! This decision allows NGOs to access the dispute settlement process and to introduce their arguments to the panel, and the Appellate Body. It is not beyond the Appellate Body to second-guess the panel's report.

This new role for NGOs allows their participation in all disputes, including antidumping, TRIPs and subsidies. This is a major breakthrough for NGOs – and, given the 'civil society' agenda mentioned above, it opens many doors by which WTO processes can be disrupted for non-trade reasons.

Many WTO members are disturbed by these latest legal interpretations. They represent a major change between GATT and the WTO. Articles in agreements are being interpreted by lawyers, without regard for the understandings and objectives of the trading system. The only way to overcome the Appellate Board decision on *shrimp-turtle* would be to reopen the issue in the General Council. Sitting as the Dispute Settlement Board, that body has already adopted that decision by consensus. The only way to reverse it would be to call for a vote on the interpretation of the understanding on dispute settlement, according to WTO article IX. But the WTO, like GATT before, operates by consensus. Once a vote is taken, all kinds of other differences could be subject to voting, and the strength of the rules-based system would be undermined. It is not an option to take lightly.

The strongest argument against allowing NGOs to have a role in WTO decisions is that they should act through national governments, like other interested parties. This is the reason, of course, why civil society advocates exaggerate the supra-national powers of the WTO, OECD, etc. It plays down the link from NGOs to government. Another reason to be wary of 'civil society' is its ill-defined composition. Who are members? What are their 'manifestos'? How are they financed? Where are their offices located? Their legitimacy and capacity to represent public opinion has to be established.

For NGOs to expand their role in WTO decisions beyond submitting reports to dispute panels will require WTO members to change the rules of the game. That is perhaps the toughest hurdle because governments are unlikely to relinquish their decision-making powers. Another problem for NGOs is that negotiated solutions require trading-off interests to achieve a compromise. The MAI experience showed that NGOs find concessions impossible to make.

THE NEW ROUND

Despite the many uncertainties surrounding the agenda, ministers were expected to initiate a new round of negotiations in Seattle in December 1999. The scope of the 'built-in' agenda ensured that. However, the 'link issues' did not seem likely to feature on the agenda because significant differences exist between members. Some, like trade and development, will intrude into negotiations at different points but not probably as an individual topic. Most remain too controversial to be included in a negotiation scheduled to be completed in three years (although, of course, that was also the target set in the Uruguay Round!)

A review of the 'link issues' reveals some hidden agendas that have been occurring in the multilateral trading system – 'colonisation by harmonisation'! Extending WTO agreements 'beyond the borders' coincides with attempts to establish public participation by means of NGOs. This conjunction will play a significant role in negotiations in the new round.

The common element underlying all the 'link issues' is the drive towards harmonised standards. Such common standards were introduced in the Uruguay Round using the agreements on TBT-SPS (*codex alimentarius*, ISO etc.) and TRIPs, backed up by the dispute settlement process. As remarked earlier, there are different motives behind attempts to integrate national economies in this way. It is also consistent with the favourable attitude towards regionalism.

Governments' acceptance of internationalisation has encouraged 'civil society' to promote an independent role in international agencies. NGOs have become the channels for independent views claiming to represent public interests, as an alternative to democratically elected governments. Governments seem to be confused about 'civil society', first seeing it as an institution to improve social cohesion and to promote the political message of 'The Third Way'. Then they saw it as an instrument for shifting difficult social/environmental problems into the international arena and out of national politics where they might cause embarrassment. The dangers this can create have already been manifested in the OECD (MAI negotiations) and the WTO (*amicus* briefs in the dispute settlement process). This ambivalent attitude by governments could create serious difficulties in future negotiations, where single interest groups will be vocal and uncompromising. The success of the NGOs in bringing the MAI negotiations to a halt is recent enough to have fed the appetites of NGOs in current negotiations,

The principal objectives of even the most serious NGOs is to place the environment and labour standards (human rights) on the trade agenda. Some OECD countries (including the US, the host country of the 1999 Seattle

Ministerials) have declared in favour of this. The majority of non-OECD countries are opposed to their inclusion in the negotiations. Already these countries are concerned about the distribution of benefits from the Uruguay Round agreements and their outstanding obligations. This makes them reluctant to make new concessions, even in the 'built-in' agenda. Before new concessions are considered many of these countries will want some trade rules reviewed, such as contingency protection and agricultural subsidies. For those countries facing economic uncertainties and poverty, the environment and labour standards are not a priority for the trade agenda.

Although the 'link issues' will not feature on the immediate negotiation agenda, the forces that are behind them will have a significant influence on current and future discussions and on the agenda agreed for any new round of trade liberalisation talks.

REFERENCES

Bhagwati, J.D. and A.D. Krueger (1995), *The Dangerous Drift to Preferential Trade Agreements*, Washington, DC: American Enterprise Institute.

Helliwell, John F. (1998), *How Much Do National Borders Matter?*, Washington DC: Brookings Institution.

Henderson, D. (1999), 'The MAI Affair: A Story and its Lessons', *Pelham Paper No. 5*, Melbourne Business School.

Marceau, G., and P.N. Pedersen (1999), 'Is the WTO Open and Transparent?', *Journal of World Trade*, **33**, 5–49.

OECD (1998), OECD *Council Meeting at Ministerial Level: communiqué*, Paris: OECD Secretariat (28 April).

Robertson, D. (1994), 'New burdens for trade policy' in R. O'Brien (ed.) *Finance and the International Economy, 8*, Oxford: Oxford University Press, pp. 108–19.

Robertson, D. (1996), 'The OECD investment mandate: Catching up with the market', *Towards Multilateral Investment Rules*, Paris: OECD Secretariat.

Sampson, G.P. (1996), 'Compatibility of regional and multilateral trading agreements: Reforming the WTO process', *American Economic Review* **86** (*Papers and Proceedings*), 88–92.

Scholte, J.A., R. O'Brien and M. Williams (1999), 'The WTO and civil society', *Journal of World Trade*, **33**, 107–123.

UNCTAD (1998), *World Investment Report*, New York: United Nations.

Wonnacott, R.J. (1996), 'Trade and investment in a hub-and-spoke system versus a free trade area', *The World Economy*, **19**, 237–252.

WTO (1996), *Annual Report 1996*, Geneva: WTO Secretariat.

WTO (1998), *Annual Report 1998*, Geneva: WTO Secretariat.

9.   Multilateralism and Minilateralism: on a Collision Course? Or can Trade Policy Practitioners Walk and Chew Gum at the Same Time?

Tim Groser

When considering the theme of 'Multilateralism and Minilateralism: on a collision course?' I had two immediate reactions:

- First, different people mean different things by 'mini-lateralism' but I shall use it to refer to regional trade agreements that are bilateral or plurilateral free trade areas (FTAs) or customs unions – subsets, as it were, of the multilateral trading system;
- Accordingly, I thought the title of such an address should extend beyond the disaster 'collision course' scenario to encompass another, rather sunnier alternative: namely, the two may be perfectly compatible.

My original and more scholarly suggestion to get that balance therefore was, after the words 'on a collision course', to add the words – 'or a false dichotomy'. Then I thought, why be so formal? I am not writing a speech for somebody else. Why not put what I think in plain language?

To state my conclusion at the outset: I am convinced that provided some simple principles – I call them the basic grammar of trade policy – are kept uppermost in mind in designing the architecture of such agreements, trade policy can indeed have it both ways – people, like the practitioners, can quite easily walk and chew gum at the same time. We can pursue sub-regional trade agreements while pushing forward with the first-best option of multilateral trade liberalisation.

I am of course aware that I am taking a relatively benign – one could say optimistic – view of a matter that has created a great deal of angst among analysts over the years. I take a stochastic view of events. Over the years, so it seems to me, more things in the world of trade policy muddle through rather than crash. Yet in this area of world politics there seems an unmitigated market for pessimism.

I have come to the view that most analysts underestimate the power of political and commercial markets to solve problems. In politics this is called a compromise; in economics it is called a new equilibrium. They may not be stable, but they are (a) vastly superior outcomes to downward spirals and (b) vastly more common outcomes than disaster scenarios.

The standard technique of many analysts is to lay out what the problems are and extrapolate them into ruinous but ripping yarns. I understand that the British economist Wilfred Beckerman, when trying to deal in the early 1970s with the Club of Rome predictions that the world was going to run out of resources in 25 years, got hold of the records of the City of London in the nineteenth century. At that stage, London was one of the world's most rapidly growing cities. The number one environmental problem for nineteenth century London was of course: horse manure.

Professor Beckerman then calculated that if you assumed a continuation of the secular rate of economic growth then being achieved in the world's first industrial nation, and you assumed (as one has to) that no forecaster had the capacity to invent inventions that had not yet been invented or could have foreseen the impact of inventions that had not yet been invented, London was now buried under 30 cubic yards of horse manure. I think it is worth reflecting carefully on this – both in terms of the rather significant methodological point he is making and his implied metaphor about a large proportion of such disaster predictions.

Second, I believe there is an in-built bias towards pessimism in political analysis because of reputational risks. What I have observed is that in all markets except pure commercial markets, there are no penalties for erring on the side of pessimism – in fact you can quickly attain a reputation for sagacity by putting all the problems together in a logical sequence. There are penalties, however, for erring on the side of optimism – few can survive the charge of being shown to have been 'a little too optimistic, I fear'. In my profession, that is the kiss of death.

Commercial markets are different, because if you tend to pessimism there you will end up with a rate of return on your capital that is way below the median and you will lose your job. The bias in commercial markets is probably the opposite: excessive optimism underlies bubbles.

Let me give you two practical examples from NZ trade policy: the Closer Economic Relations agreement with Australia (CER) and the Uruguay Round of the GATT. Concerning CER, that was going to fail because there was no way NZ Prime Minister Muldoon would agree to eliminate import licensing with respect to goods of Australian origin. According to conventional wisdom, he didn't like Australians, couldn't talk to Australian PM Malcolm

Fraser, and was a dyed-in-the-wool believer in a comprehensive protectionist import licensing system.

It was exactly the same in the Uruguay round: we were being constantly told that the only people who could not see reality – i.e. that the GATT was no more than the General Agreement to Talk and Talk – were one or two politicians in NZ, and a small number of naive NZ officials in Geneva. There was no way the French were ever going to agree to include agriculture. And imagine if we had added: 'And do you think the French will actively campaign for the Rt Hon. Mike Moore, to head up the new World Trade Organisation?' They would have thought we were barking mad.

Now consider the essence of our topic: the supposed clash between multilateralism and minilateralism.

This was a great theme of the international debate on the nature of the international trade system in the mid to late 1980s. The world, it was confidently predicted, was going to collapse into three competing trade blocs: one based around the EU, the other based on the US and the spread of FTAs into neighbouring North American countries, and one based around Japan. Under this model, multilateralism would take second place at best. At worst, the very system would be undermined.

Behind this view that regional trade agreements posed a dire threat to multilateralism lay a long-standing academic ambivalence about the role of regional trade agreements.

Academic economists have long been divided into two schools on the subject of regional trade agreements. As far as my understanding of the literature is concerned, the theoretical case for advancing the cause of trade liberalisation through regional trade arrangements came out of the theory of the second best via game theory. Put in simple terms, the argument was:

- multilateral trade liberalisation is the first best option; unilateral trade liberalisation – if you can sustain it politically given, by definition, the lack of reciprocity for your export industries – stands to one side;
- But there are circumstances where the politics of multilateral trade liberalisation are so difficult that it may be more politically feasible to advance the frontier of liberalisation with a smaller set of negotiating partners. In that way, regional trade agreements may be building blocks for subsequent trade liberalisation.

This, of course, is an economic perspective and thus to stop there is quite incomplete. As you all know, rather more than anticipated economic welfare gains lie behind most regional trade agreements, of which the most important by far is the European Union in its various guises running from the original European Coal and Steel Agreement of the 1950s through to Maastricht and beyond. That is, the politics of regional integration is an even more powerful driver.

From that standpoint, regional trade agreements have been outstandingly successful, although I am bound to observe that we do lack the counterfactual. However, after three great wars between France and Germany since 1870, the last two of which became global conflagrations, it seems churlish, to say the least, to demand evidence of a counterfactual to sustain the proposition that the EC has been a 'good thing' from a broader perspective.

This is an important component to my generally positive view of the topic I am addressing. To see 'minilateralism' solely in terms of its relationship to the multilateral trading system is certainly a large part of the issue, but it is not the sole issue. I see that these regional trade arrangements – and I very much include APEC in this – also have a vital political role and that generally that role has been very positive.

To return to the world of economics: while some early theoreticians saw the case for regional trade agreements, others have been adamantly opposed. Bhagwati is probably the best known of these opponents. I am probably not doing justice to their views, but the essence of the argument is as follows:

- Bilateral agreements are bad because they create an economic interest in maintaining preferences against the outside world – that is, they can quickly become 'fortresses' – hence the phrase 'fortress Europe' and, my word, New Zealanders know something about that. More on that later.
- Second, bilateral agreements are bad because of trade diversion costs. Expressed as simply as I can in a couple of sentences, importers make their sourcing decisions based on a 'cost, insurance and freight plus expected tariffs and border tax adjustments' basis. Thus, if you remove the import tax or tariffs but only for your FTA partner, you create an incentive to source from a less competitive country, unless by chance your FTA partner happens to be the most efficient international supplier. Thus, for example, if Australia can produce a tee-shirt for $15 and Indonesia can do it for $10 and we have a 100 per cent tariff on tee-shirts but exempt Australia from that tariff, then the rational importer will source from Australia and spend an additional $5 of foreign exchange in order to save herself a net $5 on the post-tariff equivalent price. That is an inefficient outcome. There is even a sophisticated argument that holds it is an inefficient outcome from a long-term Australian perspective – the perverse resource allocation argument.
- Third, bilateral agreements are bad because they detract political attention from the first-best option of forging multilateral agreements.

These are the three standard arguments against 'minilateralism'. Furthermore, I suspect that at least until recently, they would have represented the consensus view.

To illustrate my point, I would like to borrow a device used or at least popularised in Mancur Olsen's writings – one of my favourite theoreticians, but I am probably showing my age here, and certainly my outdated reading lists. It is what he called 'a thought experiment'. My thought experiment is the following. Imagine we are all advisers to the Australian or NZ Governments on trade policy in 1980. The Tokyo Round of multilateral negotiations has just ended with extremely limited results for our two countries. Europe has once again successfully maintained the distinctive and non-liberal treatment of agriculture from the global system of trade rules.

Meantime, there are murmurings within Washington that the US may abandon its historic policy position of refusing to enter into regional trade agreements. The beauty of thought experiments is precisely that you have the benefit of hindsight – the world's most powerful analytical tool. And thus I know that these early 'murmurings' would soon be translated into a landmark speech in 1982 by US Trade Representative Bill Brock in which for the first time the US expressed its readiness to engage in bilateral trade agreements – the US/Israel FTA being the first, and by some standards oddest, fruit of that shift in policy.

According to my 'thought experiment' we as the Government's trade policy advisers are asked a simple question: 'What would be the consequences for the multilateral trading system of a major proliferation in bilateral or regional trade agreements?'. It is entirely reasonable to suppose that we would have responded almost in one voice: 'In our opinion, Ministers, a breakdown in multilateralism would be the most likely underlying cause of a huge proliferation in bilateralism from today (1980) to the year 2000. Further, we must advise Ministers that were that to occur, such a proliferation of minilateralism would in turn accelerate the decline of multilateralism'. In other words, the answer defines a vicious circle.

True to the spirit of the time, the assumption behind the question would be that such a development – a vast proliferation of bilateralism or minilateralism – would be a deplorable development. Some twenty years ago the dominant perception amongst officials who would have considered themselves economic rationalists was 'multilateral good, bilateral bad'. This (then) prevailing liberal ideology behind the response in our thought experiment would be easily explained by reference to (a) the standard view in the economic literature which I have described above and (b) the empirical evidence of RTAs to 1980.

With respect to the second influence on our thought experiment – the empirical evidence *circa* 1980 – there were very few RTAs in our 1980 world – the European Community (EC, by far the dominant role model), EFTA (deeply protectionist on goods where EFTA countries were inefficient) and our own deeply flawed FTA with Australia. With role models like this, no wonder RTAs seemed every liberal economist's nightmare trade policy instrument.

The European experiment would have dominated our thinking on 'bilateralism' *circa* 1980. Since nearly 70 per cent of EC expenditure in 1980 was on the Common Agricultural Policy (the CAP), one could say with only a little exaggeration, that the CAP was the heart and soul of European economic integration. And we all know about the CAP – the single most important obstacle to the integration of a comprehensive system of global rules for agriculture. The CAP was the underlying reason for foot-dragging by the world's most important trading entity for many Rounds of multilateral negotiations, including the Uruguay Round. So if the model for RTAs was the EC, no wonder liberal economists felt that the theory of the second best had proved in practice to be a serious mistake.

Of course, we now know that our putative answer to our imagined Ministerial question about what might cause a proliferation of bilateralism would have been one hundred per cent wrong. There has been a vast proliferation of bilateral and plurilateral regional trading arrangements – minilateralism if you prefer – particularly since 1990. Since then, APEC has come into being, MERCOSUR has started its slow path of trying to integrate four Latin American economies including the dominant regional economy of Brazil. The NAFTA has created one giant free trade zone across North America. The ASEAN, through the AFTA agreement, looks like it is following the Australian/NZ regional path of converting a sub-optimal trade agreement (in our case it was NAFTA65) into a genuine FTA as we did with CER. There are numerous others under negotiation. Even Japan and Korea, the only two significant trading economies that are not party to such trading arrangements (leaving APEC to one side as *sui generis*), are now exploring possible FTA partners.

But, and this is the key point, the growth of bilateralism has not been sparked by a failure of multilateralism in the last twenty years. On the contrary, the growth of bilateralism has been accompanied by a significant advance of the multilateral framework. The Uruguay Round finally answered the most divisive trade policy question facing OECD countries over the previous 25 years: would the world accommodate itself to the CAP or the CAP accommodate itself to multilateralism?

In case readers feel this strong emphasis on agriculture is the product of a particularly NZ perspective, they should go back and read the history of EC/US trade relations from 1970 to 1986. It was dominated by deep differences over agriculture and prior to the Uruguay Round there were two or three times that both stepped back from the brink of trade war (publishing counter-counter retaliation lists) – all over principles (or rather, the lack of them) governing very unimportant bilateral agricultural trade flows. The underlying issue here was of course the same issue of 'comprehensiveness' – but the largest sub-set in that universe: the exclusion of agriculture from an otherwise comprehensive system of global trade rules.

The principle was settled decisively in favour of multilateralism – the CAP was accommodated to multilateralism, not vice versa. Further, the frontier of multilateralism has expanded in non-agriculture areas too. The Uruguay Round, for example, eliminating the infamous 'Grey Area' (i.e. the network of 'voluntary' export restraints, orderly marketing arrangements and other substitutes for emergency protection) brought trade in intellectual property and services within a multilateral framework (i.e. the Trade Related Intellectual Property issues (TRIPs) and the General Agreement on Trade in Services (GATS).

As the private sector has marched towards global solutions, so too has the scope of multilateralism broadened. In 1999 at Seattle, and without US Fast Track negotiating authority, it was always highly likely we would launch the next phase. Of course, launching a negotiation is the easy part, defining the conditions and implementing them in anything approaching reasonable time is quite another matter. That, I assure you, will be extremely difficult.

However, to return to the point of the thought experiment. Whatever the prevailing view amongst 'respectable' people might have been 20 years ago about the so-called inherent conflict between minilateralism and multilateralism, the political market place has clearly decided otherwise: we can and should have both. The prevailing view of 1980 – understandable in view of the appalling role models for bilateralism at that time and the ambiguity of the theoretical economic underpinning behind RTAs – has been overtaken by events.

There is, however, a critical footnote to this thought experiment that must be borne in mind. It is central to the foundation of NZ trade policy on FTAs. That footnote or qualification is that the older liberal view could still be correct in the future. The real lesson arising from the empirical evidence surrounding FTAs, at least in my opinion, is that it is meaningless to have a general view or a general policy on the desirability of FTAs, customs unions (or any RTAs). Whether they help or harm the first-best cause of multilateralism depends entirely on their technical construction.

Clearly, the CAP – with its political commitment to maintain a margin of preference for those within the fortress – represents an RTA which has been proven to be inimical to multilateralism. Equally clearly, the CER was hugely important in allowing one small country hitherto deeply addicted to protectionism – NZ – to participate in multilateralism, because CER was the first critical step to destroying our import licensing system.

We can now revisit the two other objections to RTAs I described above. The first was the 'diversion of attention' argument.   New Zealand is a small country. In 1999 it hosted APEC and there was a huge diversion of expert resources into that endeavour. Yet at the same time, because not everyone is involved, and in terms of resources at official level in Wellington, NZ has one person handling its FTA strategy (the author) and this is quite sufficient to handle the brief until such time as something real is on the table.

More importantly, NZ has a significant team which is focused on the multilateral system. One or two of the team play a significant role on the harder-edged APEC trade liberalisation issues. NZ has a tiny number of its international lawyers who have completed two outstandingly successful WTO cases, both of which were about holding on to the policy gains achieved in the Uruguay Round.

Additionally, NZ people have heavy international obligations: an unusually high percentage of WTO trade disputes involve a NZ official on the panel (the jury). This is the less public side of what seems to be NZ's fate: to make an international significant contribution to peace-keeping, except that this time, unlike Bougainville or the Sinai, it has no military character and is NZ's contribution to economic peace-keeping. Mike Moore has an opportunity to take this to a new plane. Don McKinnon will, it is very much hoped, do the same in the context of the Commonwealth.

So it seems NZ can maintain a policy of being open to minilateralism, including running APEC in 1999, while playing a role in the multilateralist system that is clearly punching above its weight. The evidence, I suggest, is clear: if countries as small as NZ can walk and chew gum at the same time, why can't others?

The political version of this argument – 'RTAs divert attention from/send the wrong signals to our top order priority: the multilateral system' is more than misplaced – the proponents of the argument have got it round the wrong way.

The premise is correct: we must ensure that whatever we do helps multilateralism, but the reasoning from the premise is clearly flawed. Having alternative trade policy outcomes – i.e. RTAs based on the same consistent underlying WTO trade policy principles – helps rather than hurts multilateralism. If the argument were actually true, then why on earth did Australia pull off one of its greatest diplomatic achievements right in the middle of the Uruguay Round – establishing APEC? Everybody agreed at the time that it was essential to complete the multilateral round. If the 'political divergence' argument had any truth to it, then forging a huge new plurilateral negotiating process right in the middle of the Uruguay Round would have been a terrible strategic blunder.

Actually the opposite is the case. Launching APEC was enormously useful to maintaining pressure on those who were holding up the multilateral system – i.e. the EC, as it then was. They realised that a number of other countries had alternatives if the Uruguay Round collapsed. In my view, having high quality RTAs creates a degree of 'healthy competition' amongst trade policy instruments. It is a matter of constructive pressure.

Trade diversion costs was the final argument used to oppose even the 'building block' FTAs. Trade diversion is an implied quantitative problem. To say that the problem exists, is to say very little. What matters is the dimension of the problem.

As MFN tariffs decline in industrial goods (from about an average of 50 per cent in 1947 when the GATT came into effect to around three to five per cent today) the margin between the MFN and preferential rates also declines. The welfare loss for participants through trade diversion becomes smaller and smaller. A genuine, CER-type FTA involves temporary but not necessarily permanent welfare losses through trade diversion. When NZ signed CER in 1982, it looked as if we were signing a document that said 'and NZ is prepared to accept massive trade diversion costs'. But other developments – the reduction in Australia's and NZ's MFN frontier protection policies – will have reduced this progressively. By 2006, when the last tariff in NZ goes, trade diversion will be zero and the CER will cease to have any preferential benefits for Australian exporters.

So, to sum up:

- Regional trading arrangements are proliferating around the world: the number has almost doubled since 1990. They are agents of regional economic and political integration – MERCOSUR being a classic example. But they also have an overt political role and that, I would assert, has been strongly positive. The EC/EU is the main example in terms of that broader political dimension and this is an important, though less obvious, component to APEC's contribution.
- Second, this explosion of minilateralism has been accompanied by a successful extension, not a contraction, of the frontiers of multilateralism.
- Third, the classic economic argument against regional trade agreements – trade diversion – is, because it is an implied quantitative question, becoming more and more trivial given the sharp decline in MFN tariff rates. One major possible exception: agricultural tariffs. They remain very high in certain pockets following the successful process of converting all non-tariff measures into tariff equivalents in the Uruguay Round. That is

potentially a significant problem, both for importers and exporters like NZ.

- Fourth, my position is that it is meaningless to have a general view on the relationship between minilateralism and multilateralism. Some regional trading arrangements have clearly been inimical to the multilateral trading system – the old CAP being the main example. But the CAP in that rigid form has gone and the key CAP frontier policy measures are negotiable, which was not the case with the variable levy and export restitutions. Moreover, I see few traces of 'fortress mentality' in the new generation regional trade agreements. They are there, but they are weak, compared with the older and malignant models of minilateralism. Broadly speaking, all countries bar a few still wedded to autarkic thinking, are following the path of liberalisation, and their design of regional trade agreements reflects that political choice.

So, to try to answer the question that was posed in my title: Is minilateralism on a collision course with multilateralism? No, the balance of the evidence suggests not, contrary to the overwhelming and pessimistic consensus view of 20 years ago – a view, incidentally, you can still hear echoed in some surprising official circles. But the old 'fortress' model is still there, so it is something that needs to be watched. The way to ensure there is a virtuous circle between minilateralism and multilateralism is to ensure a certain number of basic principles of trade policy are followed. The most important, by far, is that there is no commitment, either contractual or political, to maintain a margin of preference over non-members.

Finally, and most important of all, one needs to see trade policy as a continuum, not as a series of compartmentalised frameworks. The trade agenda of APEC over recent years has been heavily influenced by the WTO in a symmetrical sense. The sectoral liberalisation deals we have been discussing in APEC – referred to in impenetrable APEC jargon as 'EVSL', or 'Early Voluntary Sectoral Liberalisation' (if that makes it any clearer) – largely came out of what we could not pull off in the Uruguay Round.

Trade negotiations are like a game of high stake musical chairs. You go round and round while the music goes on while the negotiation slowly but surely removes some of the chairs in the room. When the music stops – and it always stops for some combination of largely extraneous political reasons (exogenous variables, if you prefer the language of economists) – you sit down wherever you can. If you have been too ambitious, dancing an extremely elaborate dance to entertain your domestic audience, you may find there is no chair to sit on. In my experience as a negotiator, so-called 'tough' negotiators who can only say no in order to please their domestic lobbies usually turn out to be useless negotiators.

So, at the end of the Uruguay Round, a whole series of sectoral deals could not be completed because we ran out of time. APEC has made excellent progress on some, less progress on others. In due course, these issues will come back into the multilateral framework once a formal negotiating process has been initiated – that is the subject of Mr Moore's chapter in this volume.

CONCLUSION

I have presented an optimistic view, but I think the balance of evidence suggests an optimistic view of these developments is a more realistic proposition than a pessimistic view. Trade policy is quite a painful process: it is a matter of making incremental steps. This is not a field for those who demand instant gratification.

Further, never expect a total consistency. At any one time, often within the same country, decisions will be taken that pull their economies away from the globalisation paradigm while other decisions are being taken in the opposite direction. How one nets these matters out is a matter on which academic economists have long debated.

If we look first, then, at multilateralism, my sense is that the system is moving forward, albeit in an imperfect way. The Uruguay Round was a major systemic step forward, dealing not only with the old problems in agriculture, the grey area and, to a much lesser extent, textiles and clothing – all of which had been effectively put into the 'too hard basket' for many previous Rounds. The Uruguay Round also 'brought the GATT up to date' by developing some outlines and frameworks in trade in intellectual property rights and trade in services and by developing an integrated Dispute Settlement System that may have its flaws but is a considerable improvement over the system it replaced.

The other side of the equation – minilateralism – is also moving forward at an accelerated pace. I do not see this historical tendency on a collision course with multilateralism, provided the same underlying philosophy shapes the architecture of all such trade policy instruments.

10. Multilateralism and the WTO

Mike Moore

Last year was the 50th Anniversary of the multilateral trading system. Recently I read a number of speeches by world leaders at that celebration. From President Clinton to President Castro, Prime Minister Blair to President Mandela, President Cardoso to then-Prime Minister Prodi – all saw this system as central to development and stability in our interdependent world. Each stressed the reality of the globalisation process and the need to improve its governance.

Why does this consensus exist? Because the history of the latter half of this century has taught us that there is really no rational alternative. The post-war architects were guided by a central idea – that a durable international peace must be built on the foundations of progressive liberalisation and economic interdependence. They knew that the Great Depression was made deeper and more prolonged because of extreme protectionist policies, which bolstered the twin tyrannies of our age – fascism and communism. In their vision, removing barriers to trade would lead to shared prosperity and a shared commitment to international stability. The principle of non-discrimination in trade relations would restrain destructive economic nationalism, and help prevent the resurgence of the protectionist policies which had done so much to increase interwar tensions. Theirs was a vision centred on the rule of law, not the rule of force, built on consensus among nations, binding commitments freely entered into and the settlement of disputes through procedures available to all and applicable to all. The proposed International Trade Organisation was to be a sister organisation to the UN, IMF and World Bank. With all their imperfections the world would be a more dangerous, less predictable place without them.

As it happened only part of the trade vision, the GATT, came into being. It took us until 1994 and the Uruguay Round to transform the GATT into the WTO. But the principles underpinning international trade have remained constant over that time.

I see this international architecture as advancing the independence and sovereignty of the nation state. Far from being a threat to the nation state, the opposite is the truth. Our independence is best guaranteed by interdependence. Globalisation is with us; it cannot be uninvented. No nation, great or small, in the world of today and tomorrow can secure its future alone. No nation can run a tax system, cure cancer, or aids, or enjoy clean air and water without the cooperation of others.

Alas, in many countries, including my own country of New Zealand, there are an increasing number of citizens who feel locked out, forgotten, angry and hurt, believing falsely that globalisation is the cause of all their problems. They sit waiting for a train that may never come, their faces pressed against the window, easy victims to old and dangerous songs that 'yesterday was better'.

We must be strong and proud advocates of the benefits that a more open multilateral trading system can have for all peoples. Thus the advocacy role of leadership must be advanced to support the actions of sovereign states who, on every continent, have taken brave and bold reforms. Yet when they are making successful adjustments, they can often find the door closed to their products, and minds closed to their problems.

Ambassadors in Geneva representing developing countries tell me about the contradictory obligations and advice their Governments have sometimes had from the IMF, World Bank and the WTO. The WTO has no power over debt reduction, nor can it guarantee development funds or infrastructural spending to assist development, to take advantage of open markets. However, and it's plain to see, it's clear that trade and development policies are linked. There has been a false separation between these policies and between organisations like UNCTAD, the WTO, IMF and the World Bank. We need to play a leadership role to ensure that ideas about the new international economic architecture that world leaders have spoken so often about, are fleshed out and have practical meaning.

The future safety, security and progress of all our peoples will be more and more based on economic diplomacy. If we fail to provide a fairer, more even result we risk outbreaks of dangerous, inward-looking, costly protectionism, which so often, sadly, turns into something more dreadful.

While most countries have seen incomes rise, the 'gap' between the 'haves' and the 'have-nots' has also risen. People are appalled and dismayed when they see the few living in splendour and the many in squalor, with half the world dieting and the other half starving. These people are not impressed by being told that on average they are better off than before. This is not the fault of the world trading system; indeed, it is an argument for making it fairer, stronger, and advancing the multilateral principles of trade. Indeed, those countries that have liberalised have done the best. We must say so.

We must make our case, otherwise the WTO will continue to meet, and Ministers assemble, behind barricades, ringed by the police. In the absence of other 'isms' to vent frustration upon, globalism is the only 'ism' left.

The WTO has already attracted the kind of abuse and demonstrations that the IMF attracted in the 1970s. The words 'Free Trade' are now negatives in many nations. The irony is that if free trade existed at all before the WTO and GATT, it was because the powerful did what they liked. The WTO, on the other hand, is about fair rules, contractual obligations and binding dispute resolution mechanisms. It's the rule of law, not the rule of force. It's about consensus decision making, and not forcing decisions by a vote. Not perfect. Not good enough. It can be improved.

We must show leadership, explain ourselves, involve the people, not be frightened by civil society, and set out to win the political debate with rational argument, or the doors of the wealthy nations could be slammed shut to poor countries. In wealthy countries, opinion polls reflect concern about 'so called' cheap imports. Whether we like it or not, this impacts upon politicians and their policies.

But let's celebrate that this system has delivered higher living standards, for most, than at any time in human history.

We ought also to celebrate that there has never been a time in the history of our species where more people have enjoyed freedom in the polling place and the marketplace. Twenty years ago most of South America was in the tyrant's grip, so was half of Europe, and most of Africa. Why is it, that when the smoke cleared from Cambodia to Chile to South Africa, people chose freedom? Economic freedom cannot be separated from political freedom. They are each other's guarantors.

Freedom and democracy is now the only valid revolution. At the dawn of the new millennium, the rule of law must be the main pillar of an improved, civilised management of our globalising world.

These values now find a consensus of support from practically every part of the world. The Berlin Wall fell because millions of people rebelled, not only against the loss of their political freedom, but against the loss of their material and economic freedom as well. With the end of the Cold War came the end of any pretence of a viable competition between state-planned and free market economies. Equally significant is the economic revolution which has been unfolding in much of the developing world, and the changing dynamic of North–South relations. Countries in Latin America, Asia, and now Africa, have moved, or are moving, from a world of import substitution and protectionism towards a world of freer markets and more open, rules-based trade. This change in outlook has, in turn, had a profound effect on the multilateral trading system. Whereas only 23 economies participated in the first GATT negotiation in 1947, in 1999 the WTO had 135 members, with 30 candidates waiting to join – ranging from giants like China and Russia, to small island states in New Zealand's region. This impressive number of members and candidates in the WTO is an unmistakable sign of the validity of this system.

The point is not that the global economy is somehow perfect – or that the widening range of public concerns are without substance or validity. The point, rather, is that the challenges we face can only realistically be addressed inside this global system – not outside of it. If people, especially young people, say that unemployment is too high, they are right. If environmentalists say that growth must be sustainable – and not destroy the planet's essential equilibrium – they are right. When developing countries say they are not getting fair access and justice, they are right. But none of these international – and national – problems will be resolved any more easily by restricting trade, closing borders, or undermining the international rule of law as embodied in the WTO. Just the opposite. As President Castro reminded demonstrators in Geneva, 'It is unemployment we are fighting, not the WTO'.

Of course the world we live in is still full of injustices. As Renato Ruggiero, the former WTO Director General, said:

> [F]ar too many people lack proper access to food, water, health care, education, or justice. The benefits of development are not evenly shared, and marginalisation remains a real threat for too many. To deny these realities is not an option. But it is equally not an option to deny the reality of globalisation, or the reality of the great opportunities it opens up to find answers to our shared global problems. ('The multilateral trading system at 50: meeting the challenges of a globalized economy'. Address to Norwegian Institute of International Affairs, Oslo, March 1998.)

The reality of globalisation is the reality of interdependence, an interdependence that, as I said at the outset, extends far beyond trade or strictly economic criteria. But trade remains a key element in sustaining and spreading the benefits of interdependence.

Over the past 50 years, trade has been a powerful engine for development. In 1950 its ratio to global GDP was seven per cent. Now it represents 23 per cent, and a third of the 25 largest trading countries are now developing countries. Between 1948 and 1997, merchandise trade increased 14 times, while world production increased 5.5 times. In the same period world GDP increased by 1.9 per cent per year at constant prices and taking account of overall population growth. Seen in an historical context, this figure is extremely high.

In particular, over the past 10 to 15 years, when developing countries have more and more embraced trade liberalising policies, the benefits have been clear. The share of developing countries in world trade overall has increased from 20 to 25 per cent. For the manufactured sector it has doubled from 10 to 20 per cent, and on current trends could exceed 50 per cent by the year 2020. Furthermore, in this same period of time, *10 developing countries with a combined population of 1.5 billion people have doubled their per capita income*. The World Bank reports that 25 years ago 70 per cent of Indonesians lived in what could be called extreme poverty, now, despite all their problems, the figure is less than 10 per cent.

South Korea's capital, Seoul, has been levelled to the ground three times this century. It now boasts rising living standards, which in turn have lifted human rights. Contrast this with North Korea: famine and fear. Night and day. Mirror opposites.

Take the stark contrasts in Europe today. On one hand a united Europe, where people respect each other's culture, and religion, and where people, ideas, information and commerce travel freely. A European Union. A force for good. Then there's the Balkans, where tribal hatred, and insular, inward looking policies have reached their natural extreme of ethnic cleansing. The lessons are clear.

For me it's always been more than trade – it's about peace, security and development. But trade is an important part of that. Trade in itself will not solve the entire world's problems, yet the absence of trade and commerce will make the world's problems worse. Imagine how much worse the economic problems of our region would be if the markets of the wealthy nations were not open to products from developing countries.

On the surface there seems to be an historic contradiction at work. As the world globalises and regionalises, new life is being given to ancient cultures, not the least in the old ex-Soviet republics. Scotland has its own Parliament for the first time in 400 years. Czechoslovakia divided into two separate nations, and both want to join the EU and NATO. People want to assert their cultural identity. Indigenous rights are on the agenda. Therefore issues of culture will be important. Solving this without distorting trade is a complex but achievable objective. Perhaps the new age of technology, with dedicated TV channels and radio stations by the hundreds, will assist.

This chapter was supposed to be about the future of the multilateral system. I have made the case historically for the system. I have argued for confident leadership to advance that proposition. There needs to be progress, a broad-based new round beginning at the end of 1999. We know that in the modern economy standing still means going backwards, and that the status quo is just yesterday's compromise.

To gain the confidence of countries and people that have yet to be convinced, we have to reform the WTO itself. It must look like the world it represents. Many countries cannot even afford to have representatives in Geneva. Others are overwhelmed by the technical details and thousands of pieces of paper. One ambassador from an economy in transition, when I asked him what he did, replied: 'Everything, therefore nothing.' Equipping smaller economies with the technical and research capacity cannot wait until the next ministerial meeting. That's the down payment they want now. Capacity to engage must be built up. That's in everybody's interest, the mighty and the modest. There can be no back-tracking on agreements already entered into.   That is equally true of the biggest and the smallest nation involved.

We are proud of our disputes settlement system, where contracting parties commit themselves to the outcome. That's something we could wish were a model for other areas of international conflict. But some small economies cannot afford, nor do they have the technical skills, to pursue their legitimate self-interest. The powerful can say they are free to do so. They are. We are all free to shop at Tiffany's, but some never will.

A World Trade Organisation should represent the world. Therefore, getting China, Saudi Arabia and others into full and engaged membership and partnership is a priority.   It would have been splendid if this were done before Seattle. Alas, the delay in appointing a new Director General made that very difficult.

We have an in-built agenda that can, and should, be added to. Some of the possibilities are well known and others are just emerging.   I would do neither myself, nor anyone else any favours if at this time I went into a personal agenda. There's no place for that in the WTO anyway.   I'm frequently asked 'what will be the issues of the future?' I say 'Issues we have not thought of'. At the beginning, indeed, at the end of the Uruguay round, no one had heard of the Internet. Now e-business is doubling every 100 days. Twelve months ago few had heard of genetically modified food. Yet, without commitment to rules and respect for objective standards these types of issues can derail all our best endeavours.

Remember when fears of cloning – Dollyphobia – swept the world. If only the breakthrough had been done in China with pandas. I have read that Chinese scientists are almost there. Good people fear what science may do.

New Zealanders must prepare for a different future. What the computer chip did for manufacturing and information, biotechnology will do for farming.

The New World will be about 'pharming', a combination of high tech science and agriculture. A drug Antitrypsin is used to fight emphysema and is now extracted from human blood.   Prices are high.   Scientists have worked a process of inserting human genes into sheep. Now a thousand ewes could produce the world's needs at a low price. By splicing a 'fish' gene into tomatoes we have a frost-free tomato that doesn't need fertilisers, and saves on pollution and energy. 98 per cent of the world's vanilla is grown in small island nations.   It costs NZ$2,200 per pound.   Patents are pending for a substitute – costing NZ$50 per pound. 100,000 poor farmers could lose a predictable income. Science is progressing quicker than our ethical, legal and social comfort zones can cope with.

The future is not to be feared, it is to be faced. Remember George Orwell's book '1984' and how technology would imprison us? I believed that in the 1970s. I was wrong. The opposite is the truth. Relative to income the cost of technology has fallen dramatically. The US uses less steel now than it did in 1960, yet its GNP has gone up 250 per cent. Super rice and super wheat now feed the world. When I was a boy it cost a working class parent almost a year's wages to purchase the Encyclopaedia Britannica. Now, it's a week's wages on a CD. 100 years ago it took almost a month's wages to put one word on a cable to London. Now e-mail is almost costless. Nobody is a racist, or an ultra nationalist, or a protectionist when their child is sick. They want the best the world can offer, and why not?

An interesting book I read recently, 'The Wealth and Poverty of Nations' (Landes, 1998) claimed that positive people and places win. It concluded, 'In this world, the optimists have it, not because they are always right, but because they are positive. Even when wrong, they are positive, and that is the way of achievement, correction, improvement and success. Educated, eyes-open optimism pays; pessimism can only offer the empty consolation of being right. The one lesson that emerges is the need to keep trying. No miracles. No perfection. No millennium. No apocalypse. We must cultivate a sceptical faith, avoid dogma, listen and watch well, try to clarify and define ends, the better to choose means'.

REFERENCES

Landes, D. (1998), *The Wealth and Poverty of Nations*, New York: W. W. Norton & Company.

11. The WTO's Dispute Settlement Mechanism: A Crack in the Cornerstone?

Patrick Lane

When Peter Sutherland, the last director-general of the General Agreement on Tariffs and Trade (GATT), brought down the gavel on the Uruguay round of global trade talks in December 1993, he and the trade negotiators of over 100 countries could look back on a job well done. After seven and a half years of talking – and sometimes not talking – they had left world commerce on a much sounder footing than when the round began in 1986.

The most obvious achievement of the Uruguay round, besides the reductions in tariffs that had been a feature of the previous seven GATT rounds, was an enormous extension of the scope of global trade accords. The old GATT had, as its name suggests, been largely confined to tariffs on internationally traded goods, although prior to the Uruguay round some progress had been made in reducing non-tariff barriers to trade. After the Uruguay round, the scope of trade agreements widened enormously. There were new agreements on trade in services and trade in agriculture, on foreign direct investment, on technical barriers to trade, on intellectual property, on sanitary and phytosanitary measures (SPS), and so on. Even textiles, long governed by a lunatic system of rules designed to choke trade rather than to permit it, was to be brought into the GATT system – albeit over a ten-year period ending in 2005. And to oversee all these new arrangements, a new club was created, the World Trade Organisation (WTO), with a proper foundation in international law; the GATT, technically, had only ever been a temporary arrangement. Members of the WTO, moreover, could not choose which parts of the Uruguay round agreements they signed. If you're in the club, you have to accept all its rules.

Arguably, however, the most important element of the Uruguay round agreements was the creation of a new mechanism for settling disputes between WTO members. In creating such a huge range of accords, the Uruguay round negotiators had also created lots of rules for governments to break, and plenty of room for argument over whether the rules had been broken or not. A dispute settlement system had existed under the GATT, but (for reasons which will be explained below) it needed reform. So a new system of dispute settlement was devised. Its importance to the whole WTO edifice is hard to overstate. Impressive as the scale and scope of the WTO agreements are, they would be worth nothing if governments were not prepared to abide by them. Renato Ruggiero, the WTO's director-general between April 1995 and April 1999, once said that the dispute settlement system is 'in many ways the central pillar of the multilateral trading system and the WTO's most individual contribution to the stability of the global economy' (April 17th 1997: see www.wto.org/wto/about/dispute1.htm). Mr Ruggiero is much given to grand phrases, but this is no exaggeration. Respect for the Uruguay round accords, and hence for the dispute settlement mechanism, is the cornerstone of rules-based trade.

However, even cornerstones can crack. The rock from which it is fashioned may be flawed. It may be vandalised. Or it may simply be bearing too much weight. This chapter will argue that all three of these things are true, up to a point, of the WTO dispute settlement mechanism. This is a long way from saying that the cornerstone, and the edifice it supports, is about to crumble. It isn't. The system is a big improvement on the old GATT arrangement. Plenty of disputes have been successfully settled, and plenty more will be. Nevertheless, any masonry needs maintenance.

There are flaws in any system of rules. The flaw in the WTO's dispute settlement system is that it is not intended to be tested to the full. The purpose of the WTO is to commit governments to remove trade barriers. If they do not, other governments can bring cases to the dispute settlement system. Ultimately, this system is underpinned by the threat of trade sanctions against countries that do not honour their trade commitments. That is to say, in extreme cases protection may be fought with protection – a curious result for a system that is supposed to guarantee free trade. This extreme is never supposed to be reached. It is hoped that disputes will be settled before that stage. Unfortunately, the extreme has been reached, with the imposition of sanctions, approved by the WTO, by the United States on goods from the European Union at the end of a long dispute over bananas.

As for the vandalism, the dispute settlement system has not always been treated with the reverence it deserves. The EU blatantly refused to comply with panel decisions over bananas. But others have dragged their feet, too: there are appeals against panel decisions almost as a matter of routine.

In addition, the system is at risk of being asked to bear too much weight. The dispute settlement mechanism is not the right place to determine the propriety of national environmental policies, say; it is qualified to rule only on their consequences for trade. Yet it is increasingly hard to separate trade from subjects that were once the fief of national governments. Trade policy is now intertwined with health regulations, labour standards and national security, as well as the environment.

The rest of the chapter is divided into three sections. The first explains how the WTO's dispute settlement system differs from and improves on what went before it. The second explains, using basic game theory, why we need a WTO and a dispute settlement mechanism at all. And the third considers the stresses on the dispute settlement system in the wake of the banana case mentioned above. A brief conclusion follows.

THE WTO'S DISPUTE SETTLEMENT SYSTEM

The WTO's dispute settlement system was not created out of thin air. Under the GATT, too, there was a system for sorting out trade disputes, but it left much to be desired. If one country thought that another was not meeting its obligations under the GATT – for example, maintaining tariffs at above their 'bound' level (GATT-speak for the maximum promised) – then it could ask for a panel to be set up to adjudicate. But if the panel decided that the 'defendant' was not playing fair, not much could be done about it. Panel decisions could only be 'adopted' by consensus. In other words, any GATT member, including a party to a dispute, could veto a panel report. Clearly, countries had an interest in blocking reports that found that they had transgressed.

Worse, frustration at the weakness of the GATT system led some countries to take the law into their own hands. In addition, this frustration stemmed from the narrowness of GATT's remit. Disputes over farm and service trade, intellectual property and so forth were not covered simply because GATT itself did not cover them. The United States, in particular, relied heavily on the threat of unilateral trade sanctions, especially its 'Section 301' legislation and variants thereupon.

The WTO system has two big advantages over its predecessor. First, it covers a far broader class of trade disputes, because the WTO's reach is so much broader than that of the GATT. So the mechanism can be invoked not only for alleged breaches of the General Agreement on Tariffs on Trade, but also for violations of the new agreements covering services, agriculture, intellectual property and so forth.

Second, the new system is far stronger than the old. The usual metaphor is that it has 'teeth'. Suppose that one WTO member – call it East – believes that the trade regime in another – call it West – discriminates against imports from East. East's first step is to ask West for 'consultations', which can last for up to 60 days. If the two countries' differences cannot be resolved in this way, then East can ask the WTO's dispute settlement body (DSB – which in fact consists of all 135 members) for a panel, usually of three people, to be set up to adjudicate. The creation of a panel can only be blocked by consensus. The WTO has 45 days to establish a panel. The panel has six months to produce a report. Its verdict is given to the parties 21 days before it is handed over to the DSB, and must be adopted within 60 days. It can be rejected only by consensus: this is an important difference from the old GATT system. Either side can appeal. Appeals panels consist of three members. They must report within 60 days (90 days in special cases). Their decisions are final, must be adopted within 30 days and, like the decisions of the original panels, can be turned down only by consensus. In all, the process should last no more than 15 months.

Suppose that the panel finds in East's favour – i.e. it decides that West is in breach of its WTO obligations. Suppose also that West appeals, and that the appeals panel upholds the original panel's verdict. West is supposed to amend its trade regime so that it falls into line with WTO rules. If it does not, East is entitled to compensation. This is supposed to be agreed between the parties. But if agreement cannot be reached, then East can extract compensation by imposing tariffs on imports from West.

The dispute settlement mechanism's teeth bite in three ways. First, because there is a strict timetable and panel reports cannot be vetoed, countries cannot postpone a verdict indefinitely. Second, because in extreme cases rule breakers can be punished by sanctions, failure to live up to WTO promises carries a financial penalty. And third, the rules are only as good as governments' willingness to abide by them, and to accept the decisions emerging from the dispute settlement system, even when those decisions go against them. Failure to comply sets a bad example that, if followed widely, would harm all the WTO's members.

By the beginning of June 1999, there had been 175 requests for consultations. Some of these duplicated one another, because more than one country made the same complaint about the trade regime of another: for instance, five countries complained about the European Union's banana-import rules, and these were later joined by a sixth. Even so, these 175 requests covered 134 distinct matters.

This is a much bigger caseload than under the old GATT system. In part, it reflects the broader remit of the WTO. But the number of cases also suggests that WTO members have confidence in it. Countries whose exports are denied entry to a foreign market, or are discriminated against, have more chance of redress under the WTO system than they did before. Therefore, they are more inclined to bring their grievances to it.

In some cases, the very act of starting consultations is enough to sort out the dispute. Of the 134 distinct matters, 37 (i.e. more than a quarter) have been settled out of court, or are 'inactive'. In others, it takes a panel decision, and usually an appeal, before a settlement is reached. Sometimes the matter of dispute is a dead letter by the time the case is completed – for instance, the American petrol import rules against which Venezuela brought the very first WTO panel case in 1995 were due to expire in any case in 1997. By June, 23 cases were still active and 21 had been completed.

THE DISPUTE SETTLEMENT MECHANISM AND THE PRISONERS' DILEMMA

Were governments true believers in free trade, there would be no need for a WTO at all, and therefore no need for a dispute settlement mechanism. It is almost always true that trade liberalisation is beneficial to a country's economy. Indeed, it is almost always true that unilateral trade liberalisation is good for you – i.e. regardless of whether other countries liberalise or not. But the world, as we all know, does not work that way. True, countries sometimes do liberalise unilaterally. It is not hard to think of examples, and it would be churlish, while in Dunedin, not to cite New Zealand. But unilateral liberalisation is still the exception, not the rule. It is far more common for governments to think of trade liberalisation as a means of getting exports into foreign markets, not of letting imports into their own. Trade negotiations still tend to be along the same old lines: 'I will open my market if you open yours', or even simply 'open yours'. That is the stance of the mercantilist, not the free-trader.

The WTO is the product of this mercantilist way of looking at the world. Governments know that trade liberalisation is a good thing – at any rate, economists have said so often enough – but cannot quite trust themselves to act as if they really believed it. The political pressures would be too great. Lobbies against imports, whether from producers or trade unions in industries making competing goods, are always far more coherent than the many disparate people who benefit from freer trade, often without even knowing it. So the WTO, with its collection of trading agreements, is the way in which governments have committed themselves to resisting mercantilist tendencies and protectionist temptations. The dispute settlement mechanism is the way in which this commitment is supposed to be enforced.

One way of illustrating how the WTO and the dispute settlement mechanism works is as a game played by governments. It can be thought of as an example of the well-known 'prisoners' dilemma'. Two prisoners are kept in separate cells, unable to communicate with each other. The police have enough evidence to convict them of a lesser crime, worth five years in prison. However, they are suspected of something worse. They are each given the opportunity to confess. The first prisoner, Smith, is told that if he confesses and shops the other, Jones, he will spend only two years inside. However if he keeps quiet and Jones shops him, Smith will go down for 15 years. Jones is given the same bargain. They both know that if they keep quiet, they will only be convicted of the lesser offence. But if they both sing, the confession of one will not be necessary to secure the conviction of the other, and they will both go down for 10 years. The options facing Smith and Jones are shown in Figure 11.1. Smith's sentence is the first number in each cell.

Figure 11.1. The Prisoners' Dilemma

| | | Jones's choice: | |
		Say nothing	Confess
Smith's choice:	Say nothing	-5, -5	-15, -2
	Confess	-2, -15	-10, -10

Consider Smith's dilemma. Suppose Jones keeps quiet. Then Smith will spend five years in jail if he too says nothing, but only two if he confesses. Suppose Jones squeals. Then Smith goes down for 15 years if he keeps quiet, but only ten if he confesses. Whatever Jones does, it is better for Smith to confess. The dilemma facing Jones, of course, is exactly the same. So it is better for him to confess too. The result: they both squeal, and spend ten years at Her Majesty's pleasure even though they both know that had they both kept quiet they would have gone down for only five years.

The prisoners' dilemma occurs in many contexts – at any rate, in many economics textbooks and journals. A common example is that of two firms in an industry each trying to choose between a mutually beneficial high price and a profit-reducing low price. The prisoners' dilemma implies that they have their work cut out trying to sustain high prices, because of the temptation to break ranks and start a price war. Game theorists and economists have spent a lot of effort trying to devise ways in which prisoners can be coaxed into cooperating, or duopolists can be persuaded to keep prices high. One way is to repeat the game over and over again. The players learn to trust each other. They also learn to punish non-cooperation in kind, increasing the incentive to cooperate.

Trade policy is another case in point. Suppose there are two countries, East and West. They both know that if they behave like free traders and keep their tariffs low, they both gain, say by $10m a year. They also know that high tariffs will wipe out these gains. However, they have a mercantilist view of the world, not a free trader's view. East thinks that it will be better off if it can keep its tariffs up (and West's goods out). West thinks the same way (see Figure 11.2; West's payoff is in the left of each cell). An alternative rationalisation is that the two governments might be in the grip of industrial lobbies at home, which want to see their goods sold overseas but want to keep imports out. Either way, the result is the same. East reasons that it would be better off with high tariffs whatever West does; West thinks the same way. Result: both set their tariffs high, and both lose.

Figure 11.2. Trade Policy as a (False) Prisoners' Dilemma

		East's choice:	
		Low tariffs	High tariffs
West's choice:	Low tariffs	+10, +10	+2, +15
	High tariffs	+15, +2	+5, +5

To economists, of course, this game is founded on a misconception. Unilateral trade liberalisation brings its own reward. So East, if it knows what is good for it, will cut its tariffs anyway, as will West. Unfortunately, not enough governments think or act this way. The WTO is, in effect, a means by which governments commit themselves to choose the free-trade option and resist mercantilism. They shouldn't need it, but they do. They ought to be taught international economics and insulated from the devilry of interest groups, but they are not. Hence, the WTO.

The dispute settlement mechanism is a mechanism for keeping trade policy in the top left-hand corner of the diagrams. It does so in three ways. The first is that it encourages cooperation. Remember that the prisoners in the original game are undone because they cannot communicate and so cannot make a pact of silence. The opening stage in any WTO dispute settlement case is consultation. Face-to-face negotiation, it is hoped, will help countries to resolve their differences. Between themselves, they can sort out whether trade barriers exist, how they can be removed and so forth. Without talks, an aggrieved party might retaliate straight away, dragging the outcome into the bottom right-hand corner.

The second way in which the dispute settlement mechanism keeps governments trading freely is by threatening political penalties for breaking WTO commitments. If a country is found to have broken its promises, it is expected to amend its trade practices. If it does not comply, it sets a bad example. Others might also treat their WTO commitments with contempt, and all would lose.

Third, it threatens financial penalties for countries that break their WTO commitments and then fail to comply with panels' decisions. If, say, East is found not to have kept a promise to cut its tariffs, and refuses to cut them, then West may be authorised to raise its tariffs in retaliation. Fail to keep your promise to stay in the top left-hand corner, and you risk dragging the world to the bottom right.

The hope is, of course, that this threat will never have to be carried out. Governments are supposed to be so fearful of a return to high trade barriers that they will never defy the dispute settlement system, nor will they risk incurring retaliatory tariffs. The problem is that there is no guarantee that the dispute settlement mechanism will be sufficient to keep governments on the straight and narrow. There may well be political and financial penalties to be paid for defying panels; but there may also be domestic political penalties to be suffered for compliance.

What makes this especially worrying is that if a country defies the dispute settlement mechanism, it faces sanctions authorised by the WTO itself. This is an outcome which the WTO desperately hoped would never come to pass: it is undesirable that the body which is supposed to be the guardian of free trade should itself authorise trade sanctions. Yet this outcome is embodied in the dispute settlement system itself. There is always the risk that consultations or panel decisions will not be enough to resolve disputes, and hence that the WTO will end up authorising limited trade wars. Trade wars? Yes, for how else do you describe the launch of retaliatory tariffs by one WTO member against another's (albeit illegal) trade barriers?

In fact, this is more than a theoretical risk. It has happened already. In April 1999, the WTO approved the levying of tariffs worth US$191m by the government of the United States on imports from the European Union. This was the final act of a protracted dispute over the EU's banana-import regime. It is hard to believe that this will be the only such incident. There are much nastier conflicts than the banana battle ahead.

BANANAS AND BEYOND

Like almost every other tale of trade politics, the story of the Great Banana War is a long one. Neither of the main protagonists, the United States and the European Union, grows bananas. But the EU has long admitted bananas from the former colonies of France and Britain on better terms than those from other countries. Among these others are Ecuador, and a number of other Latin American countries in which Chiquita, an American company, has plantations.

The Americans and Latin Americans have long complained about the EU's Caribbean preferences. Indeed, a GATT panel found against the EU's regime in 1993. The EU changed its regime – and another panel ruled against that in 1994. Its report was not adopted by the GATT, because the EU blocked it.

Enter the WTO. In 1996 the United States, Ecuador, Guatemala, Honduras and Mexico brought a WTO case. After formal consultations, a panel was established, which found against the EU regime in May 1997. The EU appealed, but the WTO appellate body upheld the panel's findings that September.

Some nine months later, in June 1998, the EU adopted a new banana regime. The United States and the other complainants had already seen drafts and had said that they thought it did not comply with WTO rules. They said that another panel should arbitrate. The Europeans replied that there was no need. The Americans responded in December by drawing up a list of products that would be hit by tariffs of 100 per cent, raising some US$500m. The Europeans said that this was itself WTO-illegal, and asked the WTO to rule on it. Undaunted, the US imposed sanctions in March, by requiring importers to post bonds. Finally, in April the WTO said that the United States was within its rights to impose sanctions – but only of US$191m.

It would be comforting to think that the banana war was a one-off and that future disputes will be resolved before trade wars begin. It might even be argued that the banana war will have a beneficial, salutary effect. Having seen that if they do not comply with panel decisions, they can suffer sanctions, they will do everything to ensure that it does not happen again.

It is more likely that this is wishful thinking and that the banana war will be repeated. Far from having a salutary effect, it may simply set a precedent. The precedent is that governments may think it all right to ignore panel decisions they do not like, as long as they are prepared to accept the sanctions that follow. But if the dispute settlement system is to uphold and extend the free flow of goods and services around the world, this is not all right at all. Trade barriers are supposed to be torn down, not reflected by other, retaliatory trade restraints. The banana war was a step, albeit a small one, towards the return of beggar-thy-neighbour trade policies – blessed by the WTO itself.

But the fear that the banana war was not a one-off rests on more than the power of precedent. On the face of it, the dispute settlement mechanism should have been well equipped to sort the banana case out. This was a trade dispute in which neither the United States nor the European Union had any great economic interest. Nor was any great moral or political cause at stake, although each claimed to be fighting a noble cause. The US said it was championing plucky Latin American banana growers; the Europeans claimed to be fighting for poor Caribbean farmers. Neither is convincing. The main beneficiaries of the EU's banana regime are the companies who hold import quotas; the main beneficiary of opening the market, apart from European consumers, is Chiquita. In short, this was exactly the sort of dispute that the

WTO system should have been able to resolve before the shooting started. It was about the technicalities of trade, not about morals or high politics. True, had the Europeans caved in, they (and the WTO) would have come in for ferocious criticism from the political left and from environmental and development groups for their supposed cruelty to the Caribbean farmers. But it is hard to believe that on this occasion fear of such criticism was the main reason for the EU's stubbornness.

The trouble is that in future disputes trade is more likely to be intertwined with moral and political issues. The list of such issues is easy to rattle off: food safety; the environment; labour standards; and national security. Moreover, at least some of these issues have hitherto been in the domestic political domain – rules on what can and cannot be injected into cattle, for instance. In each of these categories, it is easy to envisage countries imposing trade sanctions for 'non-trade' reasons and falling foul of a WTO dispute panel. Indeed, in one instance the European Union (again) has already been put in the dock and found guilty. It is also not hard to envisage countries, having lost WTO dispute settlement cases, refusing to amend their trade policies – preferring, in effect, to run the risk that other countries will impose retaliatory sanctions on them.

I will restrict myself here to two of the areas in which the dispute settlement mechanism is likely to be tested – food safety and the environment – and mention the others only briefly. On food safety, a good example of such a case is another long-running battle between the European Union and the United States over beef hormones. In the US, it is common for beef cattle to be fed growth hormones that are illegal in the EU. The US wants to export its beef to the EU. The Europeans say that it is not safe – or at any rate, that they are not sure that it is safe. And in any case, they add, European consumers want their beef to be free of hormones. The Americans say that there is no risk to health, pointing to the lack of convincing scientific evidence to the contrary, and accuse the Europeans of naked protectionism.

This dispute, like the one over bananas, has gone to a WTO dispute settlement panel. It found for the Americans, and once again the Europeans stood pat. The US drew up a list of sanctions, worth US$202m in the likelihood that at least some of them would be approved by the WTO.

Why have the Europeans not accepted the panel's ruling? Doubtless, pure protectionism has played an important part. This is European agriculture, after all. But there is an extra factor at work. Such is the fear of bad food in the European Union that – whatever the scientific evidence says – to allow hormone-fed beef into the EU would court big political trouble. It seems that the EU would rather keep the market closed, and keep the food-safety lobby quiet, than allow its consumers to buy American meat.

There is a better example brewing, over genetically modified (GM) food. In Britain, especially, there is a huge scare over GM food – the fact that tabloid newspapers call it 'Frankenstein food' illustrates both the intensity of feeling and the level of argument. Other Europeans share this concern. In fact, any suggestion that any food is not safe makes front-page news in Europe. Witness the furore over Belgian chicken, pork, and so forth. In part, of course, this is a product of the scare over bovine spongiform encephalopathy, better known as mad-cow disease.

It would be a surprise if European countries continued to import GM food from the United States, where such food has been produced for several years without (until very recently) causing any unrest among consumers. Several other countries are now using GM technology. It would be an even bigger surprise if this did not cause a trade dispute. If it ended up at the WTO, it is hard to see how the Europeans could defend discrimination against GM food imports. The scientific evidence against GM food is said to be weak. Assuming that the current fear of GM food in Europe continues, however, it seems unlikely that the EU would import GM food simply because the WTO said so. The probable result would be that the US would impose tariffs on European goods.

The overlap between trade and the environment raises two difficulties for the WTO and dispute settlement. The first is the same as in the difficulties over food safety. Protection of the environment matters politically. So it may be that one country wants to ban imports from another because it is produced in an environmentally damaging way. More sinisterly, some countries want to use 'environmental dumping' – the supposed cost advantage that come from slack environmental standards – as an excuse to keep some imports out. It is likely that such a trade ban would fall foul of WTO rules. By and large, countries cannot discriminate against imports because of how they are made; like products are supposed to be treated alike, regardless of the process by which they are made.

Again, in theory it is possible to imagine that a government that had banned an import on environmental grounds would defy a WTO ruling. Sanctions may follow. In practice, this has not yet happened: presumably, the political pressure on governments has not yet been strong enough. The WTO's efforts to become more sensitive to environmental causes may also have helped to stave off trouble. The closest call since the WTO was set up was the dispute over shrimp-fishing methods in India, Pakistan, Thailand and Malaysia. Because these countries did not insist that fishermen used nets that excluded sea turtles, the United States went to war for the turtles – but only after being prodded by a marine-environment research institute in California. The US lost the case, and little has been heard since it did.

The second difficulty is arguably more serious. Whereas the first is a conflict between political calculations and WTO agreements, the second is a conflict between two sets of international treaty obligations. The WTO agreements are not the only international political commitments made by its member governments. There are many 'multilateral environmental agreements' (MEAs), some of which permit the use of trade sanctions against countries that do not abide by the MEA. These trade sanctions are likely to be contrary to WTO rules and so in principle could face a dispute settlement challenge. Again, this is still only a theoretical possibility. The best-known MEA, the Montreal Protocol, required the banning of imports of goods made with chlorofluorocarbons (CFCs). So important was the phasing out of CFCs considered to be that the trade sanctions were not used, and not seriously challenged. But there may come a time when a signatory of an MEA bans an import from a non-signatory, and the non-signatory launches a WTO case. Because the WTO will worry only about whether WTO rules have been broken and not about the MEA, governments' trade and environmental commitments will be brought into sharp, legal conflict.

Briefly, what are the risks in other areas? It is possible that a western country will pass a law banning the import of goods made with child labour – which would be WTO-illegal, whether the motivation was protectionist or humanitarian. We have also had a near-miss over national security. When the United States took action against foreign companies with interests in Cuba, Iraq and Libya, the European Union began a dispute settlement case. The Americans' reaction was that the WTO had no jurisdiction in this area. It is just as well that the case never came to court. A stand-off between the WTO and the United States would have been a distinct possibility.

CONCLUSION

The WTO's dispute settlement mechanism, after a promising start, is now looking less shiny than it once did, thanks largely to the banana war between the United States and the European Union. I have argued that this is unlikely to be an isolated incident, given the range and scale of some of the conflicts between trade and non-trade issues now brewing.

In the previous section, the possible difficulties were discussed subject by subject – food safety, the environment, and so forth. To conclude, it may be worth looking at them from another angle. Trouble may arise in one of three ways.

First is 'brazen defiance'. The worst thing for the dispute settlement mechanism is for countries to defy it openly. Confidence in the mechanism, and hence in the WTO itself, depends on all its members treating it with respect. The most damaging aspect of the banana dispute has been that the European Union has at the very least come close to brazen defiance. Now that trade regulations impinge on areas of policy that were once considered purely domestic, it is a fair bet that brazen defiance will pay domestic political dividends, regardless of WTO obligations.

Second is 'confusion'. During the banana dispute, it was never clear exactly what the European Union would have to do to meet the dispute settlement panel's criticisms. The EU was able to exploit this lack of clarity to drag its feet in reforming the banana regime. This in turn helped precipitate the case's unhappy conclusion. One of the few encouraging results of the banana case is that the WTO seems to have learned how damaging a lack of clarity can be. Countries ought to be sure, once their trade regimes have been found to be at fault, how they should reform.

Finally, there is 'overstretch'. One of the problems with the WTO dispute settlement mechanism is that it is simply being asked to do too much. This is most obvious in environmental cases: by default, it is being asked to rule on the legitimacy of countries' environmental regulations. In any conflict between trade and the environment, WTO panels are likely to come down on the side of trade. That is not necessarily wrong; but it is not necessarily right either. And the conflict is not the fault of panels, but of those who bring the cases and who make the WTO's rules. It would be better if these disputes could be resolved outside the dispute settlement mechanism, or if WTO members could decide how to deal with environmental cases within the WTO, perhaps by amending Article XX of the GATT explicitly to recognise MEAs.

This may sound pessimistic about the WTO and the dispute settlement system. It is, but only up to a point. The WTO is a great advance on the GATT, and the dispute settlement system has worked well in many cases. But the credibility of the organisation depends largely on the dispute settlement system being used with respect – and that means resolving disputes before sanctions are imposed. If sanctions are used, then protectionism is not being eradicated, but met with more protectionism. And that, surely, was what the GATT and the WTO were established to avoid. It would be better still if governments realised that they are not playing a prisoners' dilemma game, and saw that in opening their markets they were not giving a concession to foreigners but prosperity to their own people. Despite the great steps taken towards freer trade in recent years, such a change of heart is still far from complete.

12. The Future of International Financial Institutions: Do they Add Value in a Turbulent World?

Alex Sundakov

The International Monetary Fund (IMF) and other international financial institutions have come under close scrutiny in recent years, given their significant role in the former Soviet Union, and in the Asian crises of the last year. On the one hand, the IMF and the World Bank have been heavily criticised for their failings. On the other hand, there have been numerous proposals to create alternative institutions with similar characteristics, such as an Asian Monetary Fund. In fact, a European Bank for Reconstruction and Development was created in the early 1990s.

This chapter attempts to take a systematic look at the value of such institutions both from the point of view of their ability to contribute to international financial stability, and from the point of view of economic development. While I inevitably draw on my own experience of working for the IMF, as well as my research into the operations of the international financial institutions, the questions I ask are more generic. I am less interested in the particular successes and failures, and more concerned with what organisations of such type can do given their inherent characteristics.

FINANCIAL STABILITY

Emergency Lending

The original vision behind the IMF was that it would provide emergency finance to underpin financial adjustment and stabilisation. However, the Bretton Woods model envisaged a very particular type of emergency: a balance of payments crisis under the conditions of fixed exchange rates. Periodic balance of payments problems were almost inevitable under that regime – even with the most prudent macroeconomic management, the only signal that was available to decision-makers that their domestic policies were inconsistent with the exchange rate regime was the appearance of an external imbalance. Since cyclical imbalances were commonplace, only reasonably large and persistent current account deficits could be interpreted unequivocally as demanding a change in policy settings. In other words, by the time the evidence emerged to recognise that a problem existed, it was already of sufficient magnitude to require both major policy adjustment and considerable financial flows.

There is no doubt that an international financial institution made sense at the core of a fixed exchange rate system. However, this is not how the problem presents itself now. It is true that many countries maintain fixed exchange rate regimes, and very few floating arrangements around the world are as pure as the one in New Zealand. However, countries' financial difficulties tend to be associated not with slowly evolving balance of payments imbalances, but with financial crises stemming from loss of confidence and rapid reversals of capital flows. The key point is that, unlike 50 years ago, capital flows now dominate trade flows both in magnitude and in the relative influence on exchange rates.

This change in the underlying causes of financial instability presents us with three issues:

- First, reversals in capital flows are much more sudden than evolving trade imbalances. The causes of such reversals are frequently less obvious and it is often impossible to detect that anything is about to go wrong up to the very moment when it does.
- Second, the financial magnitudes involved are much greater. A deteriorating trade imbalance may involve demand for financing amounting to a few per cent of GDP over a year. A reversal of capital flows may represent twice that over a short time span. A country's international reserves amounting to, say, six months of imports, could be consumed within days.
- Finally, financial crises originating in capital flows pose problems of moral hazard. Capital flows out because investors realise that they underestimated the risks of investing in that country. The availability of emergency lending from the international financial organisations makes risks appear lower. Hence, it encourages more risky behaviour by investors and may lead to crises of greater magnitude.

There are, therefore, two key questions that need to be answered:

1. Can the international financial institutions make a difference given a realistic amount of resources available to them?

2. And even if they can, could their very existence be causing the problems they are required to address?

In reply to the first question, it is obvious that the IMF resources are increasingly stretched. The World Bank, which is in principle a development institution rather than an emergency financier, has been drafted to provide adjustment assistance alongside the IMF. But even their joint resources are insufficient. Both during the Mexican crisis and in the Asian crises of the late 1990s, bilateral financing from countries such as the US and Japan represented more than half of all emergency funds that were made available. And the situation is only going to get worse. As world private capital flows grow, the international financial resources are likely to come under increasing strain.

Nonetheless, the international financial institutions can still perform two useful functions:

- They can act as catalysts of other finance, putting together a rescue package; and
- The very existence of an IMF/World Bank programme, even if it is not underpinned by large amounts of money, can reverse investor sentiment and restore confidence.

In practice, however, it was the US that was the catalyst of the assistance packages for Mexico and for the Asian countries. As far as the restoration of confidence is concerned, it crucially depends on how appropriate the policy prescriptions are and how likely they are to be implemented. You may recall that the announcement of an IMF programme for Indonesia was greeted by a fall in the rupiah, as investors widely regarded the IMF as addressing a wrong set of problems and imposing unnecessary fiscal restraint.

But let us assume that the international financial institutions can help. Should they? First, we must go back to the problem of moral hazard. My own experience does suggest that investors do indeed make decisions which are commercially inappropriate on the expectation that should things go wrong, they would be bailed out. In my job as an IMF Resident Representative in Ukraine, I dealt with a constant stream of private investors who assessed risk not on the basis of local economic conditions or government policies, but primarily on the basis of whether an IMF programme would ensure that there was no default.

In this regard, it is useful to consider whether a financial crisis is more like a bank run – precipitated by short term panic which is damaging an otherwise stable institution – or more like a company bankruptcy, which arises from a realisation that the business is no longer viable at existing asset values.

If it is more like a bank run, then a short term infusion of liquidity to offset financial outflows and to restore confidence makes perfect sense. In this situation, a country is borrowing from the international financial institutions to replace its other private debt, and at the end of the day, when the credibility is restored, no one is worse off. The country continues to carry the level of debt it had before, while the investors who had panicked have been paid off.

However, if a financial crisis represents a realisation that the country's assets were overvalued, then an international rescue package has the effect of paying off the investors in full, and leaving the country itself to carry the full weight of adjustment. This is unlikely to be efficient. In most corporate bankruptcies, the burden of adjustment is shared out between lenders and borrowers. This creates an incentive for lenders to exercise caution, as well as ensuring that efficient economic activities continue. By forcing the bulk of adjustment on to domestic economy, international financial institutions both undermine the incentives for private lenders to take care and may suppress efficient domestic activity.

In the real world, financial crises have elements of both situations. The problem is that the international financial institutions are not flexible enough to distinguish the two settings. This clearly creates problems of its own.

Economic Surveillance

> Central to the IMF's purposes and operations is the mandate, under its Articles of Agreement, to 'exercise firm surveillance over the exchange rate policies of members'... Traditionally, the IMF's main focus in surveillance has been to encourage countries to correct macroeconomic imbalances, to reduce inflation, and undertake key exchange, trade and other market reforms. But increasingly, and depending on the situation in each country, a much broader range of institutional measures has been seen as necessary for countries to establish and maintain private sector confidence and lay the groundwork for sustained growth. (IMF Annual Report 1998, Washington DC: IMF, p. 33.)

Economic surveillance consists of:

- Annual Article IV consultations – visits by the IMF to each member country.
- Twice annual preparation of the World Economic Outlook (WEO) by the IMF. WEO is a forecast and commentary on the world economy.
- On-going discussions with member countries in particular distress.

The idea that the international institutions like the IMF can improve welfare by detecting economic problems early on, and advising countries to correct their course, is based on three main premises:

- First, it must assume that the IMF has better information and better analytical capability than the independent – particularly private sector – forecasters and commentators do. If that is not the case, than the IMF will struggle to add value.
- Second, it must assume that the IMF – which by definition can not have better information than a nation's government – has better ability to use that information, and a stronger incentive to take a critical view of the situation than local officials.
- Finally, it must assume that the IMF has more kudos and greater moral force than other independent observers, to the extent that it is in a stronger position to make governments take note of concerns.

More recently – following the Asian crises – the focus of international surveillance shifted towards developing a more immediate ability to identify and forestall financial crises. This poses a broader issue of what it is that surveillance can and can not do. Before we examine the premises of surveillance identified above, I should emphasise that in my view, even if they hold, no amount of international surveillance will ever be able to prevent sharp adjustments in financial markets. Asset values – including currency values – are based on expectations of future performance. A financial crisis is a sharp reversal of expectations, when the sentiment that underpinned asset values turns negative.

Effective surveillance – i.e. work which both identifies problems and convinces decision-makers that these problems exist and must be taken seriously – would always affect sentiment. Consequently, it will tend to precipitate the very situation that it seeks to avoid. This is precisely why the IMF has itself historically been very nervous about issuing strong statements about countries' financial problems – it does not wish to be blamed for making them worse.

The best that can be hoped for from economic surveillance is that it can cause an adjustment before the sentiment gets too far out of line with the 'fundamentals', so that the ensuing crisis is smaller in intensity than it would have been otherwise. Even that is too much to hope for. The link between the 'fundamentals' and the financial markets is tenuous at best. Economic analysis can identify degrees of concern, but little beyond that. Much learned ink has been spilled discussing whether the US stock market performance is in line with the 'real' value of those companies, but convincing arguments can be made either way, and there is no obvious single answer.   Consequently, one can be almost certain that by the time surveillance conclusively shows that a problem exists, the problem will be of such magnitude as to cause a painful adjustment.

But let us return to the three assumptions behind effective surveillance identified above. In my view, the first assumption was once true, but no longer holds for most of the world.   In part, the international financial institutions have been the victims of their own success in promoting better and more transparent economic information.   Almost all countries now produce and make public a full set of national accounts, detailed fiscal accounts and substantial amounts of banking information.   In many parts of the world – including New Zealand – many statistics are of relatively poor quality, with high margins of error and long delays in preparation. However, quality is not the issue here: whatever the quality, everyone has access to the same information. At the NZ Institute for Economic Research (NZIER), we may complain about New Zealand's GDP releases, but we know that Treasury, the Reserve Bank and the IMF have to work with the same numbers.

Moreover, private sector forecasters, given the demands on their performance, are more fleet of foot. By the time the IMF World Economic Outlook comes out, it is typically out of date, as more up-to-date private forecasts are prepared. In recent years, as most developing countries moved ahead in the sophistication of their financial markets, there has been an increase in the number of private organisations with a strong incentive to monitor their economic performance.   Both domestic and foreign banks provide high level of expertise that may have been denied to some poorer countries in the past.

Consequently, there are fewer and fewer countries left where the international financial institutions are the only independent or the most able economic commentators. More importantly, such countries are unlikely to have financial markets of any significance, making surveillance less relevant.

The other two assumptions, however, remain true. While there are some situations when government officials can clearly identify the problems of the policies they are pursuing – witness the New Zealand public service in the early 1980s – it is more common for public servants and politicians to be defensive about the current course of action, and to be caught up in the 'team spirit'.   The IMF and the World Bank (in developing countries) can add considerable value by working on the inside with officials, but presenting a dissenting view.   Moreover, particularly in smaller or culturally isolated countries (like New Zealand), the very foreignness of the IMF teams serves to convey an air of quality and influence. The IMF's approval is still keenly sought.   It would also be fair to say that the institutions like the IMF are still regarded as one of the pinnacles of an economist's career, thus attracting some high quality staff.

On balance, the IMF, with the assistance of other international financial institutions, is still able to make a modest contribution to financial stability through economic surveillance. However, the value of such a contribution is rapidly declining as many more informed independent voices are being heard.

Incentive to Stabilise

It is often argued that access to finance from the international financial institutions, primarily the IMF, can serve as an incentive to undertake stabilisation policies, which a country's government may not otherwise be willing to implement. In an extreme form, this is an odd argument, since it seems to assume that the reward for stabilisation is access to finance, rather than the benefit of stabilisation itself. Financial instability imposes significant on-going economic costs. The dangers of very high inflation are well known, but, more generally, economic research suggests that inflation rates in excess of eight per cent per annum cause lasting damage to economic growth. One would normally expect that countries would wish to achieve economic stability because it increases their own welfare.

However, there are good reasons why countries find it so difficult to undertake stabilisation programmes. First, the costs of disinflation can be quite sharp in the short term, while the benefits are spread over time. This has political consequences – the governments that reap the benefits of macroeconomic stability are typically not the ones who initiate it. This is precisely why there exists an image of a 'heroic' Minister of Finance – someone who does unpopular things even if it means sacrificing their career.

In addition, for many developing and transition economies, the politics of inflation are complicated by the fact that the elites tend to be either cushioned from inflation by indexation, or are, in fact, beneficiaries of inflation. The brunt of financial instability is borne by the very poor, who rarely figure in politics.

From that point of view, an infusion of foreign finance through the international financial institutions can serve as an incentive to undertake stabilisation, by providing an opportunity to reduce the short-term costs of adjustment, as well as offering the resources to compensate the elites. The problem, however, is that because the value of external funding is in overcoming the short-term complications of disinflation, it also creates an incentive to concentrate on short-term policy objectives. This often means that the international financial organisations tend to reinforce the short-term focus of policy-making, from which many developing countries suffer.

I would like to illustrate this with an example with which I am particularly familiar: in the late 1990s, the international financial institutions played a remarkably influential role in Ukraine. It is not even that the IMF and the World Bank were able to influence some key government decisions. In fact, many decisions were made in direct contravention to their advice. More importantly, they defined the terms of the policy debate, and set the context for the decision-making processes. Unfortunately, over this period, the international organisations have often acted to reinforce Ukraine's own habitual focus on the short-term.

One of the main culprits has been the introduction of the system of sequestration, or cash management, as the cornerstone for the financial programmes supported by the IMF. Cash management is the critical short-term instrument for the delivery of the agreed fiscal targets. In essence, what it means is that, on a virtually daily basis, the government checks to see how much money it has collected in revenue, adds to that the agreed borrowing ceiling, and then spends only that amount. In other words, expenditure is determined not by policy programmes, but by the availability of cash.

While this is an effective tool in the very short term, if retained for more than a few months it becomes extraordinarily destructive. It introduces chaos into the public sector of the economy, dramatically reduces its efficiency, and makes public sector adjustment close to impossible. In fact, it keeps generating itself the very crisis it is trying to address. There are two reasons for this. First, cash management is addictive. It divorces the underlying fiscal policy from the budget which is presented to Parliament, removes Parliamentary oversight and gives the government considerable discretion over spending priorities. The officials involved along the entire chain of command gain in stature and power from the exercise of the discretion.

Second, it creates an extreme disincentive for the administrators of spending programmes to adjust their policies. Cash management means that payments tend to be directed towards the hot spots. One can generate a hot spot by accumulating large unpaid claims on the government. Consequently, the best strategy for a programme administrator is to change as little as possible, and to keep accumulating the claims. An administrator who attempts to learn to live within the available budget does a disservice to his organisation, because it reduces the likelihood and the frequency of receiving funds.

As a result, sequestration prevents fiscal reform. While in terms of cash flows it may appear that the government is reducing its role in Ukraine, the actual range of activities and programmes remains largely unchanged. Many of these activities remain unpaid for long periods of time, but that only serves to reduce their efficiency even further. Sequestration has been a disaster for Ukraine, and its persistent use delays real fiscal reform. In fact, after almost four years of sequestration, strategic fiscal policy making has become remarkably difficult.   Over this time, the Government has lost almost all linkage between the amounts of cash it spends and the policies it finances. It is possible to say how many millions of *hryvnia* are spent on education, for example, but it is no longer possible to say what kind of education policy this buys. The only way to get back to strategic decision-making is to undertake a zero-based review of all the spending programmes. Since that is very difficult, fiscal policy making tends to revert to the short-term.

Unfortunately, the IMF has not only failed to oppose sequestration, but has, in fact, encouraged its use. The very focus on the short-term financial performance criteria has tended to divert the Government's attention from the medium-term issues. Equally, the IMF has supported the Government in its efforts to finance its spending through the short-term debt markets. Whatever the financial wisdom of such a course of action, it has served to keep the time horizon of the policy makers firmly fixed on the next debt roll-over date, preventing them from undertaking medium-term adjustments.

By contrast, while the policy programmes supported by the IMF over the last four years have included numerous structural measures, the Fund has been lukewarm in pursuing compliance with these conditions.   It was apparent to the most casual observer, and frequently a subject of comment in the Ukrainian press, that as long as the short-term financial targets were met, the Fund would either ignore the structural issues or interpret performance most generously.   Moreover, some policy conditionality developed over recent years appeared to go as far as requiring short-term solutions, such as the imposition of tax surcharges.

This may have been the right course of action to prevent the reappearance of the immediate financial instability. It has, however, acted as a powerful reinforcement of the short-term focus of the Government of Ukraine. As a result, it has delayed transition.   This is a different argument from the frequently expressed view that by providing external finance, the IMF, in fact, helps the Government to put off painful adjustments.   This paper focuses on the intellectual climate. The international financial institutions should, and probably do, exercise more influence through analysis, persuasion and by shaping the policy debate, than they do through the carrot and stick of the money they bring.   In the case of Ukraine, this kind of external influence has, unfortunately, helped to shape exactly the wrong climate for the fundamental transformation of society.   Just like the Government itself, the IMF misfired by having a day-to-day focus, which contradicted its own medium-term rhetoric.

To generalise, the incentive to stabilise can misfire by removing the international financial institutions' greatest advantage – their ability to focus on the medium term.

ECONOMIC DEVELOPMENT

Access to Capital

There is no doubt that access to capital at market rates is no longer a justification for international financial institutions. This is not just a matter of growth in private cross-border investment. Equally significant, there has been growth in private banking institutions with global reach and with skills required to finance economic development. In fact, international institutions like the International Finance Corporation (a World Bank subsidiary dedicated to investing in private sector projects) and the European Bank for Reconstruction and Development (EBRD) compete head on with private banks. The EBRD, in particular, has struggled to establish a place for itself, as its relatively slow, bureaucratic decision-making processes have resulted in many investment projects being picked out from under it by private competitors. The World Bank has, in some sense, admitted defeat by increasingly moving away from project lending towards adjustment lending, i.e. financing designed to induce and support policy change.

The international financial institutions, however, do have one advantage, which may allow them to add value. This is their semi-official status, which in many countries is a very useful tool for managing commercial risks. In countries where private property rights are poorly protected and often disregarded (this describes a large share of the developing countries), the semi-official status may allow projects to go ahead in situations where private finance could not be made available. From my own experience, the simple fact that World Bank staff members carry diplomatic passports can make all the difference in countries where foreign nationals find it difficult to operate. Corruption, which can impose enormous costs on private transactions (such as the need to clear equipment through customs), often does not extend to the representatives of the international institutions.

Finally, the ability to offer access to concessional development finance, of course, does remain a prerogative of the international financial institutions. The amounts of such finance are, however, severely restricted. The World Bank's International Development Assistance window accounts for less than 20 per cent of its operations.

Inducement to Reform

Inducement of economic reform has become a more important function of the international financial institutions than simply financing development projects, such as roads and dams. This change in emphasis partly comes from the realisation that such institutions are no longer needed to deliver capital, and their resultant search for a rationale for existence. There are, however, two further reasons for the change in emphasis:

- Economic literature has in recent years become increasingly focused on the quality of institutions and of public policy as a pre-condition for economic growth. Some writers, such as the Nobel Prize winner Douglas North, have gone so far as to argue that most economic growth is explained by the gradual evolution of social institutions away from an environment in which economic transactions are costly and complicated, towards settings where transactions are easier to make. Even more narrowly-focused economists have emphasised the importance of economic regulation, as well as the efficiency of the public sector, for growth. In this intellectual environment, getting the policy infrastructure right is seen as at least as important, if not more so, than building up a physical infrastructure.
- In an increasingly inter-connected world, 'rogue' policy by some countries can have negative consequences beyond the borders of that country. For example, the existence of some countries with very high trade barriers complicates the process of liberalising trade for other nations. Consequently, there is a view that it makes sense for the international community to 'purchase' the establishment of good policies in some countries. This approach is perhaps most clearly seen with respect to the former Soviet Union, where the international financial institutions were given an explicit mandate to ensure the re-entry of those states into the international trade and finance system after a long period of self-induced isolation.

In general, there is little evidence that the World Bank and others have been successful in financing 'good policy'. There are a number of reasons for this, which are generic, rather than to do with the particular quality of the work or the staff of these institutions:

- First, in-house research and loan review by the IMF and the World Bank clearly indicates that reform programmes succeed only when they are 'owned' by the country authorities. This is jargon for saying that outsiders cannot induce change. Change is achieved when it is driven from within, although external financing may often be useful as a means of achieving such change.

- Second, much of adjustment lending is used to fund technical assistance. In my view, it is rarely clever to borrow money to finance external advice. I am speaking here from the experience of someone who has been involved in numerous technical assistance projects. Invariably, there are cheaper and more lasting ways to achieve the transfer of human capital.

- Finally, the international financial institutions are at their worst when they are required to perform a political function for which they are not equipped. Policy conditionality depends for its success on consistency, and the application of stringent economic criteria. All this goes out of the window when political imperatives are involved. For example, it undoubtedly makes a lot of political sense to support the transition of the former Soviet Union into a more open society, even if such transition is halting, and is accompanied by very poor economic policies. However, the international financial institutions cannot make such explicitly political decisions. Consequently, when they are put under pressure to provide support for political reasons, they have to find economically plausible grounds to justify what they are doing. The result is that bad policy often gets re-defined as good policy (such as in the example of sequestration presented above). This can, in itself, be very damaging for the recipient countries.

Overall, political inducements are best left to bilateral relations (this includes relations with the European Union, to the extent that it has common external interests). If financial support is granted for political reasons (e.g. to finance President Yeltsin's re-election) then it is best dealt with on such terms. Attempts to present it as supporting good policy are themselves likely to precipitate future economic problems (in this example, the fiscal debt accumulated during Yeltsin's campaign directly caused last year's Russian crisis).

Global Consensus

The World Bank and the IMF have played an important role in the emergence of the global consensus about what constitutes good economic policy (the 'Washington consensus'). It is difficult to know if the same would have happened without these institutions. Their value is not just in the fact that they research and promote similar policies around the world, but also in providing opportunities for regular interactions by senior economic officials from around the world, as well as in the cycling of officials between national governments and the staffs of the Bank and the Fund.

I will leave it to readers to decide whether they think this consensus is desirable or not. I would suggest, however, that it played an important role in New Zealand's economic history, as it provided support to New Zealand government officials during the Muldoon governments of the 1970s and 1980s, who had an opportunity to think through, discuss and prepare a reform package.

CONCLUSION

On balance, the arguments presented above suggest that the international financial institutions may still be able to offer some value. This is not the value which they were originally created to provide, nor do the arguments necessarily support the continuation of some of their present activities. My concerns outlined above are, however, somewhat different from the criticisms traditionally levelled at these organisations.

New Zealand is a shareholder in most of the international financial organisations (with the exception of the Inter-American Development Bank, the African Development Bank and the Arab Development Bank). More significantly, New Zealanders are stakeholders in the outcomes created by such institutions. As New Zealand often has a voice that is disproportionate to its economic size, it is worth thinking strategically about the position it should adopt as a country in the process which will undoubtedly lead to a significant reform of the international financial system in the next few years.

13. Polanyi Revisited: Globalisation and its Contradictions in the New Millennium

Jane Kelsey

For 15 years after 1984 the twin images that the global free market was the key to prosperity and that New Zealand was leading the world down that path went largely unchallenged. Globalisation was represented as inevitable and irreversible. Even if the results were disappointing or unfair, there was no alternative. Enthusiasts sought to advance the process more swiftly. 'Realistic' critics suggested ways to mitigate the adverse effects of globalisation, especially on labour and the environment. 'Unrealistic' critics denounced the growing inequalities and poverty, and warned of the erosion of democracy and the potential for unregulated capitalism to suffer a systemic collapse.

Free-marketeers had a vested interest in promoting the belief that globalisation is invincible. Critics could be summarily dismissed; opposition was futile. I will argue that at the cusp of the millennium such claims are untenable and New Zealanders from diverse walks of life, and many others around the world, are saying so. It is no longer enough for true believers in the virtues of globalisation simply to claim that people do not understand what is good for them.

To understand these developments it is essential to distinguish between economic globalisation as ideology and globalisation in practice. *Globalisation as ideology* is the grand vision, a meta-narrative that imagines an interdependent and self-regulating global economy where goods, capital and ideas flow freely, irrespective of national borders, social formations, cultures or politics. *Globalisation in practice* describes a highly contested process where the competing interests of people, companies, *iwi* (tribe) governments and other groupings overlap and collide; alliances form; accommodations and more drastic revisions are made; and new contradictions arise. The process is dynamic, and the outcome is far from certain. New Zealand is one of very few countries where successive governments have tried to put the ideology of globalisation into practice.

In the late 1990s numerous free market initiatives in NZ became unstuck. In 1998 the National government pushed through legislation to remove tariff protection for local car assembly, but had to defer similar moves for clothing and textiles after employers, unions and local communities jointly mobilised. At the same time, farmers who traditionally supported National turned against 'their own' government, refusing to support the effective privatisation of the statutory producer and marketing boards. In 1997 and 1998, negotiations for a Multilateral Agreement on Investment (MAI) at the OECD, which would have given foreign investors powerful new rights, drew protests from such diverse quarters as Maori, Grey Power, radio talkback callers and city councils; the government eventually supported a moratorium before negotiations broke down completely. After initially dismissing the issue, Local Government New Zealand challenged the failure of central government to consult them over the erosion of their power to regulate under the MAI. Environmentalists forced mining companies to take some responsibility for the hazards they created. General practitioners challenged the right of Australian authorities to decide whether New Zealanders should know their food was genetically modified. New Zealanders from all walks of life opposed greater foreign investment for sound economic, social and cultural reasons, not just xenophobia. As farmers protested US hypocrisy over 'free trade' in mid-1999, pig farmers sought the use of temporary safeguards. Even Michael Barnett from the Auckland Chamber of Commerce suggested a more 'middle of the road' position: 'By promoting a free-trade economy, we bared our soul to the world. But the reality is that while we went down the road first, the rest of the world is slower and this is turning to a disadvantage for New Zealand'.[1]

Meanwhile, Maori have asserted their *tino rangatiratanga* (independent authority) in ways that are consistent with the history of colonisation and class. They have insisted on a constitutional role in both domestic governance and international policy arenas, forcing government to hold nation-wide *hui* (meetings) on the MAI, although the effectiveness of these led to more selective dialogues on APEC. Maori have defended their *taonga* (treasures, tangible and intangible) from transnational aspirations to commodify them as intellectual property and opposed the cultural anathema of genetic manipulation. They have actively campaigned for deregulation of the Pakeha-dominated producer boards, but resisted the elimination of motor vehicle and textile tariffs because of the impact on Maori workers and communities.

Other chapters in this volume relate to tensions in the 2000 WTO negotiations and remark on moves to re-regulate electricity prices in NZ and review the Commerce Act; on the rejection of proposals to replace trade remedies with competition law; on the failure of the MAI; and on NGO pressures on the WTO.

These developments were mainly a defence of the status quo, a belated drawing of the line in the sand. Most were ad hoc responses to specific proposals by pragmatic coalitions that included business people, unions, farmers, local communities, the elderly and Maori – a residue of the historic compromise of the Keynesian welfare state, combined with Maori aspirations for economic survival and self-determination. Cumulatively, however, they represented a nascent backlash against the neo-liberal revolution.

The government, bureaucracy, trade economists and the NZ Business Roundtable chose to attack these responses as misguided and have maintained their pure free market line. Leading free traders overseas have taken a similar approach. At a seminar on the future of the multilateral trading system in Geneva in May 1998, a panel of free trade gurus conceded their bicycle was getting wobbly.[2] In the past year the Asian tiger economies had collapsed. The US President had lost his 'fast-track' authority to negotiate trade treaties; Congress could now pick and choose which parts to accept. Discussions on the controversial MAI had been suspended. People were raising irresoluble concerns about the erosion of national democracy and state sovereignty. There was pressure to reintroduce regulation of capital flows, and more protectionist approaches to trade. The panel could have added that the International Monetary Fund (IMF) was being blamed for making the Asian crisis worse and the chief economist in its sister institution the World Bank had challenged the 'Washington consensus' on structural adjustment, which both institutions had implemented for fifteen years.

The panel's solution was to peddle the bicycle faster. They warned that any moves to regulate short-term financial flows must not hinder progress in freeing up international trade and investment. Meanwhile, governments had to educate their people better about the benefits of global free markets. The international institutions should restore confidence by making their documents and decisions more transparent. They might even show a social face, and invite responsible members of 'civil society' to participate on the fringe. But there was no hint of recognition that their economic model needed to be debated and rethought; it was inconceivable that it might have failed.

My empirical work leads me to conclude that three related forces are causing these fractures in the global economic policy-making process (Kelsey, 1999). The first is internal, as disagreements between states threaten the claim to institutional consensus and make it difficult to maintain, let alone advance, the policy agenda. The second is the systemic breakdown of the economic model which these agreements require governments to advance, most notably the recent run of financial crises. The third is the mobilisation of people and communities at local, national and international levels in opposition to the procedures and substantive policies of states and the international institutions as they seek to advance this agenda. That argument centres on two themes: the problems that arise where economic theory is de-linked from people's economic and social realities; and the conflict between globalisation and sovereignty, democracy and *tino rangatiratanga*. This chapter addresses the first of those themes.

LESSONS FROM HISTORY

The proponents of globalisation in New Zealand and elsewhere make a fundamental mistake when they focus only on the future and ignore the lessons of history. Karl Polanyi's incisive account of the rise and collapse of the laissez-faire economy in Europe in the late nineteenth and early twentieth century, called *The Great Transformation* (Polanyi, 1957), records the folly of free-marketeers who insisted they could judge social events solely from the economic viewpoint, and discredited, then forgot, 'the elementary truths of political science and statecraft' (Polanyi, 1957, p. 33). Their approach was novel: 'Normally, the economic order is merely a function of the social, in which it is contained . . . Nineteenth century society, in which economic activity was isolated and imputed to a distinctive economic motive, was . . . a singular departure' (Polanyi, 1957, p. 71). Relations between families, communities, workers and businesses existed only within markets. But although the ideal of a self-regulating market system attempted to delink economic activity from society and politics, social relations did not disappear. Unregulated markets produced socially unacceptable outcomes, which in turn had political consequences.

The backlash created by treating people and nature as mere commodities 'was more than the usual defensive behaviour of a society faced with change; it was a reaction against a dislocation which attacked the fabric of society' (Polanyi, 1957, p. 130). It occurred in all three markets: for land, labour and capital. Not only human beings and natural resources, 'but also the organization of capitalistic production itself had to be sheltered from the devastating effects of a self-regulating market' (Polanyi, 1957, p. 132). Polanyi described this as a 'double movement': 'The market expanded continuously but this movement was met by a countermovement checking the expansion in definite directions. Vital though such a countermovement was for the protection of society, in the last analysis it was incompatible with the self-regulation of the market, and thus with the market system itself' (Polanyi, 1957, p. 143).

The breakdown of the market system intensified from 1916 on. Pressures to re-regulate reflected ad hoc responses to specific situations, and were supported by pragmatic alliances of those affected in each case. Opposition was not based on ideology, but on practicality. Significant new players emerged, especially workers and women. The true believers in *laissez faire* insisted it was the interventions that caused the problem and the answer lay in further deregulation (Polanyi, 1957, p. 143). They failed. The economy became embedded in social relations once more, although the new society that emerged was quite different from the one that existed before.

In time and against the backdrop of the 1929 Wall Street crash and the Depression, new forms of regulation, policy and law were introduced. Economies were rebuilt from within, nurtured by governments through financial assistance and active regulation, and protected from external competition through border controls. New social structures emerged. In some countries, these embodied a crude form of national interest and identity that laid the foundations for fascism. In other places, social reconstruction created new roles for classes and groups who had previously been excluded, new political dynamics and parties, and a more interventionist role for the state. The rise of extreme forms of economic protectionism and nationalism erupted as a collision of national economic and political interests in the Second World War.

Out of this turmoil and transformation emerged the era of welfare interventionism, in different forms and to varying degrees across the countries of industrial capitalism. States secured their legitimacy through a domestic compromise: capitalism required an environment conducive to profitability, while people demanded policies of redistribution and welfare to mitigate the harshest effects of capitalism, and democratic participation in determining those policies (see Offe, 1985).

Governments also moved internationally to restore stability to currencies through the IMF, and to the world's trading system through GATT. Both regimes were subject to manipulation by the major powers. They also reflected tension and compromises between the state's sovereignty authority to set its national priorities and the stability and expansion of international capital. The IMF's powers over currency devaluations were the subject of ongoing controversy. The GATT compromise produced a multilateral trade regime that was predicated on a degree of domestic interventionism and a shared commitment to a set of social objectives, the most important of which was full employment. Writing in 1982, John Gerard Ruggie suggests the rise of protectionism during the 1970s reflected a rebalancing within that broad norm, as governments moved to minimise the social costs of making domestic adjustments to changing economic conditions. He predicted that the greatest threat to the GATT compromise regime would come not from protectionism, but from 'the resurgent ethos of neo-*laissez-faire*' (Ruggie, 1998 p. 84).

Over time, the post-war compromise created new contradictions. The expanding menu of government services, state support for the domestic economy and social welfare provision meant that the size of public administration and demands on government revenue continued to grow. But domestic capital had a limited capacity to absorb these costs, especially when it could expand only within its borders.

From the 1970s, capital in North America, Europe and Japan actively searched beyond its national boundaries for new markets, lower production costs and new synergies. Economic activity focused increasingly on regional and international markets. Corporations restructured their production and distribution on a transnational basis, taking diverse forms. Financiers sought and created new opportunities for investment in this more fluid and complex environment. To facilitate these developments, barriers to the effective, efficient and profitable international operation of capital had to be reduced, and preferably removed. Demands from business and supportive governments for coordinated commitments to economic liberalisation at a global level saw the rapid expansion of international agreements and agencies such as the GATT/WTO, the North American Free Trade Agreement (NAFTA), APEC and much later the ill-fated MAI. Intergovernmental financial institutions, notably the IMF and World Bank, promoted the 'Washington consensus' to poor countries, often as conditions attached to loans. At the domestic level, the global free market agenda meant rolling back the size, cost and regulatory role of the nation-state. Gaining the consent of the populace to do so was difficult; hence the opening of markets tended to coincide with 'strong government', which circumvented the democratic process and sought to insulate key economic activities from political intervention.

By the 1990s, a number of developments – the end of the Cold War, the conclusion of the Uruguay Round of GATT and formation of the WTO, the emergence of regional economic integration agreements, the information technology revolution, the expansion of transnational enterprise and the surge in financial flows and foreign direct investment – made the global economy appear almost omnipotent. That resurgence was hailed as an irresistible and irreversible progression towards a self-regulating global market-place.

Yet this vision contained all the contradictions Polanyi had identified in the previous century. Its economic landscape was devoid of social and political relations, and of cultural and national identity. The social consequences of free markets in labour, natural resources and capital were ignored, creating social conditions and political pressures that made the vision unsustainable at the national level. The institutional vehicles for global economic policy-making, driven by the same neo-liberal theories, were equally detached from the requirements of real economies; they too suffered mounting challenges to the social impacts of the free market, and to their lack of political legitimacy. Governments who turned their back on these realities and imposed a pure free market agenda without popular consent put the legitimacy of their political system at risk.

Few Western governments could put the ideology of global free markets into practice for a sustained period of time, even if they wanted to. Some did make radical moves to deregulate, notably the governments of Margaret Thatcher in the UK and Ronald Reagan in the US, but their rhetoric was often purer than their practice. These moves were superseded by a new compromise. Tony Blair's 'third way' in the UK and former Secretary for Labor Robert Reich's 'reinventing government' in the US offered adjustments which left the market regime largely intact. It remains to be seen how successful these compromises will be in defusing the pressures that brought them about.

In New Zealand, the aim of successive governments since 1984 and their supporters had been to put 'globalisation as ideology' into practice. After 15 years the contradictions Polanyi identified had visibly emerged – the dysfunctional domestic economy, the unacceptable social cost, and the stubborn survival of values that are irreconcilable with the self-regulating market place. Compounding that was the irreconcilable collision between the universalising project of globalisation and people's deep-seated notions of sovereignty, democratic government and *tino rangatiratanga*.

ECONOMY

As NZ Minister of Foreign Affairs Don McKinnon observed at the University of Otago Foreign Policy School in 1996, 'increasing interdependence must give people results, if not they find an external force to blame and the events of the past twenty years will be reversed.' (McKinnon, 1997 pp.7, 12). Talking up the economic returns has been central to the free market project's survival. This meant focusing on the positive indicators: very low inflation since 1991, successive budget surpluses since 1994, repayment of government debt, significant reductions in government expenditure to GDP. But structurally the economy was in serious trouble.

In an article entitled 'New Zealand's Economic Reform Programme was a Failure', Paul Dalziel examined whether New Zealand's real gross domestic product was higher than it would have been under likely plausible alternative policies, and whether all households were better off than before 1984. Comparing the growth rates of Australia and New Zealand, Dalziel notes a striking similarity between the two countries' GDP paths from 1978 until

1984, and a striking divergence after that. He concludes that, 'if New Zealand had continued to grow at approximately the same rate as Australia (as it did between 1978 and 1984), it would have produced extra output between 1985 and 1998 amounting to more than NZ$210 billion in 1995/96 prices, or well over *twice* New Zealand's total GDP in 1998. Although it would be unreasonable to lay all the blame for this dismal performance at the door of the reforms . . . even if only half this lost production was due to "the special character of New Zealand's reform programme", it still amounts to more than a year's worth of income having been sacrificed.'

The problems facing New Zealand's domestic economy were compounded by the international economic indicators. The deficit in the external current account of the balance of payments for the year to March 1999 was NZ$6.4 billion – about 6.4 per cent of GDP. The deficit had to be covered by a combination of asset sales and borrowing. New Zealand's total foreign debt had reached 103.6 per cent of GDP in March 1999 or about three years and five months' worth of exports of goods and services. Interest and repayments were a massive drag on the productive economy. Long-term servicing of this debt would be a serious problem, because the borrowing had not gone into building New Zealand's productive capacity.

Two main factors accounted for the deficit: the net outflow of investment earnings, and the country's poor international trade performance. By 1998 New Zealand had twice the level of foreign direct investment of Australia or Canada. Yet levels of reinvestment were very low. In the year to September 1998, foreign direct investors earned NZ$3.2 billion profit – but there was *no* net reinvestment in New Zealand. The second factor was the deterioration in New Zealand's international trading position. In 1998 a J. P. Morgan survey of 45 countries showed that New Zealand was one of five to have lost market share over the past six years; this was expected to continue for another two years.[3] New Zealand was ranked 20th out of 25 OECD countries on export growth performance indicators. The terms of trade also deteriorated in the 1990s. In the March 1999 quarter, the terms of trade index fell another 2.1 per cent, putting the index at the lowest point since the September 1987 quarter.

Many structural problems contributed to New Zealand's poor trade performance, including distance, size and access to heavily guarded agricultural markets. There had been external shocks (global recessions, the Asian crisis) and natural disasters (drought, electricity outages) that were beyond government control. But the Darwinist approach to the domestic economy and the Reserve Bank's use of the exchange rate to control inflation were the major reason for the loss of domestic competitiveness, as Brian Easton (among others) has documented (Easton, 1997).

In other countries, these external economic indicators would have caused grave concern. New Zealand officials insisted that there was no problem because of the 'quality' of the deficit.[4] New debt was being incurred by the private sector while the government was repaying public debt. If private debt and current account deficit got too high, the market would lose confidence and make firms 'adjust' (as happened in Asia). NZ Reserve Bank Governor Don Brash argued that the best the government could do to address the balance of payments was to maintain fiscal surpluses as a contribution to domestic saving.

By the later 1990s prominent voices in the business community, such as Hugh Fletcher, Gilbert Ulrich and Jim Scott, were calling for government to relink economic policy with domestic economic reality. Their proposals ranged from balancing monetary policy objectives of price stability with economic growth to compulsory superannuation that could build a domestic investment pool to promoting strategic investment in promising export industries. Other economic commentators, such as Tim Hazledine, questioned whether the export sector could provide a long-term foundation for a remote country like New Zealand. He urged a greater emphasis on restoring the capacity of New Zealand's economy to service the country's needs from within (Hazledine, 1998). The search for alternatives to the self-regulating marketplace was under way.

SOCIETY

Economic debate has re-emerged in response to the damage the free market experiment has caused to New Zealand's real economy. The social costs have also become unsustainable. Over a decade and a half, countless New Zealand communities have been shattered by free market policies that were imposed with little or no warning and with callous disregard for their human consequences.

A major redistribution of wealth has taken place. Recent research shows that between 1984 and 1996 the richest five per cent of the population increased their share of national income by 25 per cent and the top ten per cent by 15 per cent (Chatterjee and Podder, 1998). The share of national income for the bottom 50 per cent of New Zealanders fell; the poorest proportionally lost most. When Statistics New Zealand released a report in March 1999 on long-term trends in national income from 1982 to 1996 (Statistics NZ, 1999) the chief statistician remarked that, 'the results are unequivocal: income inequality has increased substantially'. The cost was borne unevenly. Some 28 per cent of Maori were in the bottom fifth of income earners, and over one quarter of the country's children. Average personal market income (based on 1996 figures) for Maori fell from NZ$16,800 in 1982 to NZ$11,900 in 1991 and only recovered to NZ$14,400 by 1996. The comparison for Pakeha was NZ$20,700 in 1982, NZ$19,500 in 1991 and NZ$21,000 in 1996.

The *Closing the Gaps* report to the Minister of Maori Affairs in 1998 showed the gap between Maori and non-Maori had widened (Ministry of Maori Development, 1998). Almost half of Maori households earned less than NZ$27,800, compared to two-fifths of non-Maori. Over one-third of Maori were now primarily dependent on government benefits for income (non-Maori 14.3 per cent); at the same time, benefits payments were being reduced. Maori rental housing became less affordable. Maori were almost twice as likely to be admitted to hospital. The health gap widened on key poverty-related illnesses like glue ear, youth suicide, diabetes, pneumonia and mental health. There was also a marked increase in the feminisation of poverty, especially for elderly women and sole parents who were affected disproportionately by cuts to public services, user charges and effective reductions in the value of pensions and benefits.

Overall the median personal income of all New Zealand adults declined by 13.4 per cent between 1986 and 1996. Most job growth in the 1990s was part time. In November 1998 there were still 34,400 (or 3.2 per cent) fewer full-time filled jobs than in February 1987, when the household labour force surveys began, but 243,900 (or over 100 per cent) more part-time filled jobs. Brian Easton describes the emergence of a dual employment market – a top tier of high status, high income earners in relatively secure employment, and a bottom tier (mainly young, Maori, Pacific Islanders and women) who range between low-quality, low-paid and part-time or insecure jobs and unemployment (Easton, 1997).

The Economist acknowledged in 1994 that increased poverty and inequality between and within countries are intrinsic features of free markets and observed it was 'no coincidence that the biggest increases in income inequalities have occurred in economies such as those of America, Britain and New Zealand, where free-market economic policies have been pursued most zealously.' (*The Economist* 5 November 1994, p.19). Not only were such results expected; those responsible have positively welcomed them. Finance Minister Bill Birch was reported in July 1998 as saying, 'The fact that incomes at the top of the ladder have grown more than those at the bottom is not a bad thing. I think it's an inevitable part of increasing rewards for effort . . . You've got to send the right signal'. Such detachment from people's struggle to survive assumes that the globalisation project can be sustained irrespective of the social dislocation and human pain it causes, that free markets can dictate the terms of social existence, and that those who suffer will grudgingly adapt to their new mode of existence.

VALUES

The same assumption applies to New Zealanders' values. The crude model of structural adjustment adopted in New Zealand assumes that people will embrace the market model once the changes are made and the benefits are properly explained. More sophisticated theorists distinguish between a rapid implementation phase, through insulated change teams, followed by consolidation that combines construction of a support base among the élite and 'social learning' where the remainder adjust their expectations and lifestyle to their new circumstances (see Haggard and Kaufman, 1992; Williamson and Haggard, 1994; and Nelson, 1992). But they stop short of requiring the mass of people to embrace the new regime. Indeed, they seek to entrench the free market system against any resurgence of conflicting values and political programmes.

Social values are notoriously difficult to assess. But surveys of New Zealanders' social attitudes and values conducted by Massey University researchers Paul Perry and Alan Webster in 1989, 1993 and 1998 suggest that conservative welfare state values are still dominant within New Zealand (Perry and Webster, 1999). Those surveyed were prepared to pay more tax to increase government spending on health and education, had major concerns about pensions and environmental protection, and supported not only government redistribution of wealth, but also stricter limits on selling foreign goods in New Zealand to protect local jobs and tighter regulation of big business and multinationals. Almost 70 per cent felt the country was 'run by a few big interests looking out for themselves'; less than 20 per cent believed it was run for the benefit of all the people. Three quarters of those surveyed believed that poverty had increased, a majority said the government was not doing enough in response to it, and 40 per cent believed that some people had no chance to escape poverty. A majority also supported tariffs to protect local industry. However, the overwhelming rejection of any obligation on government to break the poverty trap facing Maori and Pacific Island people, and to address Treaty of Waitangi grievances – let alone confront the vexed question of Maori political autonomy – shows colonial attitudes remain very much alive.

Globalisers tend to ignore this conflict of values and treat people as bystanders in the societies and economies, which they comprise. Yet people's sense of identity and of values shapes their view of the world, their responses to adverse situations, and their degree of politicisation. If, as John Helliwell has argued in this volume, they are also a central feature of social capital, this disjuncture will have serious economic as well as political consequences.

Just as Polanyi found with nineteenth century *laissez faire*, pretending that economic and social reality can be reconstructed to fit the free market model creates practical problems for the productive economy, and social costs that become unacceptable. People, faced with governance by the market, demand an effective say in the decisions that directly affect them, and new forms of intervention, regulation and support to address the new problems they encounter.

After a decade of radical, theory-driven change, New Zealanders have begun to reassert the relevance of their social and political world in the decisions that government makes. It is clear that New Zealand cannot simply go back to what existed prior to 1984, even if people wanted to. Society has changed; the new generation of 'children of the market' has known nothing else. Agriculture, industry and services have been substantially restructured and the capacity and functions of the state have been fundamentally altered. Different groups have become empowered, and there are new communities of poor and dispossessed. Maori have reasserted their role in political and economic life, variously supporting aspects of deregulation, suffering disproportionately from its impacts, and continuing to confront Pakeha society with its failure to redress the wrongs of the colonial past.

The free market revolution began in NZ in 1984 with a clear blueprint and a committed team of politicians, officials and private players who shared broadly common goals. In 1999 there are growing signs of resistance; but demands that a new direction for the country be explored have been unsystematic and unorganised. There is no alternative template, no coherent vision of the kind of society in which people want to live, or the kind of state they wish to empower. These pressures have been resisted by those in business, politics, the public service, academia and the media who have an economic interest in, and/or an ideological commitment to, the free market agenda. They reassert the inherent validity of their economic model, and blame the failures on a refusal to 'finish the business'.

However, the state cannot permanently abdicate its responsibility for the country's economic and social well-being by leaving those outcomes to be determined by competitive markets. Just as governments are the vehicles through which deregulation is pursued, they also retain the authority to reassert some control. Despite attempts to insulate economic policy from political reality, governments are the subjects of political pressure. Acquiescence is only sustainable if people are prepared to continue absorbing the cost of free markets on their lives or can be pacified by new policies that ameliorate their worst effects. There are signs that both major NZ parties are seeking to defuse these tensions within the existing globalisation paradigm – Labour with its local version of Blair's Third Way, National with its more activist approach to the 'knowledge economy'. Many critics of the free market within the business sector, the CTU unions and Maori entrepreneurs have seemed content to accept that new compromise. However, the sequence of policy rejections and reversals suffered by the government in recent years, coupled with the structural problems facing the economy, suggest there is a potential to move beyond a 'grumbling acquiescence' to demand for a more fundamental reconsideration of New Zealand's future direction.

NOTES

[1] Press release, 17 June 1999.
[2] Seminar on the Future of the Multilateral Trading System, Asian Development Bank Meeting, Geneva, May 1998; panelists were Renato Ruggiero, Director General of the WTO; the Deputy Prime Minister of Thailand; leading trade economist Jagdish Bhagwati; Fred Bergsten, Director of the Institute for International Economics; and Martin Wolfe, deputy editor of the *Financial Times*.
[3] *NZ Herald*, 3 February 1998.
[4] D. Brash, speech hosted by Chatham House, London, July 1998.

REFERENCES

Chatterjee, S. and N. Podder (1998), 'Sharing the national cake in post reform New Zealand: income inequality trends in terms of income sources', presented to the Annual Conference of NZ Association of Economists, Wellington, 2–4 September.

Easton, B. (1997), 'Why has New Zealand's Economic Performance been so Disappointing?', paper for Economic and Social Research Trust on New Zealand, Wellington.

Haggard, S. and R. Kaufman (1992), 'Institution and Economic Adjustment', in S. Haggard and R. Kaufman (eds), *The Politics of Economic Adjustment*, Princeton NJ: Princeton University Press.

Hazledine, T. (1998), *Taking New Zealand Seriously*, Auckland: Harper Collins.

Kelsey, J. (1999), *Reclaiming the Future: New Zealand and the Global Economy*, Wellington: Bridget Williams Books.

McKinnon, D. (1997), 'New Zealand Sovereignty in an Interdependent World', in G. Wood and L. Leland (eds), *State and Sovereignty: Is the State in Retreat?*, Dunedin NZ: Otago University Press.

Ministry of Maori Development (1998), *Progress Towards Closing the Social and Economic Gaps Between Maori and Non-Maori*, Wellington.

Nelson, J. (1992), 'Poverty, Equity and the Politics of Adjustment', in S. Haggard and R. Kaufman (eds), *The Politics of Economic Adjustment*, Princeton NJ: Princeton University Press.

Offe, C. (1985), 'Legitimacy Through Majority Rule' in J. Keane (ed.), *Claus Offe: Disorganised Capitalism*, Oxford: Polity Press.

Perry, P. and A. Webster (1999) *New Zealand Politics at the Turn of the Millennium: Attitudes and Values About Politics and Government*, Auckland: Alpha Publishers.

Polanyi, K. (1957), *The Great Transformation: The Political and Economic Origins of our Times*, Boston: Beacon Press.

Ruggie, J.G. (1998), *Constructing the World Polity: Essays on International Institutionalization*, London: Routledge.

Statistics New Zealand (1999), *New Zealand Now: Incomes*, Wellington, NZ: Statistics NZ.

Williamson, J. and S. Haggard (1994), 'The Political Conditions for Economic Reform', in J. Williamson (ed), *The Political Economy of Policy Reform*, Washington DC: Institute for International Economics, p.527.

14. Rapporteur's Report

Tim Hazledine

What is the role of the rapporteur? One possibility is simply to 'report' the entire proceedings of the conference, as they occurred, in summary form. Another possibility is to attempt to establish some 'rapport' between the papers – to bring out common themes and to contrast their differences, and so to synthesise the contributions of the authors into some sort of cohesive narrative that does not necessarily literally summarise all the information presented.

The first approach – the linear summarising report – would probably be boring for readers and it certainly would bore me to do it. So I am going to attempt to tease out a theme from the chapters in this volume, and the discussion they provoked on presentation at the Foreign Policy School. I will do so, of course, under the rubric of the overall topic established by the title of this School: *The Global Economy: Continuity and Change.*

I have to forecast that my *rapport* will bear some bias towards the economic issues around globalisation, at the expense of the procedural and technical matters of the actual international policy process. This is partly in reflection of my own expertise and interests, which of course lie in economics rather than politics or international affairs. But it also, I believe, quite fairly represents a natural intellectual bias generated by the content of our proceedings. All the papers were good and interesting and we – certainly I – benefited from listening to them. But there was one paper that I would judge, on the basis of the discussion it provoked at the time and since, to contain the highest ratio of things you didn't know to things you did know, and furthermore, those things you didn't know could turn out to be terrifically important – potentially even revolutionary – to our understanding of the workings of the international economy in particular and of economic affairs in general. That paper was an economics paper.

There is a chance I am quite wrong about this, and, even if I am not, there is a very good chance that I will turn out to have exaggerated the importance of the new ideas. But I think it better to commit a Type II error than a Type I. Or is it the other way around? Anyway, I mean that you would probably rather want to be told about a really Big Idea that turns out to be wrong, than not be informed about a Big Idea that turns out to be right.

Now, in June 1999 we had a seminar at the University of Auckland given by Professor Jagdish Bhagwati, of Columbia University, New York. Although Bhagwati has not yet received the Nobel Prize, he may very well get one eventually, and he is undoubtedly a most eminent trade theorist. Professor Bhagwati began his talk with an anecdote. He said that a reporter in America had recently asked him whether he (the reporter) could label him (Bhagwati) as a 'free trader'.

'What are my choices?' responded Bhagwati.

'Free trader or Protectionist,' said the reporter.

'Oh well, in that case you'd better put me down as a free trader,' said the professor.

How would I respond to this question? I am to the left of Bhagwati, but not that far to the left. I think my response would be the same as to the question: 'Name your favourite New Zealand city: Whangarei or Invercargill.' I would refuse to answer the question as posed – my true answer lies somewhere in between.

The point here – and it is the point that Jagdish Bhagwati went on to make in his talk – is that it really isn't very helpful to restrict the debate on trade to a binary choice between two extremes. Such restrictions, unfortunately, have been a feature of the debate in New Zealand (to the extent that there has even been this limited choice offered), and they haven't got us very far. I would argue that we need to put matters into a more realistic context. Here we are, on the eve of the millennium, after four decades or so of fairly steady liberalisations of tariffs and other restrictions on international commerce, following a programme set down by Keynes and a few other far-sighted economists and statesmen after the last World War. This programme, which is not going to be rolled back, leaves the world still short of what most analysts would describe as full integration.

So where do we go from here? That is both a positive and a normative question: where will the inherent massive momentum of the forces of globalisation take us, and what, if anything, should governments and international agencies do about it? Now, the orthodox response – and this orthodoxy has been ably represented at this conference – is to charge right on; to something which might indeed be well described as an extreme: full free trade, deep integration, globalisation (whatever that means – and I will offer definitions later).

This is the standard neoclassical economic model, and we all know it well – perhaps too well! It tells us that free trade is the only way to maximise efficiency and GDP. And what if that process throws up losers as well as winners, as just about every participant in this conference concedes that it does? Well, then, use some direct redistribution policy to ameliorate this, to the extent that large and systematic inequalities are involved. But don't kill the goose that lays the golden egg – that (to switch metaphors) maximises the size of the pie available for redistribution.

Allan Mendelowitz warned that protection is a very inefficient way of redistributing income, because it shrinks the pie, and because it encourages wasteful rent-seeking activities. So too may other redistributive policies and it was suggested from the floor that it may be better if the winners don't actually compensate the losers, so long as it is possible that they could. This is not as hard-hearted as it sounds, if the economic game is open and fair enough that everyone gets enough chances to win and lose for the probabilities to come out in their favour in the long run.

Now, this is quite extreme, and other economists would not go so far, which is partly why Jagdish Bhagwati is not comfortable with the label of full-fledged free trader. Doug Irwin offered in his paper a rationale for stopping short of full integration: 'Contingent protection may prevent the full gains from trade from being realised, but it at least sustains a critical mass of political support for open markets'.

This is actually a heavily loaded statement, provoking at least two important questions: what are the 'full gains from free trade', and why is it politically unpopular? I will return to the second question, but let us first scrutinise those free-trade gains, on which so much is being wagered by the supporters of full integration.

The news is not great. It is what Paul Krugman called 'economics' dirty little secret' that the 'static' or immediate gains from moderate trade liberalisation – which is all that is now available to us at the present quite low rates of tariffs set by almost all developed countries on most goods – are disappointingly tiny. Consumers gain, producers and taxpayers lose, and the net difference (the 'allocative efficiency triangle') is worth no more than a small fraction of a percentage point of GDP – well within the margin of error of any economic model. New Zealand's Minister of Foreign Affairs and Trade, Mr McKinnon, referred in his paper to a recent study by the NZ Institute of Economic Research (NZIER, 1999) documenting consumer benefits in New Zealand in 1998 from tariff cuts on cars, household appliances, shoes and clothes at around NZ$350 per person, but after you net out the losses to taxpayers and producers, which were ignored by the NZIER (though many consumers do pay taxes and earn wages or profits!), you are left with a net efficiency gain of about $30 – truly 'a case of beer each', as one economist dubbed the typical magnitude of these allocative triangle gains.[1]

And the list of possible errors in static free trade theory is rather long, with any of these having the potential to more than wipe out allocative efficiency gains.[2]

But what about the 'dynamic' or long-term gains from higher economic growth spurred by more open and competitive markets? Much effort has gone into tracking down such effects in the data, and we have the now famous study by Sachs and Warner which did establish an empirical relationship between differences in rates of growth across countries, and a measure of their 'openness'.

A worry with this is that the measure of 'openness' is quite problematic – it was constructed by the authors of the study, and shows signs (in my opinion) of having been rather massaged to fit the (strong) priors of Sachs and Warner that a relationship between openness and growth indeed exists. For example, Korea, which we saw in an overhead (put up by John Helliwell) to be just about the fastest growing developing economy, is classified as 'open'. Korea has had one of the most protectionist and mercantilist trade/industrial policy regimes ever seen.

In response to a question from Rod Deane, Douglas Irwin was very frank on the issue of a growth/openness link. He said: 'Most economists would like to find it, but we are still looking for strong compelling evidence', and then cited a 'devastating' critique of Sachs and Warner by Dani Rodrik, to which I could add a reference to a study by Ann Harrison and Gordon Hanson (1999) in the *Journal of Development Economics*.

And do not forget this: Mike Moore, documenting the 'clear' benefits for developing countries of trade liberalising policies writes that: 'ten developing countries with a combined population of 1.5 billion people have doubled their per capita income' over the past 10–15 years. But he did not point out that most – more than a billion – of those fast-growing people live in the Peoples' Republic of China – then as now a Communist dictatorship.

So maybe there *are* other paths to economic progress, after all, as Jane Kelsey suggested in her paper. But how could there be? Surely there is no respectable alternative to the neoclassical free trade model? Here is where the New Economics comes in: our paper with the high surprise/knew-that ratio. This paper is, of course, John Helliwell's 'The scope for national policies in a global economy.'

To summarise, Helliwell builds on work by John McCallum which found, for example, that a business person in Ontario is about *twenty times* more likely to do business with someone in British Columbia than with someone over the border (but no further away) in the US state of Washington, despite the near absence of trade barriers and the many evident similarities between the two countries. This implies that national borders really do matter – a lot! – even with the abolition of formal barriers to trade.

I was not surprised by this finding on Saturday, but I certainly was the first time I heard it, which was at the Canadian Economics Association annual conference, in Montreal, in June 1995, at a session which must have been one of the earliest at which John Helliwell told his (and John McCallum's) intriguing tale. I was then struck both by the number itself, and also how it fitted with another striking number that I had recently come across as a Discussant in a Toronto trade conference, of one of the papers by Jeffrey Frankel and his co-authors, to the effect that countries with a common linguistic and/or colonial past trade about two thirds more with each other than do other country pairs, *ceteris paribus*. (See Frankel *et al*., 1994 and Hazledine, 1994).

To these, I would add another striking number, which has long been lying, almost unnoticed, in the 'gravity model' used to explain international trade flows. The actual physical gravity model – Newton's law – predicts that the attraction between two bodies is proportional to the product of their masses, and inversely proportional to the distance between them. In the trade version, mass is proxied by the GDP of each trading partner, and distance is distance. Distance 'works' in the trade gravity model, such that the amount of trade between two economies of given sizes just about halves as distance doubles. This is the same as the physical gravity model, which is probably why it hasn't been remarked on, but it is actually much too large to be consistent with neoclassical trade theory – implying, basically, that transport costs just about double the cost of a good for each doubling of distance. Actual transport costs are only a small fraction of this.

Well, what does this ail mean? Early in the conference I asked Doug Irwin for a definition of globalisation. He defined it as full integration. But what is the definition of integration? The Helliwell paper suggests a definition. Full international integration between nations holds if and only if the border-augmented gravity model does not hold.

Let us examine this proposition. Fairly clearly, the border effect must go if we are to have integration – the nationality of who you are dealing with cannot matter. But this is necessary, not sufficient for global integration. We could have no border effect, but still very strong distance effects, such that people prefer to do business with people close to them. This would hardly be globalisation. So the distance effect in the gravity model must go, too (or at least, its coefficient must drop by an order of magnitude to be consistent with objective trade costs, such as transportation).

Now what John Helliwell tells us, very firmly, is that border and distance effects are a very long way from disappearing. The 'end of geography' (in the Minister's striking phrase) is not yet nigh. Even between free trade Canada and the United States, trade flows are much too small – by at least an order of magnitude – to be consistent with the neoclassical trade model. Free trade does not bring full integration.

Why not? The concept which Helliwell brings in to explain this is called 'social capital'. In economists' terms, it is the measure of the trust between participants in markets which allows them to escape from non-cooperative Nash equilibria (or 'prisoners' dilemmas', in the term used by Patrick Lane) and exploit the full gains from cooperation and exchange. It is all about the transaction costs of economic life – an utterly neglected topic in neoclassical theory, including orthodox trade theory. Our capacity to build trusting relationships is probably limited like everything else in life, and it seems very plausible that both shared values and 'culture' as well as physical proximity are important determinants. Thus, we have an explanation for the border and distance effects that so dominate the data on trade flows.

This could be very important because social capital may be not just a useful supplement to the explanatory power of neoclassical theory, but it may, rather, be fundamentally subversive of it! Take the big issue, mentioned above, of income distribution. In the standard welfare economics approach, as noted, this is quite separate from the 'allocative' matters that determine growth and productivity (except to the extent that mis-conceived redistributionary policies may blunt the incentives to produce). But in the social capital model, income distribution may be a key determinant of trust. Specifically (as John Helliwell noted in discussion), the empathy and sympathy that are conducive to two agents trusting each other may be depreciated when their incomes are far apart, for a number of possible reasons. We heard that there does appear to be an inverse relationship between income inequality and economic growth: this could be why.

All this means that 'Third Way' approaches ('For the market economy; against the market society', in the words of French Prime Minister Lionel Jospin) are misconceived. *Ex post* 'safety nets' don't hold water: you just can't separate economy and society – the terms on which we engage each other socially are actually fundamental to our success in operating a civilised and productive market system. I expect that my insights into this matter will be sharpened by following Jane Kelsey into an examination of the ideas of Karl Polanyi.

Evidence for the importance of social capital has been provided in the most appalling fashion by the post-Soviet experience of Russia after it was liberalised: output halved! This, we now see, shows the importance of building the institutions (which are not just formal institutions, such as legal systems) of the 'civil society' in which social capital grows and trust flourishes.

I would suggest that New Zealand's very disappointing economic performance since 1984 shows the other side of the civil-society coin: unlike

Russia, NZ had the social capital, the trust, the informal institutions, but NZ has been neglecting them – even, tearing them down, in its own drastic 'liberalisation' experiment. John Helliwell spoke of the 'bottom-feeders' – the Mafia; the criminals – who move in and flourish in an institution-impoverished society like Russia: but in New Zealand after 1984 you didn't need to use force to misappropriate large sums of money – it was just sitting there for the taking (as the fates of many of our high-flying entrepreneurs after the 1987 stock market crash revealed all too clearly).

In his talk to the conference, Roderick Deane spoke of New Zealand multimillionaires driven into exile (I paraphrase) by local hostility or indifference to their talents. I think it a mistake to confuse popular hostility towards certain businessmen with hostility towards business. On the contrary, the people may know something very important about what it takes to operate a successful market economy, and that is that very large income differentials are counterproductive.

This is not the 'politics of envy' as Tim Groser put it, but the down-to-earth economics of social capital. I fear – I hope wrongly – that the really quite violent wrenching apart of the distribution of earned income seen in New Zealand, the United States and elsewhere is a time-bomb, threatening to explode not just into civil strife but also striking at the social capital core of market capitalism. As the great Yogi Berra said,[3] towards the end of a long baseball season in the days before floodlit grounds: 'It is sure is getting later earlier these days!' I think that the income distribution issue is getting very late on us all.

This starts to move us from the positive to the normative. Social capital and the border (and distance) effects may well be indispensable analytical tools to explain why market participants will not *choose* full integration, but so what, from a policy perspective? Should we not continue to work towards eliminating those barriers that do have their constraining effect on trade? Well, perhaps we should, but social capital, and transaction costs considerations in general, can also explain why there might be (as Jane Kelsey urges) different paths to prosperity – different cultures form different institutions and rules of economic engagement. So long as the people in a nation understand their own rules (so that they manage enough cooperation to solve their prisoners' dilemmas), it may not matter crucially exactly what they are.

Such is truly very subversive of There-Is-No-Alternative (TINA) -style neoclassical doctrine because it causes us to question the very basis for policy harmonisation – what David Robertson, in his process-oriented definition,[4] calls 'positive' or 'deep' integration, and sees as the next big step in international policy negotiations, after the 'negative' (why negative?) or 'shallow' integration of previous GATT rounds based on tariff reductions. This is the territory of the 'link' issues: 'trade and. . .'[5]

Now, we can all easily appreciate the case for harmonisation, and I will not stress it here. What needs to be flagged is the case against. For example, nations differ enormously in the financial and governance structures they provide and permit for their private sector firms. Should such structures be 'harmonised'? Well, perhaps there could beneficially be some narrowing of the range, lopping off the extremes of 'crony capitalism' at one end of the spectrum, and 'rampant short-termism' (driven by stock market performance) at the other. But the social capital perspective tempers this with an appreciation that the institutions developed in one cultural setting may (a) suit that setting quite well, in terms of fostering cooperative exchange; yet (b) be not productively transplantable to other settings.

We have to ask 'to whom the good?' from forced harmonisation. Is the whole process just a euphemism for 'Americanization', as some participants in the School suggested? We can admit that homogenising the international institutional landscape will make the world a safer and simpler place for multinational enterprises to roam in, but we still require some demonstration of the gains from such an outcome. There is some irony here in the increasing obtrusiveness of supra-national NGO (non-government organisation) single-issue pressure groups in the WTO negotiating process. These unelected bodies have apparently hijacked for their own use the phrase 'civil society', and their agenda of achieving 'post-sovereign governance' that bypasses elected national governments provokes some comment from David Robertson in his paper. But isn't the bypassing of national government just what globalisation is all about? Whence comes the political legitimacy of multinational business?

Continuing on the theme of political legitimacy, could social capital illuminate the issue – a frustrating puzzle to well-meaning neoclassicists – of the undoubted general unpopularity of free trade – the other loaded proposition in my quote above from Doug Irwin's paper? Do the people – stalwart mercantilists, as Patrick Lane reminds us – know something here, too, that we don't? Well, they just might. It might be true that those last liberalising steps have a significant disruptive effect on the social networks of trust underpinning successful gains from trade and exchange more generally. This is quite speculative on my part (though see Dani Rodrik's (1998) recent article interpreting the surprising fact – as it seems to be – that, cross-sectionally, greater openness is associated with a higher share of government in GDP, which Rodrik interprets as the result of populaces demanding more (income-stabilising) public expenditure as compensation for greater instability of their incomes due to openness). However, it may be relevant to the information given to us in the Helliwell paper, to the effect that the very large (unforecast) increases in Canada–US trade flows since free trade was implemented apparently have not shown the promised productivity pay-off for the smaller economy.

These considerations suggest a case for (moderate) tariffs as a 'sand tax': perhaps of no direct benefit in itself, but acting as an irritant or friction to the flow of commerce, sufficient to discourage destabilising in-and-out transactions, but not enough to prevent productive long-term commitments to setting up in markets.[6] The case applies too to other national policies or institutions which may seem irrational and unnecessary at face value, such as differences in product labelling requirements, or even what side of the road cars are driven on (and thus what side of the car the steering wheel is placed) – which was once seriously raised by the United States as a trade barrier unfairly impeding the export of American-made automobiles to Japan!

The people's voice has also long been heard in the stubborn persistence of that oldest (more than a century, in the US and Canada) system of major regulatory interventions in markets: anti-trust or competition policy, the international dimensions of which are expertly explained to us in Kerrin Vautier's paper, based on her new book with Peter Lloyd. Although the teeth of anti-trust have been drawn somewhat by the move – which Vautier supports – towards a more efficiency-based competition policy (over the old due-process orientation based on deterring substantial lessenings of competition), the popularity of competition regulation seems still pretty secure, and it will likely remain an important institution qualifying globalisation and international and national commerce.

Now I wish to focus on the nature of the globalisation process itself, responding to the excellent papers and informal contributions of Allan Mendelowitz and Douglas Irwin. John Helliwell showed us how far we are from full economic integration, but we do still seem to have gone a long way along that path. Have the impact of liberalisation and accompanying changes in information technology compounded themselves by now into a major qualitative and/or quantitative change in our economic lives?

This is a big and fascinating question, and rather difficult to answer from within – as a participant in the ongoing process, as am I and all of us. If only some economic genius like Keynes could suddenly emerge from a fifty-year sojourn in the jungle, have a bit of a look around, and then tell us whether the modern world *really* is different, or whether what seems like fundamental change is really just 'churning' – endless but ultimately pointless rearrangements of ephemera! I am currently happily working my way through the five volumes of autobiography of Keynes' contemporary and friend, Leonard Woolf, whose memories extend from soon after 1880, when he was born, to the 1960s, when he wrote these volumes (obit. 1969).

Admittedly, this lengthy life span just misses computers and modern telecommunications, but, still, rather a lot happened over those eighty years.

Yet, and although Woolf was a successful practical businessman amongst his other activities, it is remarkable how 'timeless' is his narrative. He writes penetratingly about the things that mattered to him, as they still do to us – love, literature, politics, life – in terms in which 'technology' barely gets a look in. The only exception I can recall is that people like Leonard Woolf who grew up in a London of horse-drawn carriages apparently carried through life a sense of the proper pace of city life inaccessible to the children of the motor age.

In Victorian London, you could post a letter in the morning, and receive its reply in the afternoon post. Is that really *fundamentally* different from e-mail? Isn't the message really still the message? Is Internet shopping fundamentally different from ordering from the old Sears Roebuck catalogue? Is the 'mass customisation' of products forecast by Allan Mendelowitz fundamentally different from the old days of bespoke tailoring and made-to-order coachbuilding? Allan would argue that the differences are fundamental, and perhaps he is right: what we might more easily agree on is that, intriguingly, the differences between today/tomorrow's technologies and those of, say, Leonard Woolf's time are less in some sense than the differences between all of these and the dominating technologies of the mid-twentieth century: telephones, shopping malls, mass production.

This 'back to the future' theme is explored in Douglas Irwin's paper, which explores the big numbers of world trade flows. Certainly, these numbers have increased substantially in the post-war decades, but this was from a base of barriers and protectionism that grew up in the turmoil of two world wars and a global depression. Some influential economists (Krugman; Sachs and Warner; Rodrik) have suggested that today's trade and financial flows no more than recover the degree of integration found in the world economy of one hundred years ago (when Leonard Woolf was a young man).

Irwin and his co-authors challenge this view, in a long and scholarly paper that focuses on the United States economy. They concede that the ratio of merchandise exports to GDP is not much different now (about eight per cent) than it was in the late nineteenth century (about seven per cent), but point out that the share in total GDP of the tradeable goods sector has about halved, so that the ratio of merchandise trade to merchandise GDP has actually gone up a lot. The US tradeables sector is much more into actual trading than it used to be.

But, still, if the domestic sectoral composition of output has shifted away from 'tradeable' merchandise production to 'non-traded' service industries (of which the actual trade share is small, though rising fast), why should we say that the overall economy has become significantly more globally integrated?[7]

And, the actual nature of modern merchandise trade has features that, in my view, are not consistent with true long-run integration. The cost and time for transporting goods internationally has fallen, a great deal.   One consequence is this.   Whereas in the olden days a commodity made at most two trips across the ocean   – first as a raw material and then, possibly, embedded in a manufactured export – nowadays it is not uncommon for three or four or more trips to be made before the end user is finally reached.

Now, about 40 per cent of world trade is intra-firm, and much of those transactions, and much of trade between firms, is of semi-finished components.   Such trade is facilitated by cheap transport and motivated (often) by cheap labour – by the opportunities for 'mining' labour in plentiful supply in developing economies.   Allan Mendelowitz's paper gives a striking illustration: out-of-work Indian physicians being used to transcribe American doctors' dictated patient evaluations.   Although just about all the parties involved probably benefit from this ingenious transaction (possibly excepting some of the American typists whose services are dispensed with), from a long-run global point of view it is extremely inefficient, reflecting market imperfections that prevent very large wage differentials between people of similar skills in different countries from being arbitraged away.

Now transactions like these are in fact part of the arbitrage process, and we must hope that eventually they and many other adjustments will bring Indian standards of living closer to those in the United States.   But then it will no longer be profitable to so extravagantly use trained physicians as transcribers – the work will be done at home, in both countries.   And so too will much of the other current trade in semi-finished goods[8] also become unprofitable (given the quite substantial transport and other transaction costs incurred). The point is that perhaps the long-run prospects are for less, not more trade, and that countries allowing their manufacturing industries to be sacrificed to cheap-now imports might come to regret this.

The bottom line?   At the very least, we do seem to have found that there is more to free trade and globalisation that perhaps some of us (including your *rapporteur)* thought before. We really do have something to discuss and debate. How well have we been doing this in New Zealand – before, of course, this excellent conference?   In discussing the multilateral trade negotiation process, and why this country has been quite effective at it (very effective given our size), Tim Groser told us that New Zealand had been strong internationally because 'we don't have to negotiate at home'.   Tim Groser has been a very able public servant of New Zealand, and he made it clear in other remarks at the conference that he personally has concerns about the closing off or at least discouraging of debate on policy alternatives that has (I think) been a distressing outgrowth of the authoritarian and conformist strain in New Zealand culture and institutions that has caused us trouble at least since the late 1970s.

But others have tried to discourage 'negotiation at home', and even go so far, as Jane Kelsey pointed out, as to do their best to entrench trade and other agreements, so as to foreclose any changes of heart by future governments straying from the true free trade religion. I see this is as deeply undemocratic, and to any proposition that we should refrain from internal debate in order to strengthen our bargaining position in the multilateral halls, I would say, and I hope most of you would too, in the words of the great Yogi Berra: 'Include me out!'[9]

NOTES

[1] I calculated this as 0.5x0.15x0.15x2700, using the NZIER's average price cut figure of about 15 per cent, their elasticity of demand assumption (-1), and average annual expenditure on these items of $2700 per person.

[2] Perhaps it is worthwhile listing the possible sources of reversal of free trade welfare or policy implications. Standard or neoclassical trade theory is vulnerable because it assumes: (1) *No distortions* in markets which could generate '2nd best' problems [for example, the NZIER's econometric pricing equation shown in the study cited above implies the existence of market power in the import market such that each New Zealander in 1998 *lost*, on average, about NZ$100 – several cases of beer! – from paying higher foreign supply prices for imports as a result of the tariff cuts]; (2) *No unemployment* – but in reality 'resources released' (eg, labour laid-off) as a result of tariff cuts may not all be quickly or satisfactorily redeployed; (3) *No externalities* such as arising from economies of scale so that, say, an otherwise efficient NZ autoparts manufacturer may not be viable if it loses its original equipment customers as a result of the free-trade induced closing of local car assembly plants; (4) *No history* – everything is fully reversible in neoclassical theory; (5) *No future,* so that there is no account of the role of protection (for good or ill) in economic growth.

[3] In case it doesn't survive in the written record of the conference proceedings, I should perhaps explain that there was an informal competition between certain participants to insert at least one Yogi Berra quote into their presentation.

[4] Process-oriented in contrast (or complementary) to the outcome-oriented economists' definition offered above in terms of actual trade flows being unaffected by geography, apart from objective transportation costs.

[5] Robertson lists seven such link issues: trade and: (1) government procurement; (2) investment; (3) competition; (4) economic integration (regionalism); (5) development; (6) environment; (7) labour standards. Most progress has been made on the first three of these; the last two are the most controversial.

[6] An often-discussed example of a sand tax is the 'Tobin tax' on international financial transactions, set low enough (say at 1/4 per cent of the value of the transaction) to be insignificant to, for example, long-term foreign direct investment, but enough to strip the profit from very short-term speculative and arbitraging capital flows.

[7] Especially given that the pre-1914 United States trade shares were achieved in a world with much higher tariffs, on average, than now (cf. Irwin's Table 3.3).

[8] The typing-up of doctor's patient evaluations is of course an intermediate input or unfinished good in the production of health care services.

[9] Actually, I think this remark belongs to another unintentionally very funny man, Sam Goldwyn.

REFERENCES

Frankel, J.A., S-J. Wei and E. Stein (1994), 'APEC and Regional Trading Arrangements in the Pacific', in W. Dobson and F. Flatters (eds), *Pacific Trade and Investment: Options for the 90s*, Kingston, Ontario: John Deutsch Institute for the Study of Economic Policy, Queen's University.

Harrison, A. and G. Hanson (1999), 'Who gains from trade reform? Some remaining puzzles', *The Journal of Development Economics, 59*, 125–54.

Hazledine, T. (1994), 'Comment', in W. Dobson and F. Flatters (eds), *Pacific Trade and Investment: Options for the 90s*, Kingston, Ontario: John Deutsch Institute for the Study of Economic Policy, Queen's University.

NZIER (1999), *Consumer Benefits from Import Liberalisation: A New Zealand Case Study*, Wellington, NZ: Ministry of Foreign Affairs and Trade.

Rodrik, D. (1998), 'Why do more open economies have bigger governments?', *Journal of Political Economy,* **106**, 997–1032.

Index